A Student's Guide to History

NINTH EDITION

A Student's Guide to History

Jules R. Benjamin

Ithaca College

Bedford/St. Martin's

Boston ◆ New York

For Bedford/St. Martin's

Publisher for History: Patricia A. Rossi
Director of Development for History: Jane Knetzger
Developmental Editor: Rachel L. Safer
Production Editor: Arthur Johnson
Production Supervisor: Christie Gross
Marketing Manager: Jenna Bookin Barry
Production Assistant: Kristen Merrill
Copyeditor: Patricia Herbst
Indexer: Steve Csipke
Cover Design: Hannus Design Associates
Cover Art: World map from *Novus Atlas* published by Willem Janszoom Blaeu and Iohannem Blaeu, Amsterdam, 1649. Courtesy of the Harvard Map Collection.
Composition: Pine Tree Composition, Inc.
Printing and Binding: Haddon Craftsmen, Inc., an R.R. Donnelley & Sons Company

President: Joan E. Feinberg
Editorial Director: Denise B. Wydra
Director of Marketing: Karen Melton
Director of Editing, Design, and Production: Marcia Cohen
Managing Editor: Elizabeth M. Schaaf

For information, write: Bedford/St. Martin's, 75 Arlington Street, Boston, MA 02116 (617-399-4000)

ISBN: 0–312–40356–9

Acknowledgments

From *Libraries through the Ages* by Fred Lerner. Copyright © 1999, Continuum International Publishing Group. Reprinted by permission.

From *The Limits of Power: The World and United States Foreign Policy, 1945–1954* by Joyce Kolko and Gabriel Kolko. Reprinted by permission of Joyce and Gabriel Kolko and HarperCollins Publishers, Inc.

From *The Marked Men* by Aris Fakinos. Copyright © 1971 by Liveright Publishing Corporation. Originally published as *Les Derniers Barbares,* Éditions du Seuil, 1968. Reprinted by permission of Georges Borchardt, Inc., for the author.

From *Rise to Globalism* by Stephen E. Ambrose, copyright 1971, 1976, 1980, 1983, 1985, 1988 by Stephen E. Ambrose. Used by permission of Viking Penguin, a division of Penguin Putnam Inc.

Acknowledgments and copyrights are continued at the back of the book on page 242, which constitutes an extension of the copyright page. It is a violation of the law to reproduce these selections by any means whatsoever without the written permission of the copyright holder.

To Elaine, Aaron, and Adam

Preface

I was motivated to write *A Student's Guide to History* almost thirty years ago in response to a barrier I noticed between my students and the historical material I was teaching. Although this barrier differed somewhat from one student to the next, the need of individuals to learn basic study, research, and writing skills was consistently the core issue. If my students could not take concise notes, tackle common assignments, write clearly, or understand what an exam question required of them, then my efforts to explain the meaning of the past ran up against their inability to respond. Today, the situation remains much the same, but by attacking this skills barrier outside the classroom, I have been able to devote my classroom time to teaching history.

In my ongoing effort to overcome this obstacle, I have turned to my students and to students across the country, asking them what they need to know to demonstrate their understanding of historical material. The original structure of the first edition, still discernible in this ninth edition, took the form of responses to these needs. Over the past three decades, some needs have changed, particularly as new technologies have arisen to facilitate teaching and learning. Today, writing requires skills not only with language but also with word-processing programs, and research requires knowledge not only of the organization of a college library but also of electronic databases and the Internet. Thus recent editions of *A Student's Guide to History* have sought to provide students with skills appropriate to the digital age.

My goal has been to equip students with all the skills they need to succeed in a history course by providing concrete advice and annotated examples that teach students to read critically, discern key concepts, and synthesize information into coherent notes and written assignments. *A Student's Guide to History* discusses the discipline of history; reviews basic study, research, and writing skills; explains how to approach common assignments; offers test-taking strategies; and includes extensive coverage of the Web as a research tool.

Chapter 1 discusses why people study history, how historians go about their investigations, and how to distinguish between primary and secondary sources, as well as how the study of history can prepare students for a variety of careers. It also examines differing interpretations of history and the directions of historical research. Chapter 2 teaches fundamental skills that students need to read a variety of history assignments, take notes in class, and study for exams. This chapter includes annotated examples guiding students to the main ideas of a text; a section on reading maps, charts, graphs, illustrations, and artifacts and other nonwritten materials; and information about collaborative work and communicating online. Chapter 3 focuses on writing skills and uses examples to demonstrate clear and connected writing. It takes the reader through the steps of building and revising an essay, provides guidance on matters of style and mechanics, and offers examples of writing appropriate to a variety of history assignments, including a sample book review.

Chapters 4 and 5 and the appendixes address the more complex tasks of preparing and writing a research paper. Chapter 4 helps students choose a research topic, narrow it to a practical theme, and craft a workable thesis; use library resources to gather information; and evaluate print and electronic sources and mine information from them. It also warns of the dangers of plagiarism and helps students understand how to avoid them. Chapter 5 stresses the importance of good writing skills, using quotations, and documenting sources with over forty models for footnotes or endnotes and bibliographies. The complete, annotated sample research paper that concludes the chapter illustrates how to pull together research findings, how to incorporate visual materials, and how to document sources, providing a model for students as they tackle this complex assignment. Appendix A points students toward places to start their research, highlighting the most helpful indexes, references, collections, and periodicals and hundreds of print and electronic resources. Appendix B includes sections on local and family history and provides lists of grammar and style manuals. The Glossary includes all of the key terms that appear in boldface throughout this book.

In addition, the popular guidelines boxes have been retained. The boxed guidelines, which serve as checklists for students, succinctly summarize the most helpful tips for taking lecture notes, speaking in class, giving an oral presentation, peer reviewing, writing in-class essay exams, writing clearly, writing a book review, writing a short essay, evaluating print sources, evaluating Internet sites, and avoiding plagiarism.

New to This Edition

A Student's Guide to History has been revised in ways that provide students with even more practical tools and features that reinforce basic skills and explain tricky issues:

- Evaluating visual materials and incorporating them into a research paper are given increased attention in response to student feedback.

New and expanded sections in Chapter 2 focus on interpreting maps, illustrations, photographs, and artifacts as different types of historical sources. Chapter 5 includes additional guidance on integrating visuals into research papers; the sample reseach paper at the end of that chapter provides two models for students.

- An increased emphasis on avoiding plagiarism raises students' consciousness without being negative or critical. Consolidated coverage of paraphrasing and avoiding plagiarism, new advice about plagiarism in the context of group work, and new boxed guidelines on avoiding plagiarism inform students.
- Expanded coverage of thesis statements in Chapter 4 helps students develop and craft thesis statements by encouraging them to move from a broad topic to a theme to a more narrow, workable argument. Both the introduction and the conclusion to the sample research paper have been revised to emphasize the thesis.
- New hands-on exercises encourage students to practice key history skills. Designed for student self-study and as assignments in historical methods courses, exercises on understanding various types of primary source evidence, communicating online, conducting library research, conducting Internet searches, and evaluating a Web site help students sharpen their research and writing skills.
- Thoroughly updated lists of reference sources in Appendix A guide students to some of the best tools available for the most common research areas. In addition, the nearly 250 digital reference sources have been annotated to describe each Web site's content, saving time for students exploring different research topics. An easy-to-navigate hypertext version of these digital reference sources can be found at the book's Web site, *A Student's Online Guide to History Reference Sources,* at bedfordstmartins.com/benjamin, along with complete contact information for state, local, and professional history organizations.

I am always looking for ways to improve *A Student's Guide to History* and would appreciate any suggestions that you would like to share. The e-mail address for comments is guidetohistory@bedfordstmartins.com.

Acknowledgments

Each edition has benefited from comments and suggestions made by some of the hundreds of instructors who have assigned *A Student's Guide to History* and by some of the third of a million students who have read it over the years. I particularly wish to thank the many people who reviewed the manuscript in preparation for this edition: Ted Binnema, University of Northern British Columbia; Ron Doel, Oregon State University; Alexis McCrossen, Southern Methodist University; Kenneth Orosz, University of Maine at Farmington; Jonathan Rees, University of

Southern Colorado; Tom Velek, Mississippi University for Women; Ken Wilburn, East Carolina University; an anonymous reviewer for the press; and ten student reviewers.

I would also like to thank my research assistant, Caroline Sherman, whose work found its way into many sections of this edition, most notably the detailed documentation models and the newly annotated electronic reference sources in Appendix A. And I want to express my great respect for those at Bedford/St. Martin's who have contributed to this edition of *A Student's Guide to History:* Rachel L. Safer, Patricia A. Rossi, and Arthur Johnson. I am in their debt not only for their editorial skills but also for their commitment to this book and its mission.

Jules R. Benjamin
Ithaca College

Contents

A Note to Students

Since I wrote the first edition of this book in 1975, more than a third of a million students have used it in their history classes. Each year, students have written to tell me how the book helped them to master parts of their work, as well as how I might make improvements. I have incorporated some of their ideas into the text you are about to read, and I encourage you to contact the publisher or me with your comments at guidetohistory@bedfordsmartins.com.

I have tried to make this book useful regardless of whether you are taking world history, Western civilization, ancient history, modern history, social history, economic history, or the history of a particular region or nation. This book presents all the tools you need to succeed in any history course, as well as the skills that will open the past to you.

Each section discusses how to tackle a specific kind of assignment. Clear guidelines, practical examples, concise explanations, and hands-on exercises guide you through reading, studying, researching, and writing tasks. Care has been taken to make it easy for you to find answers to your questions about history assignments and about the Web as a resource tool. The appendixes highlight the most helpful print and electronic resources for starting your research. *A Student's Online Guide to History Reference Sources,* an easy-to-navigate hypertext version of this electronic resource guide, can be found at the book's Web site, bedfordsmartins.com/benjamin, along with complete contact information for state, local, and professional history organizations.

I have also written this book to introduce you to the enormous world that is the heritage of people everywhere. This world is as fascinating as the world of today or as any vision of the future. I hope to convince you that the study of history is not a journey into a dead past but instead offers a way to understand and live in the present. You can use the tools of historical research to succeed not only in history courses but in your future career. And you can use them to answer important questions about your own life and your relationship to the rest of the world. This broader purpose is what makes the study of history so valuable.

Jules R. Benjamin
Ithaca College

CHAPTER 1

The Subject of History
and How to Use It

What History Can Tell You

The interstate highway system connects all of the major cities of the United States. The speed limits are high, and cross traffic is carried over or under the interstate. Where the interstates connect, the spaghetti-like on and off ramps form a pattern that seems to express what is most new about our society. Traveling at seventy miles per hour, you may not realize that these highways have a history—that construction of the interstate system began in the 1950s.

The car that carries you comfortably and swiftly along the highway and the music that plays on the car radio have a history even older than the highway's. Your car has the same basic components—engine, rubber tires, steering wheel, axles—as the boxy "touring" cars of the 1920s, whose design was based on the design of horse-drawn carriages. The rock or rap music playing on your car radio is a descendant of country music, folk music, and jazz with roots extending into the distant past. American folk music traces its roots to the British Isles, from which it was brought to the Appalachian Mountains of the eastern United States in the eighteenth and nineteenth centuries. Jazz traces its roots to the music of enslaved Africans brought to the American South and the Caribbean in the seventeenth and eighteenth centuries.

Looking for the marks of history in the world around us is something like the task of the geologist or archaeologist. However, instead of digging into the earth to uncover the past, the historical researcher digs into the visible, everyday elements of society to find the historical roots from which they sprang. The interstate highway system, parts of

1

which are still being built today, is in the uppermost layer of history. If a study of the newest superhighways can take us back fifty years, what about the historical roots of older highways or country roads? How far into the past can we travel on them?

Turn off the eight-lane interstate, past the gleaming gas station, past the drive-up window of the nearest fast-food restaurant, past the bright signs before the multistory motel, and onto U.S. Route 51 or 66— older highways built in the 1940s and 1950s. Being from an earlier period, perhaps they can tell us something about life in mid-twentieth-century America.

When you leave the interstate system for this older road network, you first notice that the speed limit is lower and many of the buildings are old. As you ride along at the slower pace, there are no signs saying "Downtown Freeway ½ mile" or "Indiana Turnpike—Exit 26N." They say "Lubbock 38 miles," or "Cedar Rapids 14 miles." As you approach Lubbock or Cedar Rapids, you will see small, single-story motels. They may be wooden cottages with fading paint and perhaps a sign that says "Star Motor Court" or "Stark's Tourist Cabins." Instead of fast-food restaurants, you pass "Betty's Restaurant" or "Little River Diner." If you pay close attention to these buildings, you can take a trip into history even as you ride along. All of the older restaurants, stores, and gas stations that you see were built before the large shopping centers where people usually shop today, and they provide clues to the history of the road on which you are riding. Places like the Star Motor Court and the Little River Diner probably were built when the road was new. Unless they have been modernized, they are relics of a previous historical period—when Franklin Roosevelt and Harry Truman were president and when the cars had rounded hoods, trunks, and fenders. The diner isn't air-conditioned, and the sign over the tourist cabins proudly proclaims that they are "heated." This is the world of the 1930s and 1940s.

Now turn off at State Route 104 where the sign says "Russell Springs 3 miles" or "Hughesville 6 miles." Again the speed limit drops. You are on a road built in the 1920s and 1930s or earlier (some country roads are a hundred or more years old). Time has claimed many of the buildings that once stood along this road, but if you look closely, the past is there ready to speak to you. The gas station has only one pump, and the station owner sells bread, eggs, and kerosene. Faded advertisements on the wall describe products that you may have never heard of—NeHi Orange and Red Man Chewing Tobacco. If you see a restaurant or motel, it may be boarded up because the people who used to stop in on their way to Russell Springs or Hughesville now go another way or have moved to a nearby city. However, many homes are still standing along Route 104. They were built when only farmland straddled the road, and they may date back to a time when horses pulled traffic past the front door. Relics of early technology such as wringer-washing machines and iceboxes may stand on the tilting wooden porches, and a close look behind the tall weeds beside the dirt drive-way may reveal the remains of a 1936 La Salle automobile. As you stop before one of the old farmhouses, the past is all around you. With a little imagination you can reconstruct what life was like here on the day in 1933 when President Roosevelt closed all the banks or the day in 1918 when the Great War in Europe ended.

The line linking past to present never breaks, and the house itself has a history, as do the people who once lived in it. In this sense, every house is haunted with its own past, and a keen eye can see the signs. If you enter the house, you can see the stairway that was rebuilt in 1894 and, in the main bedroom upstairs, the fireplace that was put in about 1878, the year the house was built. Perhaps the old Bible on the table near the bed notes the year the family came to the United States and the dates in the early nineteenth century when the parents of the immigrants who built the house were born.

The story could extend far back into the past, although the evidence would become slimmer and slimmer. From county records you could find out who owned the land before the house was built, going back perhaps to the time when the people who lived on the land were Native Americans. In distance you may have traveled only ten or twenty miles from the interstate highway, and the trip may have taken you less than an hour; but while looking in the present for signs of the past, you traveled more than a hundred years into history.

If you think about and study the passage of time between the old farmhouse on the country road and the gleaming service station by the interstate, you may come to understand some of the social, political, and economic forces that moved events away from the old wooden porch and sent them speeding down the superhighway. The more you know about this process, the more you will learn about the time when the farmhouse was new and the more you will understand how the interstate highway came about, what you are doing riding on it, and into what kind of a future you may be heading.

What Historians Are Trying to Do

Since the invention of writing, people have left records of their understanding of the world and of the events in their lives and how they felt about them. By studying the records left by previous generations, we can find out about the lives they led and how they faced their problems. We can use what we learn about the experiences of people who lived before us to help solve the problems we face. Though the modern world is quite different from the societies in which our ancestors lived, the story of their accomplishments and failures is the only yardstick by which we can measure the quality of our own lives and the success of our social arrangements.

All of us look into the past from time to time. We read historical novels or books about historical events. We gaze at old photographs or listen to the stories our grandparents tell. **Historians**[1] attempt to make a systematic study of the past and to use the knowledge they gain to help explain human nature and contemporary affairs. Professional historians spend their lives pursuing the meaning of the past for the present. Students too make journeys into the past that may contribute to the store of human knowledge and can greatly influence their own lives. Your study and research as a student is similar to that of the professional historian. Your examination of the past is part of the same search for knowledge carried on generation after generation.

History and the Everyday World

Most of us are curious. Children are always asking their parents the "why" of things. When we grow up, we continue to ask questions because we retain our fascination with the mysteriousness and complexity of the world. Because everything has a history, most questions can be answered, at least in part, by historical investigation.

What are some of the things about which you are curious? Have you ever wondered why women's skirts in old movies are so long, or why French men often embrace one another but English men almost never do? Perhaps you have wondered how the Kennedy or Rockefeller families came to be rich, or why the Japanese attacked Pearl Harbor. Have you thought about why most of the people of southern Europe are Catholic and most northern Europeans are not? Many Asian peoples bow when they greet one another; many Americans shake hands. The questions could go on forever; the answers are somewhere in the record of the past.

This record is not only contained in musty volumes on library shelves; it is all around us in museums, historical preservations, and the antique furnishings and utensils present in almost every household. Our minds are living museums because the ideas we hold (for example, democracy, freedom, equality, competitiveness) have come down to us by way of a long historical journey. Though we are usually unaware of the past, it is always with us.

How Historians Work

Like you, historians are challenged by the complexity of the world, and many want to use their studies of the past to help solve the problems of the present or future. The questions that can come to mind are num-

[1] Terms in **boldface** are defined in the Glossary at the back of the book.

berless, and serious historical investigators must choose wisely among them. They do not want to spend a lot of effort pursuing the kind of question to which history has no answer (for example, "What is the purpose of the Universe?" or "Who is the smartest person in the world?"). Nor do they want to struggle to achieve the solution to a problem that is not of real importance. (Historical investigation can probably tell you who wore the first pair of pants with a zipper, but that piece of information might not be worth knowing.) The main difficulty facing historians is not eliminating unanswerable or unimportant questions but choosing among the important ones.

A historian's choice among important questions is determined by personal values, by the concerns of those who support the historian's work, by the nature of the time in which the historian lives, or by a combination of all of these. The ways in which these influences operate are complex, and historians themselves often are unaware of them.

When the historian has chosen his or her subject, many questions still remain. For example, does historical evidence dealing with the subject exist, and if so, where can it be found? If someone wanted to study gypsy music from medieval Europe, and that music was never written down or mentioned in historical accounts of the Middle Ages, then little or nothing could be found about this subject through historical research. Even if records exist on a particular subject, the historian may be unaware of them or unable to locate them. Perhaps the records are in an unfamiliar language or are in the possession of individuals or governments that deny access to them. Sometimes locating historical evidence can be a problem.

Having determined that records *do* exist and that they can be located and used, the historian faces a more important problem: How complete is the evidence? Are there significant gaps in it? What is the credibility or reliability of the evidence? Is it genuine? How accurate are the records, and what biases were held by those who wrote them? If sources of information are in conflict, which source is correct? Or is it possible that most of the sources are in error? Historians must pick and choose among the sources they uncover, and that is not always easy to do. The historian's own **biases** also cloud the picture, making impartial judgment extremely difficult.

Philosophies of History

Historical investigation can lead to very different results depending on the aspect of human nature or society emphasized and the kind of information obtained. Even greater differences can result from historical investigations that employ different *philosophies* of history. A philosophy of history is an explanation not only of the most important causes of specific events but of the broadest developments in human affairs. It explains the *forces* of history, what moves them, and in what direction they are headed. The dominant philosophy of history of a particular age is the philosophy that most closely reflects the beliefs and values of that age. Most of the historians writing at that time write from the perspective of that philosophy.

Perhaps the oldest philosophy of history is the **cyclical school.** According to this view, events recur periodically—history repeats itself. The essential forces of nature and of human nature are changeless, causing past patterns of events to repeat themselves endlessly. As the saying goes, "There is nothing new under the sun." This view of history was dominant from ancient times until the rise of Christianity. The Aztecs conceived of history this way, as did the Chinese.

A central message of early Christianity was the uniqueness of the life, death, and resurrection of Jesus Christ. In societies influenced by the Christian Church—especially in Europe in the Middle Ages—the new concept of divine intervention to overthrow the past weakened the cyclical view.[2] The resulting philosophy of history, the **providential school,** held that the course of history is determined by God, and that the ebb and flow of historical events represents struggles between forces of good and evil. These struggles are protracted, but the eventual victory of good is foreseen.

That particular idea of the providential school—that history is characterized not by ceaseless repetition but by direction and purpose—became an element in the thinking of the more secular age beginning with the eighteenth century. In this new age of scientific inquiry and material advancement, there arose the **progressive school,** whose central belief was that human history illustrates neither endless cycles nor divine intervention but continual progress. According to this school, the situation of humanity is constantly improving, and this improvement results not from divine providence but from the efforts of human beings themselves. Each generation builds on the learning and improvements of prior generations and, in doing so, reaches a higher stage of civilization. The idea of history as continual progress remains powerful. Currently, many variations of the progressive philosophy share the field of historical investigation.

The newest school of history is **postmodernism.** It has not replaced the progressive school but has raised significant questions about the inherent nature of human progress. Postmodernism has influenced many academic disciplines. In history it raises the fascinating question of whether the past can truly be understood from the perspective of the present. Evidence from the past, say the postmodernists, takes on new meanings because the present is so different from the past that they cannot directly communicate with one another. According to postmodernists, when historians search the records of the past, the understanding of the past that they bring back is heavily influenced by

---

[2] An earlier development of this view is found in the Old Testament.

the methods they use or the questions they ask. They do not "find" history or discover how things really were; rather, they "create" history in the process of looking for it. Few historians wholly accept this new post-modernist view, but it has affected and weakened the older idea of objectivity—the idea that, with time and effort, the historian could avoid bias and uncover the "truth" about history.

Historiography

Another approach to the study of history is through **historiography,** the study of changes in the methods, interpretations, and conclusions of historians over time. As historians examine a subject, they become aware that earlier studies of the subject they are pursuing often came to surprising conclusions. For example, between 1920 and 1939, most of the major histories of World War I placed principal blame for the war on Germany. The prevailing view was that Germany's aggression against its neighbors caused the war. At the end of the war, the Treaty of Versailles required Germany to disarm, to accept blame, and to pay "reparations" to the countries it fought against for the great damage the war had caused—even though Germany too had suffered greatly. Despite this general agreement on the cause of World War I, the experience of World War II, lasting from 1939 to 1945, led many scholars to rethink the origins of World War I. Historians began to ask how the Nazi movement in Germany, which directed unprecedented brutality against civilians both before and during World War II, had been able to rise to power through elections. Why were so many Germans willing to follow Hitler?

Before coming to power, the Nazi Party repeatedly charged that Germany had to avenge itself for the war guilt placed on the German nation by the Treaty of Versailles. Slowly, historians of World War I realized that the idea that Germany alone was responsible for that conflict had helped the Nazi Party to exploit the patriotism of the German people. Historians looked more closely at the world of 1914 and concluded that there were *many* reasons for the erupting of World War I. Germany was no longer considered to be the sole culprit. Economic and strategic competition among the major powers (Germany, England, France, Russia, and the United States) was seen as an important factor. Intensified nationalism in all these nations—not just in Germany—had increased tensions. Also, it was realized that a series of interlocking alliances among the great powers—which turned a minor conflict in the Balkans into an all-European war—was another source of the explosion. The simplistic verdict of German guilt gave way to a complex explanation of the aims and security concerns of many nations. In this case, an attempt to understand Germany's role in World War II led to a new understanding of the German role in World War I. This kind of reinterpretation or "revision" is not uncommon in history.

Historians' views of Reconstruction, the period in U.S. history after the Civil War when the defeated South was under the military and political control of the victorious North, also changed. During Reconstruction, for the first time in U.S. history, black people, many of them former slaves, were allowed to be elected to and hold political office. Prior to the 1930s, almost all the books written on this subject (whether by northern or southern historians) concluded that southern politics was corrupted and made ineffective during the Reconstruction period by selfish northerners and ignorant black southerners. Since the 1950s, however, scholars have reached very different conclusions. Most now believe that southern blacks' participation in state and local government was a healthy development and that the standard of politics in the South was generally equal to that of other regions of the nation at that time.

One reason for this new interpretation was the later historians' more effective use of basic sources describing the work of the Reconstruction governments of the southern states. Also, historians compared southern Reconstruction politics with politics in northern and western states of the period (an example of comparative history). And after looking back over the older literature and placing it in the historical **context** of race relations existing at that particular time, most scholars now conclude that an understanding of racist attitudes toward African Americans does much to explain the negative conclusions of earlier historians. Historiography lets historians use the tools of historical research to study themselves.

Historiography also can show how historians are influenced in their interpretation of the past by the ideas and events current in their own day. Recent decades have seen the breakup of the Soviet Union, the emergence of AIDS, and the globalization of economic change. These events may spur historians to take up questions about the past that may shed light on these recent developments. The breakup of the Soviet Union, for example, might lead to deeper study of the forces that created the Russian Empire. The AIDS crisis might lead to deeper study of the origin and transmission of earlier epidemics that spread across a wide area. Globalization might lead to deeper study of the rise of international trade in the late nineteenth century or its decline in the 1930s.

Changing Directions of Historical Research

When historians investigate the questions that interest them most, they are influenced in their approach by their own values and experiences, their academic training, and their beliefs about which aspects of human nature, human institutions, and the human environment are most important in understanding those questions. As a result, histori-

ans might look at a historical question from a wide range of perspectives, including social, cultural, intellectual, political, diplomatic, economic, and scientific.

Social historians often focus their research on the development of
human communities and their interaction with the larger society. They
might study the changing role of French peasants during the 1800s or
the history of fraternal organizations over a broad region or a broad
span of time. Cultural historians focus on group attitudes and behav-
iors and how they change over time; they might research the treatment
of beggars in eighteenth-century London. Intellectual historians examine powerful ideas and how they influence beliefs and actions, such as
Charles Darwin's early ideas on evolution. Political historians look at
relations of power and how they operate in institutions such as governments, political parties, and interest groups. They might research the
role of the colonial governor in Portuguese Angola. Diplomatic historians usually deal with relations between nations and how they change
over time; they might examine the treaty system and the outbreak of
World War I. Economic historians study developments in technology,
production, transportation, consumption, and patterns of wealth and
poverty; an appropriate topic for an economic historian might be centers of Italian trade in the Renaissance. Historians of science examine
the evolution of scientific knowledge, how changes in such knowledge
arise, and how its application influences society; they might examine
the failure of German scientists to develop an atomic bomb.

Demonstrating how current issues influence the direction and subject matter of history, several new approaches have become important
in recent decades. Environmental historians, who examine the interaction between human communities and their habitat and the attitudes
of these communities toward nature, might examine what nineteenth-
century Mediterranean tidal data say about global warming. Historians
of sport, media, and other aspects of popular culture might examine
radio detective shows. Historians of the family and private life have
taken up the examination of the structural and emotional development of small, intimate groups and the interaction of these groups
with powerful social forces such as wars, depressions, class and ethnic
conflict, and technological change; they might examine children's role
in the French rural family during the eighteenth century. In contrast,
the field of world history takes in centuries of change across large areas
of the globe, and comparative historians seek to understand the significance of an institution, political system, people, or nation by comparing its history with that of others. Such historians can learn much
about Vietnam, for example, by studying the ways in which its culture
resembled or diverged from that of China.

Two of the most rapidly expanding areas of research in recent
decades have been women's history and gender studies, enormous

topics largely neglected by earlier generations of historians. Women's historians might study women in the workforce during World War II— who stayed home and who did not. Historians of gender study the ways in which ideas of masculinity and femininity have influenced history; they might study the portrayal of male and female characters in fairy tales.

Two older areas of historical research are reviving. Genealogy and local history are regaining prominence as people in countries or regions undergoing rapid change become concerned with holding onto or rediscovering their past. Genealogy traces the history of a particular family; local history examines the evolution of a town, community, or neighborhood. For more on family and local history, see "How to Research Your Family History" in Appendix B (pp. 233–35).

Methods of Historical Research

Certain kinds of historical research have been influenced by other disciplines: family history by psychology, **demography** by sociology, **ethnohistory** by anthropology, political history by political science, and economic history by economics. While still adhering to the special focus of history—examining and explaining the past—historians welcome ideas and methods of analyzing evidence from other fields. For instance, **quantitative history** (called cliometrics) uses quantitative data, such as election returns, price levels, and population figures of earlier periods, to re-create a picture of earlier times. Because quantitative data are uniform, they measure the same things—votes, prices, numbers of inhabitants—over time. Thus, comparisons can be made among **statistics** from different periods. The electoral support of a political party, the price of wheat, or the size of a town can be examined to see if it is rising or falling and at what rate.

If the uniformity of the data can be established (that is, if the numbers really *do* measure the same thing in each period), then the data can be subjected to mathematical analysis. Percentages, ratios, averages, the mean, median, and mode can be obtained. If the dataset is large, the historian may subject it to complex analyses that explore patterns within the numbers and among subgroups of them: the frequency distribution, the standard deviation, and the coefficient of variation. Elaborate statistical analyses not only can determine how fast prices are rising or where the majority of a party's voters reside but also can compare different kinds of changes—party registration with price levels, population decline with employment levels—in an attempt to describe the conditions under which certain changes occur. By noting those categories of numbers (variables) that move together, the historian can begin to explore the causes of the changes under examination. Computers make this task more manageable, allowing historians to work with very large datasets and to analyze them in new ways.

Primary and Secondary Sources of Evidence

Two basic forms of historical **evidence** help historians answer these different questions: primary and secondary. **Primary sources** (see Figure 1.1 below and Figure 1.2 on p. 12) record the actual words of

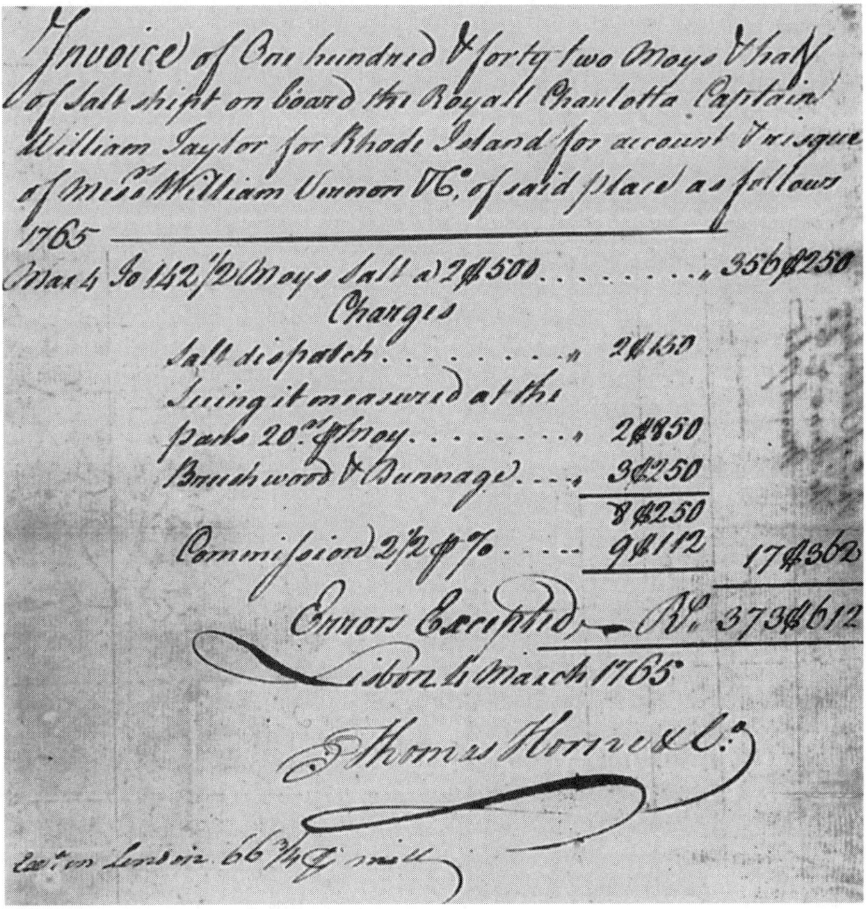
Invoice of One hundred & forty two Moys & half of Salt shipt on board the Royall Charlotta Captain William Taylor for Rhode Island for account & risque of Messrs William Vernon & Co. of said place as follows

1765

Mar 4 To 142 1/2 Moys Salt a 2$500 .... 356$250

Charges

Salt dispatch .... 2$150

Seeing it measured at the parts 20rs p Moy .... 2$850

Brushwood & Dunnage .... 3$250

8$250

Commission 2 1/2 p % .... 9$112 17$362

Errors Excepted — Rs. 373$612

Lisbon 4 March 1765

Thomas Horne & Co.

Exc on London 66 3/4 d p mill

FIGURE 1.1 Example of Primary Evidence (1765)
Primary documents are often handwritten rather than printed and reflect the vocabulary and writing style of the period in which they were created. This invoice describes a shipment of salt carried from Lisbon, Portugal, to Providence, Rhode Island, in March 1765 "on Board the Royall Charlotta Captain William Taylor for Rhode Island for account & risque of Mr. William Vernon. . . ." The value of the cargo is written in Portuguese escudos. The document was handwritten and signed by Thomas Horne just after the salt was loaded onto the ship. It brings us as close as we can come to the actual scene on the docks at Lisbon over two hundred years ago.

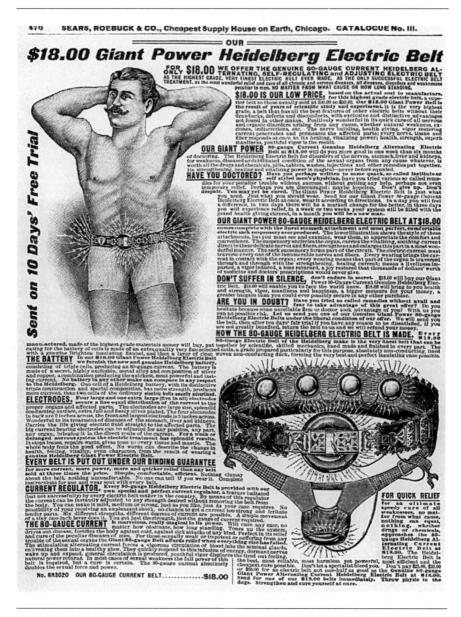

FIGURE 1.2   Example of Primary Evidence (1902)

This printed advertisement for a Heidelberg Electric Belt appeared in the 1902 Sears, Roebuck and Company catalog. If you are doing research on some of the strange medical cures sold at that time, the claims made in this advertisement would be an important piece of primary evidence. What kind of "illness" do you think this belt was supposed to cure?

someone who participated in or witnessed the events described or of someone who got his or her information from participants. Primary sources can be newspaper accounts, diaries, notebooks, letters, minutes, interviews, and any works written by persons who claim firsthand knowledge of an event. Another primary source is official statements by established organizations or significant personages — royal decrees, church edicts, political party platforms, laws, and speeches. Primary sources also include any official records and statistics, such as those concerning births, marriages, deaths, taxes, deeds, and court trials. Recent history has been recorded by photographs, films, and audio- and videotapes. These recordings of events as they actually happened are also primary sources of evidence. Artifacts are another primary source. These are things made by people in the past: houses, public buildings, tools, clothing, and much more.

EXERCISE

Understanding the Types of Primary Source Evidence

Here is a self-study assignment to help you determine whether you have mastered the different types of primary source evidence.

   a. Choose an important Civil War battle.
   b. Find at least two different kinds of primary documents from the battle.
   c. Search collections in books, Civil War Web sites, your library's collections of newspaper and magazine articles from the time of the battle, or perhaps a local historical society.
   d. Compare the documents you find. Be sure that they are referring to the same event.
   e. On what points do they agree or disagree?
   f. In what ways do they differ? In the case of disagreement or significant difference, try to account for the way that the source of each document — such as a soldier's letter home and a newspaper article — helps to explain the disagreement or difference.

Secondary sources (see Figure 1.3 on p. 14) record the findings of someone who did not observe an event but investigated primary evidence of it. Most history books and articles fall into this category, although some are actually *tertiary* (third level) evidence because they rely not on primary evidence but are themselves drawn from secondary

In continental Europe, the establishment of public libraries lagged behind developments in the English-speaking countries. The European education system emphasized the preparation of young men for their life's work rather than the production of an informed citizenry. And readers were accustomed to owning books rather than borrowing them, a practice encouraged by the comparatively low price of books on the continent.

In many countries of the nineteenth-century Europe, illiteracy was high and education opportunities limited. Even in the more literate countries of western Europe, public libraries served only a small number of people. Municipal libraries were concerned with preserving the nation's literary heritage, not with accommodating the needs of the reading public. Even in those libraries founded specifically for the use of the common people, the book collections reflected the literary standards of intellectuals and cultural bureaucrats rather than the tastes of ordinary readers. Books were chosen more for the conformity to approved political or religious doctrine than for their popular appeal. Serious literature rather than entertaining fiction was the rule. Even as late as 1952 an American visitor observed that "one simply does not find mystery stories and the like in the Parisian public libraries."[47] Subscription fees were often charged, which discouraged poor families from using the public libraries.

[47] Leon Carnovsky. "The Public Libraries of Paris," *Library Quarterly* 22 (3): 194–99 (July 1952), 196.

FIGURE 1.3   Example of Secondary Evidence

This example comes from Fred Lerner, *Libraries through the Ages* (Continuum, 1999), 103–04. Lerner gathered his evidence from a few primary but mostly secondary sources. He points the reader toward these sources by including a footnote.

sources. When your own **research paper** is finished, it will be secondary or tertiary evidence to anyone who may use it in the future.

The problem of determining the reliability of evidence is a serious one. Secondary and even primary sources can be fraudulent, inaccurate, or biased. Eyewitness accounts may be purposely distorted in order to avert blame or to bestow praise on a particular individual or group. Without intending to misinform, even on-the-scene judgments can be incorrect. Sometimes, the closer you are to an event, the more emotionally involved you are, and this involvement distorts your understanding of it. We can all recall events in which we completely misunderstood the feelings, actions, and words of another person. Historians have to weigh evidence carefully to see whether those who participated in an event understood it well enough to accurately describe it, and whether later authors understood the meaning of the primary sources they used. Official statements present another problem — that of propaganda or concealment. A government, group, or institution may make statements that it wishes others to believe but that are not true. What a group says may not be what it does. This is especially true in politics.

To check the reliability of evidence, historians use the tests of consistency and corroboration: Does the evidence contradict itself, and does it disagree with evidence from other sources? Historical research always involves checking one source against another. For example, Figure 1.4 (see p. 16) presents two primary documents that report the fighting at Lexington and Concord, Massachusetts, in 1775—battles that began the Revolutionary War. In what important ways do the two accounts differ? How do you think the conflicting goals of the colonists and the English soldiers biased each report of the battle? What phrases could you pull out of each document to highlight the bias? Note that the American version talks of "some inhabitants of the colony" who while "travelling peaceably" were "seized and greatly abused" by the English soldiers. The English officer, in contrast, says that the Americans were "drawn up in military order, with arms" and that his troops were "without any intention of injuring them." You should be able to find other important differences in the two reports of the fighting. Also, as you read the documents, consider what additional sources would help you decide which report is more accurate. The two accounts agree on some facts but disagree on the responsibility for the fighting. Eyewitness accounts from other English soldiers and from American colonials who were there will help in determining which description is more accurate. It might turn out, for example, that parts of *each* account are correct and other parts are distorted in some way. Sometimes there is no *one* true source for the history of an event. Still, the more primary sources you read, the closer you will come to knowing the event in all its details and meanings.

The bias of a source also presents difficulties. People's attitudes toward the world influence the way they interpret events. For example, you and your parents may have different attitudes toward music, sex, religion, or politics. These differences can cause you to disagree with them about the value of a rock concert, a Sunday sermon, or the president. Historians have their own attitudes toward the subjects they are investigating, and these cause them to draw different conclusions about the character and importance of religious, political, intellectual, and other movements. Later historians must take these biases into account when weighing the reliability of the primary and secondary evidence.

Interpreting and Organizing Evidence

In analyzing evidence, historians must find some way of *organizing* it so that they can make clear its meaning. A mass of facts and opinions concerning a subject is not a historical study. The task of the historian is to arrange the material so that it supports a particular conclusion. This conclusion may have been partly formed in the historian's mind at the outset, or it might be the result of investigation. If the evidence does not

By the clearest depositions relative to this transaction, it will appear that on the night preceding the nineteenth of April instant, a body of the king's troops, under the command of colonel Smith, were secretly landed at Cambridge, with an apparent design to take or destroy the military and other stores, provided for the defence of this colony, and deposited at Concord — that some inhabitants of the colony, on the night aforesaid, whilst travelling peaceably on the road, between Boston and Concord, were seized and greatly abused by armed men, who appeared to be officers of general Gage's army; that the town of Lexington, by these means, was alarmed, and a company of the inhabitants mustered on the occasion — that the regular troops on their way to Concord, marched into the said town of Lexington, and the said company, on their approach, began to disperse — that, notwithstanding this, the regulars rushed on with great violence and first began hostilities, by firing on said Lexington company, whereby they killed eight, and wounded several others — that the regulars continued their fire, until those of said company, who were neither killed nor wounded, had made their escape — that colonel Smith, with the detachment then marched to Concord, where a number of provincials were again fired on by the troops, two of them killed and several wounded, before the provincials fired on them, and provincials were again fired on by the troops, produced an engagement that lasted through the day, in which many of the provincials and more of the regular troops were killed and wounded. . . .

By order,
Joseph Warren, President.

I think it proper to observe, that when I had got some miles on the march from Boston, I detached six light infantry companies to march with all expedition to seize the two bridges on different roads beyond Concord. On these companies' arrival at Lexington, I understand, from the report of Major Pitcairn, who was with them, and from many officers, that they found on a green close to the road a body of the country people drawn up in military order, with arms and accoutrements, and, as appeared after, loaded; and that they had posted some men in a dwelling and Meeting-house. Our troops advanced towards them, without any intention of injuring them, further than to inquire the reason of their being thus assembled, and, if not satisfactory, to have secured their arms; but they in confusion went off, principally to the left, only one of them fired before he went off, and three or four more jumped over a wall and fired from behind it among the soldiers; on which the troops returned it, and killed several of them. They likewise fired on the soldiers from the Meeting and dwelling-houses. . . . While at Concord we saw vast numbers assembling in many parts; at one of the bridges they marched down, with a very considerable body, on the light infantry posted there. On their coming pretty near, one of our men fired on them, which they returned; on which an action ensued, and some few were killed and wounded. . . . On our leaving Concord to return to Boston, they began to fire on us from behind the walls, ditches, trees, &c., which, as we marched, increased to a very great degree, and continued without intermission of five minutes altogether, for, I believe, upwards of eighteen miles . . .

I have the honor, &c.,
F. Smith, Lieutenant-Colonel 10th Foot.

FIGURE 1.4   Two Conflicting Primary Documents

appear to support the conclusion, however, then the historian must either change that conclusion or seek other evidence to support it.

Once a historian is satisfied that research has uncovered sufficient evidence to support a particular conclusion, then he or she works to display the evidence in a manner that will clearly show that the conclusion drawn is a proper one. If any evidence that leads to other conclusions is uncovered, the historian has a responsibility to include it. In doing so, he or she must show how the supporting evidence is stronger than the nonsupporting evidence. There are many ways of organizing evidence in support of a conclusion. The historian's arguments in favor of a particular conclusion must be strong and convincing, and the logic of these arguments must not be faulty.

You will confront the issue faced by all historians when you conduct your own historical research, an assignment that is part of all advanced (and some beginning) history courses. (See Chapters 4 and 5 for advice on researching and writing such an assignment.)

The Computer and Historical Research

The computer is an important tool for gathering historical information across the discipline, not just in quantitative history. Historians use computers not only to analyze data but also to gain easier access to sources of historical information. Unpublished information residing in **archives** around the world can be made available online to historians and students with access to computers that are part of a network like the **World Wide Web.** Primary sources that have been entered into electronic **databases** can be read (and even printed out) by researchers anywhere. Secondary sources that are available only in special libraries can be read in this way also if they have been put into computer-readable form. History databases containing millions of individual historical statistics are available in many college libraries. The texts of documents, articles, and, in some cases, whole books can be brought to your computer screen. With Web **plug-ins,** researchers can gain access to art, maps, photographs, recordings, and even films that once resided only in faraway archives. (For more information on using computers in your own research, see pp. 93–103 and 212–31.)

How You Can Use History

Experience is said to be the best teacher. Still, our learning would be very narrow if we profited only from our own experiences. Through the study of history, we make other people's experiences our own. In this way, we touch other times and places and add to our lifetime's knowledge the knowledge gained by others.

If history is the greatest teacher, what can we do with the knowledge we draw from it? In what practical ways does knowledge of the past help us to accomplish the work we do today or will do tomorrow? History is not merely a course you take in college; it is a way of thinking about the present, one that attempts to make sense of the complexity of contemporary events by examining what lies behind them. Such an examination is intellectual (its goal is to broaden understanding in general), but it can be practical as well.

There are any number of jobs in which the tools of the historian are directly employed. You yourself could teach history at the secondary or college level. You could work in the archives of a library, museum, historical site, or large corporation with a record-keeping department. Labor unions have staffs of historians that research the history of important unions. The field of public history is a very large one, and you could be hired to the research staff of the U.S. government's National Archives and Records Administration, the Library of Congress, or any of the Cabinet departments or U.S. intelligence agencies. There are even more opportunities at the state, county, and local levels. For example, you could work for a local or county historical society. You might do archaeological research at the site of an ancient Indian village or a Civil War battlefield, or you might organize the nineteenth-century records of a great natural disaster or of a major exhibition of farm or industrial machinery. You could be hired to construct a family history from the photographs, diaries, and letters of one of the founding families of a town. Every step back in time calls on the skills of a historian.

When you learn how to read history, how to research the past, and how to write a summary of your findings, you are mastering career skills as surely as if you were taking a course in real-estate law or restaurant management. The ability to see the present in relationship to the past is a skill needed not only by academic, private, and public historians, archivists, historical novelists, and documentary producers; it is an essential preparation for almost any career. Understanding the past can be its own reward, but it pays off in other ways as well. In fact, people who think that history is irrelevant run the risk of history making that judgment of them.

How to Read
a History Assignment,
Take Notes in Class, and
Prepare for and
Take Exams

How to Read a History Assignment

Reading history can be a satisfying experience, but to enjoy the landscape you must first know where you are—you must have a general sense of the subject and of the manner in which it is being presented. If you begin reading before you get your bearings, you may become lost in a forest of unfamiliar facts and interpretations. Before beginning any reading assignment, look over the entire book. Read the preface or introduction. This should tell you something about the author and his or her purpose in writing the work. Then read the table of contents to get a sense of the way in which the author organized the subject. Next, skim the chapters themselves, reading subheadings and glancing at illustrations and graphed material. If you have the time, preread sections of the book (especially the introductory and concluding chapters) rapidly before reading the full work.

After scouting the ground, you will be ready to read. By this time, you should be familiar with the topic of the book (what aspects of history it covers), the background of the author (politician, journalist, historian, eyewitness, novelist, etc.), when the book was written (a hundred-year-old classic, the most recent book on the subject, etc.), how it is organized (chronologically, topically, etc.), and, most important of all, its **thesis** and conclusions. The thesis is the principal point that an author wishes to make on a subject: that the geography of Spain was a significant factor in that nation's failure to industrialize in the eighteenth and nineteenth centuries; that disagreement on moral issues between J. Robert Oppenheimer and Edward Teller delayed development of the hydrogen bomb. Most authors set out their thesis in a preface or introduction. If you understand the principal point the author is trying to make, then the organization and conclusions of the work will become clear to you. The author will be organizing evidence and drawing conclusions to support the thesis. The ability to recognize and describe a weak thesis or unsupportive evidence is part of learning history too. (For a discussion of the difference between a **theme** and a thesis, see Chapter 4, pp. 79–83.)

Reading a Textbook

The most common history assignment is the reading of a **textbook.** Many students hope to get by with their lecture notes, and they put off reading the textbook until right before the final exam. Reading the textbook week by week will give you the background knowledge necessary to understand the lectures and supplementary readings. In most courses the lectures embellish portions of the textbook, and lecturers assume that students are familiar with the textbook coverage. Sitting through a lecture on the economic aspects of the American Revolution may be confusing if you have not read the textbook discussion of the mercantilist theories behind many of the colonists' grievances.

Read textbook chapters in close conjunction with the lectures to which they are related. If particular passages are unclear, you might benefit from rereading the material. Underline or highlight the most prominent factual information. Also underline important generalizations, interpretations, and conclusions. In addition to underlining, look for passages emphasized by the author or passages that you feel reflect the author's viewpoint or with which you disagree, and write your reaction or a summary of these passages in the margin. All of this will come in handy when you prepare to take a test: you will be able to reread the underlined material and your comments and obtain a quick review of the chapter's contents. Before the final exam, however, you may want to reread the textbook itself. Figure 2.1 on p. 21 shows an underlined and annotated textbook page.

Reading a Monograph

Another typical reading assignment is a **monograph**—a specialized history work on a particular subject. In addition to the procedures used in reading a textbook, you will want to pay special attention to the theme and point of view of monographs because your teacher may expect you to learn not only about the subject they deal with but also about the emphasis and methods of the work. Therefore, you will need to determine the author's assumptions and values, and to understand the book's theme and conclusions. Read this kind of work not only to absorb the facts but also to analyze, question, and criticize. If you own

Civilizations in Sub-Saharan Africa

Leader of empire of Mali — Mansa Musa (1312–1337)

Under <u>Mansa Musa (1312–1337) Mali's authority</u> reached into the middle Niger city-states of Timbuktu, Djenné, and Gao. He put Mali on the European world maps by performing a stunning gold-laden pilgrimage to Mecca, Islam's spiritual capital in the Middle East. Upon returning, <u>Mansa Musa fostered the growth of Islam</u> by constructing magnificent mosques in the major urban centers. With his seemingly inexhaustible supply of gold he com-

Growing influence of Islam

missioned Spanish and Middle Eastern scholars and architects to <u>transform Malian cities into great seats of Islamic learning.</u> Leading intellectuals were sent to Morocco and Egypt for higher studies, and at Timbuktu foundations were laid for a university at the famous Sankoré mosque. For decades after Musa, Mali enjoyed a reputation in the Muslim world for <u>high standards of public morality and scholarship</u> as well as for law, order, and security. People and goods flowed freely, enabling the <u>cosmopolitan cities of Timbuktu, Djenné, and Gao to flower into major market centers.</u> Through the leadership of Sungata and Mansa Musa Islam became more deeply implanted among the elite and spread widely in the important towns.

While Mansa Musa made great advances in establishing an efficient administrative bureaucracy, he neglected to develop a for-

Leader of empire of Songhay — Sunni Ali (1464–1492)

mula for succession. <u>Court intrigue and factional disputes</u> followed the death of each Mansa. Inevitably, central authority weakened. <u>Gao seceded in 1375 and under Sunni Ali (1464–1492)</u> it blossomed into an expansive territorial <u>empire called Songhay.</u>

Important point

As in Muslim India, it was <u>not uncommon for slaves in Africa to assume considerable administrative and military reponsibilities</u> and on occasion usurp authority. This happened in Songhay in 1493 when a high-ranking Muslim slave, named Muhammad Touré, staged a brilliant palace coup. Lacking traditional legitimacy rooted in a pagan past, he promoted Islamic practices and found Islam an invaluable instrument for political and cultural

Expansion of Songhay under "Askia" Muhammad Touré (1493–1528)

control. Using the praise title of <u>"Askia," Muhammad Touré (1493–1528) extended Songhay's frontiers</u> deep into the strategic Saharan oases, across the Middle Niger to include Mali, and eastward to the emporiums of Hausaland. He then created a labyrinthine bureaucracy of ministries for the army, navy, fisheries, forests, and taxation. Songhay itself was <u>decentralized into provinces, each ruled by a governor</u> chosen from among the Askia's family or royal followers.

FIGURE 2.1 Example of an Underlined and Annotated Textbook Page
This example is from Edward McNall Burns et al., *World Civilizations,* 9th ed. (New York: W. W. Norton, 1997), 605–06.

the book, you can again do your questioning and criticizing in the margins. If the book is not yours, or if you wish to have an organized set of notes about it, summarize the contents and the author's theme on index cards or on a computer file. You can then review your underlinings or index cards before the exam. (For more on taking notes, see pp. 37–43.)

Reading an Anthology

Some courses also include an anthology—a book of readings, usually short excerpts from larger works or from **primary documents** that deal with a single subject. All of the suggestions concerning the reading of textbooks and monographs apply here as well, but this type of assignment often calls for a particular kind of reading. Each selection usually discusses a different aspect or interpretation of the subject, and some pieces are likely to be in serious disagreement. Teachers expect students to be able to assess the arguments of the various authors and on occasion to take a position in the debate. Therefore, you should read this particular kind of book with an eye to analyzing the arguments of the different authors or to comparing their different approaches to the subject. A good way to do this is to summarize briefly the argument or approach of each selection.

Reading a Historical Novel

A **historical novel** is a work of fiction based on actual occurrences and people. It is often more dramatic and more personal than a textbook or monograph and describes the feelings of those caught up in important historical events. Reading a historical novel gives you a feel for the times in which it is set and for the historical material it contains, but be cautious not to treat the text as historical truth. Nevertheless, a novelist who knows a historical period or event well can bring it to life in ways that scholarly works cannot.

Examples of Reading Assignments

To help you appreciate the differences among the four types of reading assignments, here are passages from each. The subject is the policy of the United States toward the Greek civil war of the late 1940s. As you read these passages, note the different manner in which each deals with this subject.

TEXTBOOK   The day before, 6 March, Truman had begun to prepare the ground. In a speech at Baylor University in Texas he explained that freedom was more important than peace and that freedom of worship and speech were dependent on freedom of enterprise. . . .

HOW TO READ A HISTORY ASSIGNMENT **23**

The State Department, meanwhile, was preparing a message for Truman to deliver to the full Congress. He was unhappy with the early drafts, for "I wanted no hedging in this speech. This was America's answer to the surge of expansion of Communist tyranny. It had to be clear and free of hesitation or double talk." Truman told Acheson to have the speech toughened, simplified, and expanded to cover more than just Greece and Turkey. He then made further revisions in the draft. . . .

At 1 P.M. on 12 March 1947, Truman stepped to the rostrum in the hall of the House of Representatives to address the joint session of the Congress. The speech was also carried on nationwide radio. He asked for immediate aid for Greece and Turkey, then explained the reasoning. "I believe that it must be the policy of the United States to support free peoples who are resisting attempted subjugation by armed minorities or by outside pressures."

The statement was all-encompassing. In a single sentence, Truman had defined American policy for the next twenty years. Whenever and wherever an anti-Communist government was threatened, by indigenous insurgents, foreign invasion, or even diplomatic pressure (as with Turkey), the United States would supply political, economic, and most of all, military aid. The Truman Doctrine came close to shutting the door against any revolution, since the terms "free peoples" and "anti-Communist" were assumed to be synonymous. All the Greek government, or any dictatorship, had to do to get American aid was to claim that its opponents were Communists. And the aid would be unilateral, as Truman never mentioned the United Nations, whose commission to investigate what was actually happening in Greece had not completed its study or made a report.

—From Stephen E. Ambrose, *Rise to Globalism: American Foreign Policy Since 1938* (New York: Penguin, 1971), 148, 150.

MONOGRAPH   What was really on the mind of the president and his advisers was stated less in the Truman Doctrine speech than in private memos and in Truman's March 6 address at Baylor University. Dealing with the world economic structure, the president attacked state-regulated trade, tariffs, and exchange controls—". . . the direction in which much of the world is headed at the present time." "If this trend is not reversed," he warned, ". . . the United States will be under pressure, sooner or later, to use these same devices in the fight for markets and for raw materials. . . . It is not the American way. It is not the way to peace."[16] . . .

The question of how best to sell the new crusade perplexed the administration, not the least because Greece was a paltry excuse for a vast undertaking of which it "was only a beginning," and in the end it formulated diverse reasons as the need required.[18] The many drafts that were drawn up before the final Truman Doctrine speech was delivered to Congress on March 12 are interesting in that they reveal more accurately than the speech itself the true concerns of Washington. Members of the cabinet

---

[16] DSB, March 16, 1947, 484. See also Acheson, *Present at the Creation*, 219; Jones, *Fifteen Weeks*, 139–42. . . .

[18] Acheson, *Present at the Creation*, 221.

and other top officials who considered the matter before the twelfth understood very clearly that the United States was now defining a strategy and budget appropriate to its new global commitments—interests that the collapse of British power had made even more exclusively American—and that far greater involvement in other countries was now pending, at least on the economic level.

Quite apart from the belligerent tone of the drafts were the references to ". . . a world-wide trend away from the system of free enterprise toward state-controlled economies," which the State Department's speech writers thought "gravely threatened" American interests. No less significant was the mention of the "great natural resources" of the Middle East at stake.

—From Joyce and Gabriel Kolko, *The Limits of Power: The World and United States Foreign Policy, 1945–1954* (New York: Harper & Row, 1972), 341.

ANTHOLOGY (EXCERPT FROM SPEECH)   The United States has received from the Greek government an urgent appeal for financial and economic assistance. Preliminary reports from the American Economic Mission now in Greece and reports from the American Ambassador in Greece corroborate the statement of the Greek Government that assistance is imperative if Greece is to survive as a free nation. . . .

At the present moment in world history nearly every nation must choose between alternative ways of life. The choice is too often not a free one.

One way of life is based upon the will of the majority, and is distinguished by free institutions, representative government, free elections, guarantees of individual liberty, freedom of speech and religion, and freedom from political oppression.

The second way of life is based upon the will of a minority forcibly imposed upon the majority. It relies upon terror and oppression, a controlled press and radio, fixed elections, and the suppression of personal freedoms.

I believe that it must be the policy of the United States to support free peoples who are resisting attempted subjugation by armed minorities or by outside pressures. . . .

It is necessary only to glance at a map to realize that the survival and integrity of the Greek nation are of grave importance in a much wider situation. If Greece should fall under the control of an armed minority, the effect upon its neighbor, Turkey, would be immediate and serious. Confusion and disorder might well spread throughout the entire Middle East.

Moreover, the disappearance of Greece as an independent state would have a profound effect upon those countries in Europe whose peoples are struggling against great difficulties to maintain their freedoms and their independence while they repair the damages of war. . . .

The free peoples of the world look to us for support in maintaining their freedoms.

If we falter in our leadership, we may endanger the peace of the world—and we shall surely endanger the welfare of this Nation.

Great responsibilities have been placed upon us by the swift movement of events.

I am confident that the Congress will face these responsibilities squarely.

—From an address delivered by President Harry Truman before a joint session of Congress on March 12, 1947. Reprinted from Thomas G. Paterson, *Major Problems in American Foreign Policy*, 4th ed. (Lexington: D. C. Heath, 1995), 2:259–61.

HISTORICAL NOVEL   Tzelekis was right: now it was 1949, and war was beautifully organized—things were done in an orderly fashion. Various specialists had come in, trained in "wars of movement": The British, the Americans, with a good deal of experience in such matters. They put things in their places, taught enemies and friends to recognize each other—you over here, them over there. Work with a system, no fooling around! Back in '46, you see, everything was topsy-turvy. The army was an indiscriminate herd, no organization whatever; everyone did as he pleased, everything pell-mell, all mixed up together slaughtering: EAM-ites, EDES-ites, X-ites—you didn't know who was your enemy and who your friend. At night they sent out patrols—in the morning they came back in company with the others and cut up their captains. Other times when they fought at night with knives and bayonets it was like mother losing child and child losing mother: same clothes (all the rags of the world resemble each other), same appearance— you came face to face with the enemy, you went at him with a dagger to rip out his guts, and you saw—if you had time—that he was one of your own men, so you let him go and went for the one beside him. And don't forget, what mixed things up even worse was the language; since they were all spouting Greek, who could tell them apart? . . .

Later when foreign aid began to arrive, the army got new uniforms, munitions, wireless transmitters, codes of recognition. Things were put in order, names were given to the enemy, and the radio blared them out every day, they were written on the walls and in the newspapers; and finally, for the first time in their history, the Greeks began to kill each other systematically. The solution was a very simple one; and a considerable number of people couldn't understand why they had not thought of it before.

—From Aris Fakinos, *The Marked Men* (New York: Liveright, 1971), 92–93.

Note that the textbook is general in its coverage. It does not use footnotes or quote from primary sources other than Truman's speech. It tries to summarize the content and meaning of the event without too much detail and without extensive proof for its conclusions. The monograph, in contrast, covers a small portion of the topic, gives more detail, quotes from primary materials, and uses footnotes to record its sources of information. The selection from the anthology is a primary source— the Truman speech itself. The section from the historical novel is very different from the first three passages. The author gives us the imaginary thoughts of some of the soldiers who fought in the Greek civil war, far away from the formulation of foreign policy in Washington.

No matter what kind of reading assignment you may be given, the goal is to understand the author's meaning and to relate that understanding to the content of the course.

How to "Read" Nonwritten Materials

Interpreting Maps

History is often displayed on maps. The landscape is one of history's fundamental settings. The rise and fall of empires, the course of wars, the growth of cities, the development of trade routes, and much more can be traced on maps of large areas. Figure 2.2 indicates the years in

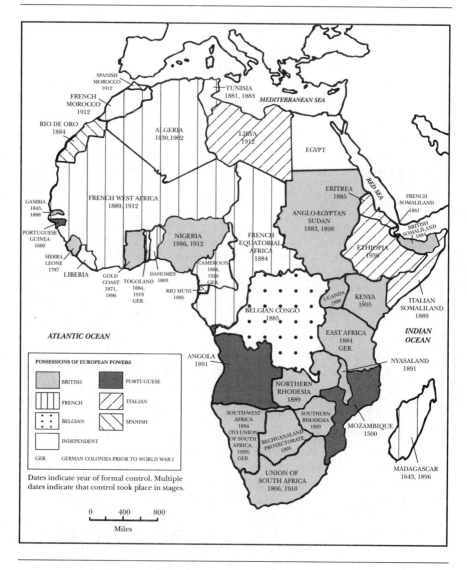

FIGURE 2.2   The March of Colonialism in Africa

which parts of Africa came under European colonial rule. This map tells you which European countries controlled which parts of Africa and when this control was established. Analyzing the map, you can see that Britain and France had the largest colonial empires in Africa and that most of Africa was free of colonial rule before the 1880s. Figure 2.3 indicates the dates on which the nations of Africa became independent. By comparing this map with Figure 2.2, you can determine which countries changed their names upon achieving independence.

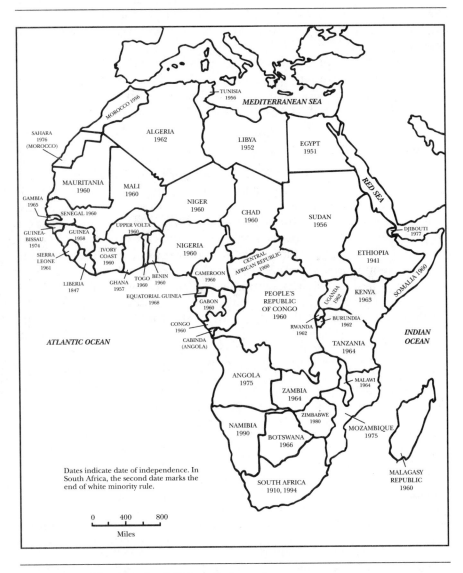

FIGURE 2.3   The March of African Independence

Comparing the dates on the two maps, you can figure out how long colonial rule lasted in different countries. Note also that the first wave of independence came in the 1960s and that the date for Namibian independence is 1990—just over a decade ago.

Small area maps can show the layout of villages, the outcome of battles, or the location of mines, canals, and railroads. To read a map, you must understand the *key*, which translates the symbols used on the map. A line on a map may be a road, a river, or a gas pipeline. The key tells you which it is. The *scale* of a map tells you the actual size of the area the map represents. Maps are an important aid in understanding history because they display the physical relationship between places. Never ignore maps in a textbook or other reading. It is also wise to put a good map of the area you are studying near your desk so that you can see the location of places mentioned in lectures and readings.

Old maps are primary documents. The way that old maps describe the territories they cover can give you clues as to what was going on in the mind of the mapmaker when the map was created.

Analyzing Statistical Data

In addition to maps, works in history often include statistical data arranged in **charts, graphs,** or **tables.** These data describe the amounts of something (such as warships, marriages, schools, bridges, or deaths from smallpox) at a specific time in the past, and usually they compare these amounts (such as the number of marriages in relation to the number of schools) or trace changes in amounts over time (such as the number of warships in 1820, 1830, and 1840). Figure 2.4 shows a tabular arrangement of statistical data with an explanation of how to read them. The table organizes population statistics from different regions of the earth and across more than three hundred years. Reading across the

	1650	1750	1850	1900	1950	1980	1996
Europe	100	140	265	400	570	730	800
United States and Canada	2	2	25	80	165	252	295
Latin America	12	10	35	65	165	362	489
Africa	100	95	95	120	220	470	732
Asia	330	480	750	940	1370	2600	3430

FIGURE 2.4   Estimated World Population

Numbers represent millions of persons. These are rough estimates only. The figures for 1650 and 1750 in particular come from a time before it was common to conduct a periodic count (*census*) of populations. There is great debate about the size of the native populations of the Western Hemisphere before 1850. (The figure is adapted from L. S. Stavrianos, *The World since 1500: A Global History,* 4th ed. [Englewood Cliffs, N.J.: Prentice-Hall, 1982], 181.)

lines allows you to trace the changes in population of a particular region (Europe, Africa, Asia) over time. By doing so, you can follow the population of each region at hundred-year intervals (the population of Latin America in 1650, 1750, 1850, and 1950). You can note the change for each region and the rate of change. For example, the population of the United States and Canada did not increase in the hundred years between 1650 and 1750, but it more than doubled in the fifty years between 1900 and 1950. Reading down the table, you can examine the population of each region during the same period. This allows you to compare the populations of the different regions. In 1650 the populations of Europe and Africa were the same, but in 1950 the European population was more than two-and-one-half times that of Africa.

More complex comparisons can be made from Figure 2.4 by combining the differences between regions (reading down) and their rates of growth over time (reading across). For example, you can discover that whereas the population of Asia grew more than that of any other region in absolute terms, its *rate* of growth from 1850 to 1980 (750 million to 2600 million, or about 350 percent) was much less than that of Latin America (35 million to 362 million, or around 1,000 percent).

Even the cold statistics of a table can provide images of the great drama of history. The decrease in African population between 1650 and 1850 may tell us something of the impact of the slave trade, and the decrease in population in Latin America between 1650 and 1750 hints at the toll taken among Native Americans by the introduction of European diseases. The large increase in the U.S. population between 1850 and 1900 tells us something about the history of European emigration.

The information in the table can be presented differently in order to highlight different aspects of the data. In Figure 2.5, the numbers for each region are represented as percentages of the total world population. By changing the numbers from absolute amounts to percentages, the new table facilitates the comparing of populations and population growth.

	1650	1750	1850	1900	1950	1980	1996
Europe	18.4	19.3	22.8	25.0	23.2	16.5	13.9
United States and Canada	0.2	0.1	2.3	5.1	6.7	5.7	5.1
Latin America	2.2	1.5	2.8	3.9	6.3	8.2	8.5
Africa	18.4	13.2	8.1	7.4	8.8	10.6	12.7
Asia	60.8	65.9	64.0	58.6	55.0	58.9	59.7

FIGURE 2.5   Estimated World Population
Numbers represent percentages. (The figure is adapted from L. S. Stavrianos, *The World since 1500: A Global History,* 4th ed. [Englewood Cliffs, N.J.: Prentice-Hall, 1982], 181.)

Another way of presenting these population data is in the form of a graph. Note that Figure 2.6 makes more obvious the differences between numbers and thus makes comparisons easier. However, ease of comparison is traded for a loss in precision; the graph gives less specific numbers (reading along the vertical axis) than the table. A graph also often requires more space than a table to convey the same information. If Figure 2.6 included all of the time periods of the table, it would be very large.

The more detailed the data and their arrangement are, the more historical information that can be displayed and the more intricate the comparisons that can be made. Figure 2.7 (p. 31) presents a table that lists the percentage of the total vote and the number of deputies elected to the German parliament (the Reichstag) by each of the major political parties in each election from 1919 to 1933. (Note that in a parliamentary system, elections do not come at regular intervals.)

This table allows you to follow the changing fortunes of each political party. A wealth of information on German political history is contained in these figures. Between the lines one can also find pieces of the social and economic history of Germany. To choose only two examples, the strength of the Communist and Social Democratic (Socialist) parties attests to the deep dissatisfaction of many German workers with the state of the economy during the period known as the Weimar

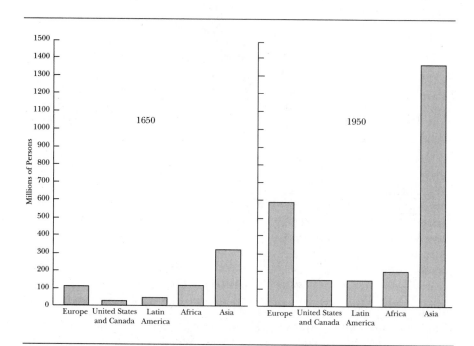

FIGURE 2.6   Estimated World Population

Republic. Even more striking is the tremendous growth of the National Socialist (Nazi) Party after 1930. This development brought Adolf Hitler to power in 1933, and the results of that event would eventually reverberate around the world. As you can see, a table is more than just numbers.

Interpreting Illustrations, Photographs, and Other Visual Material

Visual material can also present historical information. However, gathering information from old paintings, drawings, photographs, and films can be more difficult than it may seem. First, you need to

Party	1919	1920	1924	1928	1930	1932	1933
Communist							
# of deputies	0	4	45	54	77	89	81
% of total votes		2.1	9.0	10.6	13.1	14.6	12.3
Social Democratic							
# of deputies	165	102	131	153	143	133	120
% of total votes	37.9	21.6	26.0	29.8	24.5	21.6	18.3
Democratic							
# of deputies	75	39	32	25	20	4	5
% of total votes	18.6	8.3	6.3	4.9	3.8	1.0	.8
Centrum							
# of deputies	91	64	69	62	68	75	74
% of total votes	19.7	13.6	13.6	12.1	11.8	12.5	11.7
Bavarian People's							
# of deputies	0	21	19	16	19	22	18
% of total votes		4.4	3.7	3.0	3.0	3.2	2.7
German People's							
# of deputies	19	65	51	45	30	7	2
% of total votes	4.4	13.9	10.1	8.7	4.5	1.2	1.1
National People's							
# of deputies	44	71	103	73	41	37	52
% of total votes	10.3	14.9	20.5	14.2	7.0	5.9	8.0
National Socialist							
# of deputies	0	0	14	12	107	230	288
% of total votes			3.0	2.6	18.3	37.4	43.9

FIGURE 2.7   Reichstag Elections, 1919–1933
Under the electoral system provided for in the Weimar Constitution, each party received approximately one representative for every sixty thousand popular votes cast for its candidates. Various small parties, not listed here, were underrepresented in the Reichstag. (From L. S. Stavrianos, *The World since 1500: A Global History,* 4th ed. [Englewood Cliffs, N.J.: Prentice-Hall, 1982], 419.)

recognize the actual information that they present—what Columbus's ships looked like, how Hiroshima appeared after the explosion of the atomic bomb, and so on. Then you need to interpret them. This involves an effort to understand what the artist or photographer was "saying" in the work. When an artist draws something and when a photographer takes a picture, he or she is not simply recording a visual image but is sending a message to anyone who looks at the work. In this way, artists and photographers are like writers whose written work needs to be interpreted.

Figures 2.8 and 2.9 present two illustrations of the Spanish conquest of Mexico. Look at them and see whether you can detect what they are saying.

Figure 2.8 is by a European artist and shows Hernán Cortés, who conquered Mexico for Spain, being offered young Indian women by a coastal tribe. The Indians seem happy to greet the Spaniards. Figure 2.9 was drawn by an Aztec Indian and shows Cortés's soldiers (having fought their way from the coast to the Aztec capital) massacring Indians in their main temple. Not all drawings have such obvious (and opposite) messages: the Spanish as friends of the Indians and the Spanish as murderers of the Indians. The interpretation of some visual material

FIGURE 2.8 Indian Offerings to Cortés
Courtesy of the Bancroft Library, University of California, Berkeley.

FIGURE 2.9   Massacre of the Aztec Indians
From *The Broken Spears* by Miguel Leon-Portilla. Copyright © 1962, 1990 by
Miguel Leon-Portilla. Expanded and Updated Edition © 1992 by Miguel Leon-
Portilla. Reprinted by permission of Beacon Press, Boston.

requires knowledge about the subject matter, the artist, the style, and the context in which it appeared. Like written descriptions of past events, art does not simply "speak for itself."

Now look at Figure 2.10, a photograph of a clash in 1968 between Chicago police and demonstrators opposing the war in Vietnam. Like the illustrations in Figures 2.8 and 2.9, it too has information. Even a casual glance shows confusion and violence. Examining it closely, you can see the kinds of weapons used by the police and the facial expressions of some of the demonstrators. The more difficult part, again, is interpreting the photograph. Is this a scene of provocation by lawless demonstrators or an attack by the police? A careful look at the picture may help you answer this question. In any case, you need more evidence. While an unaltered photograph does show something that actually happened, another photograph—even one of the same event— might show something very different. In most cases, the person taking the photograph has made an effort to say something, and you need to take this motive into account, as well.

Not all pictures have controversial interpretations. Figure 2.11 on page 35 is a photograph of a city street in Ithaca, New York, in the 1890s. There is a wealth of information here about nineteenth-century town

FIGURE 2.10   Antiwar Demonstration at the 1968 Democratic National Convention in Chicago
Copyright © Bettmann/Corbis.

life. Note that at this early date, the town already had electric trolleys. Note also that the horses are not pulling wagons or carriages ("buggies," as they were called) but sleighs ("cutters"). This simple fact opens up a window to farm life in winter. When roads were covered with snow and ice, the flat, smooth wheels of wagons could not navigate, but the sharp runners of the cutter dug into the ice and gave it stability.

Interpreting Artifacts

An **artifact** is a physical object from the past: a radio from the 1920s; a rifle from the U.S. Civil War; the ruins of a fourteenth-century church in Paris; a 10,000-year-old arrowhead. If you have the opportunity to

FIGURE 2.11   Town Life in Ithaca, New York, during the 1890s
Courtesy of the DeWitt Historical Society of Tompkins County, Ithaca, New York, General Photo Collection.

examine an artifact in a museum or in an attic or under the foundations of an old building, do so carefully. Try to figure out how old it is and how it might have been used. (In a museum this is done for you.) Suppose you find a heavy metal object half buried in the floor of an old wooden building. First, look around the building for clues to the age and purpose of the object. If you are lucky, you may find broken bricks on the floor. If you dig down, you may find a layer of ash. Where the old wooden walls are still intact, you may find bent or broken horseshoes nailed into the beams. A few more clues, such as hammers and other tools and a stone hitching post outside the door (for tying up horses securely), may lead you to guess that you are in the ruins of a blacksmith's shop. The heavy metal object you found is an anvil.

A blacksmith was someone who heated bars of iron and hammered them into horseshoes and other useful objects. A blacksmith used many tools to flatten, round off, bend, or work the hot metal, but his principal tool was the anvil—a block of iron or steel on which he shaped the metal. Figure 2.12 shows a nineteenth-century anvil. On this flat surface the blacksmith thinned out the heated bar of metal by pounding it with special hammers. The tapered, rounded end on the right was used to bend the thinned metal to the desired shape.

After you identify the object you found, the next step is to place it in its proper historical context—in this case, a nineteenth-century black-

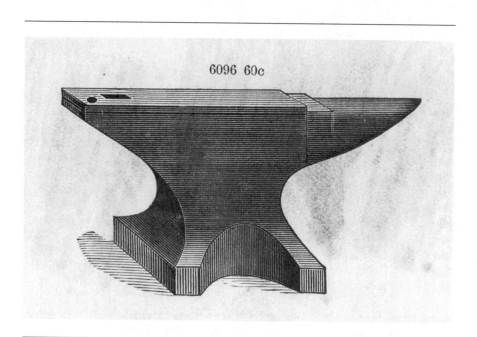

6096 60c

FIGURE 2.12 A Blacksmith's Anvil
Copyright © Bettmann/Corbis.

smith's shop. If you wish to delve deeper, you can read about the work of blacksmiths, the many kinds of objects they made, and how their work with metal contributed to the village economy.

Nonwritten materials are as vital to historians and history students as are written records. As our methods of creating and preserving visual images increase, more and more of our historical records take the form of pictures. Students need to learn to interpret these new kinds of evidence.

How to Take Notes in Class

Your time in class is vital to your learning. True, you can learn on your own outside of class, but the interaction with your instructor and other students is most intense during class time. Learning to record that interaction in your notes is an important skill.

From Class Lectures

The first rule of note taking is simple: pay attention. Learn to concentrate on what is being said. Read assigned texts before going to class so you won't end up taking notes on the material in the book. If everything the instructor says is new to you, you will spend so much time writing that you may not be able to grasp the theme of the lecture. If you have obtained some basic information from outside readings, however, you will be able to concentrate on noting points in the lecture that are new or different.

An instructor is most likely to prepare exam questions from the material that he or she considers most important. It is therefore essential in preparing notes to determine which points in the lecture are given most prominent attention. Some instructors are very open about their preferences and clearly emphasize certain points, often writing them on the blackboard. Never fail to note something that the instructor indicates is important. Other instructors are less explicit about their biases and values, and you will have to try to figure them out. Listen closely, and make note of interpretations and generalizations that seem to be stressed, especially when they differ from the approach in the textbook. You should not feel obliged to parrot your instructor's interpretations in an exam, but ignorance of them could work against you.

Your notes should be written legibly and begin with the date and subject of the lecture. They should reflect a general outline of the material covered, with emphasis on major interpretations and important facts not covered in the textbook. It is often best to write on every other line or to leave a large margin on at least one side of the page.

This will allow you to add material later and to underline your notes and write additional comments without cluttering the page.

If possible, reread your notes later in the day on which they were written. If your handwriting is poor or your notes are disorganized, it is best to rewrite them. Check the spelling and definitions of any unfamiliar words, and be sure that your notes are coherent. Remember, your notes are an important source of information in your studies.

The following guidelines summarize this advice.

Guidelines for Taking Lecture Notes

1. Prepare for a lecture by reading all related course materials ahead of time.
2. Write the course information, lecture subject, and date at the top of each page of notes.
3. Be selective—don't try to write everything a lecturer says.
4. Be sure to write anything that the instructor (a) puts on the board; (b) says is important; (c) emphasizes as he or she speaks.
5. Leave room in your notes to add material later if necessary.
6. Reread your notes later in the day on which they were written.
7. Underline especially important points.
8. Look up the meaning of any unfamiliar words.
9. Rewrite any parts of your notes that are poorly organized.
10. If something important in your notes is unclear to you, ask your instructor about it.

Examples of Note Taking

To illustrate some of the essentials of good note taking, here are portions of two sets of class notes taken from the same lecture. The first example illustrates many of the common errors of note takers, whereas the second example is a well-written set of notes. The subject of the lecture was early European contact with Africa.

POOR NOTE TAKING

Colonization of Africa—People were afraid to sail out. Afraid of sea monsters. But they liked the stories about gold in Africa. The Portuguese King Henry sailed south to find the gold mines and built a fort at Elmina.

England and France want to trade with Africa. They begin trading. Competing with Portugal. These countries got into wars. They wanted to control Africa.

China had spices. They traded with Cairo and Venice. The Asians wanted gold, but the Islams stopped all trade. They fought wars about religion for hundreds of years. Fought over Jerusalem. The Pope called for a crusade. This was in the Middle Ages.

Spices came from Asia. In Europe they were valuable because the kings used them to become rich. They also ate them.

The Portuguese wanted to explore Africa and make a way to India. Their boats couldn't get around until Bartholomew Diaz discovered the Cape of Good Hope in 1487.

Most of all, the Portuguese wanted slaves. They shipped them back from Africa. Columbus took them after he discovered America (1492). The Pope made a line in the Atlantic Ocean so the Catholics wouldn't fight. The colonies needed slaves. They sent 15 million from 1502 to the 19th century. Slaves did the hard work. They got free later after the Civil War.

Immigrants go to Africa from Europe but they don't like the hot weather and they catch diseases. The Dutch set up their own country at the Cape. Then the English conquer them.

GOOD NOTE TAKING

Early European Contact with Africa   History 200

Why Did Europeans Come to Africa?   10/22/03

1. Desire for gold
   — Medieval legends about gold in Africa.
   — Prince Henry (Portuguese navigator) sent men down coast of Africa to find source of gold. (Also to gain direct access to gold trade controlled by Muslims.)
   — Portuguese built forts along the coast. Their ships carried gold and ivory back to Portugal (16th century).
   — Then the other European states came (England, Holland, France, Spain) to set up their own trading posts.
   — Competed with each other for African trade. (Will talk about rivalry next week.)
2. Wanted to trade with Asia and weaken the Muslims
   (The Muslims had created a large empire based on the religion of Islam.)
   — Religious conflict between Christianity and Islam. Fought a religious war in the 11th–12th centuries — the Crusades.
   — The Muslims had expanded their empire when Europe was weak. In 15th century they controlled North Africa and they dominated trade in the Mediterranean. They controlled the spices coming from Asia, which were in great demand in Europe. In Europe they were used to preserve meat. So valuable, sometimes used as money.
   — Portugal and Spain were ruled by Catholic monarchs. Very religious. The Catholic monarchs wanted to force the Muslims out of Europe. (They still held part of Spain.) Wanted to convert them to Christianity.

[IMPORTANT] — The Muslims controlled North Africa and Mediterranean trade. If the Portuguese and Spanish could sail to the Indian Ocean directly, they could get goods from China and the Muslims couldn't stop them. The way to Asia was the sea route around Africa.

   3. The Europeans wanted slaves
      —When the Portuguese explored West Africa (15th century), they sent back the first slaves (around 1440).
      —The Spanish conquered the New World (Mexico, Peru, etc.). (Columbus had made several trips for Queen Isabella I of Spain.)
      —In America (the name for the New World), they needed slaves. Most slaves were sent to America.
      —Native Americans died from diseases of white men. They were also killed in the wars. There was nobody to run the mines (gold and silver).

[IMPORTANT] —Sugar plantations of the Caribbean (and Brazil) needed labor. Cotton and rice plantations in the south of U.S. also. It was hard work and nobody wanted to do it.
      —15 million slaves were brought to work the plantations starting in 1502 until mid-19th century.
   Colonization of Africa
   1. Immigration (why white people didn't come)
      —They couldn't take the climate.
      —There were a lot of tropical diseases.
      —The Europeans didn't want to live in Africa, only run it.
      —Only the Dutch settlers came. They set up the Boer states in South Africa. After them came British settlers.
      —Some French settled in Algeria.
      —Some English also moved to Rhodesia.
   2. Dividing Africa
      —Whites began exploring the interior. (Will discuss exploration next week.)

Taking notes during a lecture is difficult, and even a good set of notes can be greatly improved by being rewritten. Here is a rewriting of these notes. Note how much clearer everything becomes.

REWRITTEN GOOD NOTES

Early European Contact with Africa   History 200
What Drew Europeans to Africa?   10/22/03
   Gold
      There were medieval legends that there was a lot of gold in West Africa. Access to the gold was controlled by non-Christian powers (Muslims—believers in Islamic religion). Tales of gold lured the Portuguese (led by Prince Henry) to explore the coast of West Africa in the late 15th century. By the 16th century, the Portuguese had built several trading posts and forts along the West African coast and were bringing back gold, ivory, and pepper.
      By the 17th century, English, Dutch, French, and Spanish ships challenged the Portuguese trading monopoly and set up their own trading posts. This was the beginning of rivalry between European countries over the wealth of Africa.
   Desire to weaken the power of the Islamic Empire (Muslims) and expand trade with Asia

Conflict between Christianity and Islam was an old religious conflict (the Crusades as an example in 11th and 12th centuries). The Muslims controlled North Africa and the Mediterranean. They also controlled the spice trade from Asia. Spices were important in Europe because they were the only known way to preserve meat.

The Catholic states of Portugal and Spain wanted to fight with the Muslims. They wanted to drive them out of Spain and challenge the large Muslim empire in Africa, the Middle East, and Asia. They hoped to convert them to Christianity. *The Muslims were strong in North Africa, but if European powers could discover a way around Africa into the Indian Ocean, they could outflank the Muslims and obtain direct access to the trade with India and Asia.*

Slaves

Portuguese trading posts in Africa had sent a small number of slaves to Europe starting in the late 15th century. With the discovery and conquest of America at the turn of the 16th century, a new and larger slave trade began to European colonies in the New World (America).

The Native Americans died (they were killed in war and by European diseases in great numbers). There was a shortage of labor. In the 17th and 18th centuries, large sugar plantations were set up in the Caribbean and Brazil and rice and cotton plantations in the southern United States. *The need for laborers to do the hard agricultural work led to the importing of millions of slaves from Africa.* Approximately 15 million Africans were sent to America as slaves between 1502 and the mid-19th century. This slave trade made Africa valuable to the European powers.

The Colonization of Africa

Immigration

Because of the unsatisfactory climate and tropical diseases, there was no major European immigration to Africa. The only significant white colony was set up in South Africa by the Boers (Dutch) and later the English. There were smaller European settlements in Rhodesia (English) and Algeria (French).

Dividing up the continent

Exploration

If you reread the poor notes now, you can easily see how little of the lecture material is recorded in them and how confusing and even erroneous a picture you get from them. What is there about the poor notes that makes them inferior? First, they are not well organized. They do not even record the title of the lecture, the course number, or the date, which could be problematic if the notes get out of order. They are little more than a series of sentences about gold, trade, spices, Portugal, and slaves. The sentences are not in any particular order and do not say much of anything important. Even the factual information does not cover the major points of the lecture. By paying too much attention to trivial points about sea monsters, China, Jerusalem, Bartholomew Diaz, and Columbus, the note taker missed or did not have time to record the principal theme of the lecture—the relationship between European-Asian trade and the religious struggle between Islam and Christianity. The note taker also missed another major point—the connection between the enslavement of Africans and the need for plantation labor in the New World. Without these two points, this student cannot write a good exam essay on this subject.

The good notes, in contrast, follow the organization of the lecture and touch on the major points made in class. The notes make sense and can serve as the basis for reviewing the content of the lecture when the note taker studies for exams. These notes have a wide margin for extra comments and the marking of important passages. Notice the sections marked "important." The instructor had emphasized these points in class, and by specifically identifying them, the student will be sure to master them.

The rewritten version, which eliminates unimportant or repetitious phrases and smoothes the language into connected sentences, is even better as a study guide. The greatest value of rewriting, however, is that re-creating the lecture material in essay form helps it to become part of the note taker's own thinking. The mental effort that goes into revising lecture notes serves to impress the material and its meaning upon the mind. This makes it much easier to review the material at exam time.

From Slides and Films

Some instructors present slide lectures or show films or videotapes. Note taking in these instances presents special problems. If a lecture is accompanied by slides, you will need to include in your notes information about what the slides illustrated (for example, the Pyramid of Cheops, the novels of Willa Cather, the assassination of John F. Kennedy, the dances of Martha Graham) and anything of importance your instructor said about the slides.

Taking notes on films or videotapes also presents the unusual problem of dim lighting. The greatest problem, however, may be the film itself. In our culture, films are a medium of entertainment rather than education. Your natural response may be to sit back and relax your mind, but you will need to fight this response and learn to probe a film as you would a lecture. If a film is essentially factual (*Walled Cities of the Middle Ages*), note the major facts and interpretations as you would in a lecture. If a film is dramatic rather than documentary (*The Pianist, Citizen Kane,* or *Schindler's List*), examine the emotional message and artistic content as well as any historical facts it describes (or claims to describe). Ask yourself, What is the movie director trying to say, and what dramatic and technical devices does he or she use to say it? Your notes should record important narration and dialogue that illustrate the theme of the film. Finally, you will need to take note of cinematic elements (camera angles, sets, lighting, gestures and movements, facial expressions) because the impact of a dramatic film is essentially visual. Taking notes on slides and films takes practice, but the effort is worthwhile because photographs, films, and videotapes are used increasingly in history courses.

Classroom Participation

The modern classroom is a place where students are expected to actively participate in their own learning. This section discusses some ways of doing so.

Classroom Discussions

Many instructors encourage class participation. Some base a portion of the final grade on it. Come to class prepared to answer (and to ask) questions. Follow the discussion as it develops. If you are called on, contribute what you know. If some part of an instructor's presentation or a classmate's comments is unclear to you, don't hesitate to ask a question. If class ends and something remains unclear, raise your question with your instructor after class or during your instructor's office hours.

The following guidelines summarize this advice.

Guidelines for Speaking in Class

1. Be familiar with the subject under discussion.
2. If you are unclear about something the instructor or another student has said, compose and ask your question.
3. If you disagree with something said, make your point clearly and constructively.
4. If you don't have a chance to raise a question in class, ask your instructor after class.

Giving an Oral Presentation

Some instructors require students to give an oral presentation in class. Eloquence and effectiveness in public speaking cannot be mastered in a week or two, but you can make a start by taking such an assignment seriously and adequately preparing yourself for it. If you are allowed the option, reading from a prepared text is often the safest procedure. However, this type of delivery can lead to a dull presentation. It is usually better to speak from notes: your presentation will be livelier and more enjoyable for the class. To do a good job, you need to be fully familiar with your subject and pay close attention to getting your points across. Prepare your presentation outline as you would that of a short paper (see the section on writing short essays in Chapter 3, pp. 75–77). Be sure to cover all the important points and to present them in a logical manner.

Use short phrases rather than sentences in your presentation notes. Suppose you intend to tell the class the following: "Before 1848, most of the large landowners of California were Mexicans. In the decades after the United States annexed California, these Californios, as they were called, lost most of their lands to migrants from the eastern states." Your notes need only say: "(a) Until 1848 big landowners Californios. (b) Cal. annexed in 1848. (c) Lost land to easterners." Once you are fully prepared, do a dry run of your presentation before a relative, friend, or roommate (or even in the mirror). Be sure that you exhibit knowledge of your subject because this is most likely to determine your grade. Effective public speaking is one of the most important tools for success in many fields of work, and giving a talk in class is a good opportunity to develop your skills in this area.

Guidelines for Giving an Oral Presentation

1. Use 3-by-5 note cards, each with one or (at most) two major points on it.
2. Write neatly and use phrases, not whole sentences.
3. Put a number in the corner of each note card so that the cards will not get out of order.
4. If you have a time limit, rehearse your talk beforehand so that you won't need to rush. Pare down your notes to fit the time needed to present the material clearly.
5. Visual aids (such as overhead projections, slides, or videos) can make your presentation much more interesting. Make sure, however, that you have the resources you need beforehand and that you know how to integrate them easily and smoothly into your verbal remarks.
6. Relax! Speak slowly and clearly, and make eye contact with your audience every few sentences.

Group Work

Your instructor may ask you to be part of a small group and carry out an assignment working with members of that group. Instead of the individual oral presentation just mentioned, your group may be asked to make a presentation to the class. Conducting research and preparing a group presentation can be tricky but also rewarding. The key to success is to clarify who in the group is to do what part of the assignment and to be sure that each member is prepared when the time comes.

Another kind of group work takes place outside the classroom. Known as **peer reviewing** or peer editing, this type of work requires you to evaluate the work of a classmate. For example, you may be asked to read and comment on a student's **rough draft** of an assignment. Your peer review may take the form of an informal one-on-one review in which you go through the paper with the author point by point. Some instructors may ask you to write your evaluation; others may want your review in the form of a class presentation. No matter what the format is, remember to provide *constructive* criticism that will help your classmates develop their papers. Be sure to point out the paper's strengths in addition to any weaknesses.

If you are asked to peer edit the work of a classmate, remember also to pay particular attention to the theme and thesis of the paper. Ask yourself whether the theme and thesis are stated clearly and whether there is sufficient evidence to support them. Additionally, you should consider whether the information has been presented in an organized manner, such that your classmate's conclusions are justified.

The following guidelines summarize this advice.

Guidelines for Peer Reviewing

1. Don't be overly critical. Your goal is to assist your classmate in seeing the strengths and weaknesses in her or his draft. Your ability to do this comes from your outsider status: you have not been submerged in the research and are able to take a fresh look at the essay.
2. Pay special attention to the thesis of the essay. Is it stated in clear terms?
3. Does the body of the paper provide important evidence to support the thesis?
4. Are the points made in support of the thesis well organized, and are they clear to you as a reader?
5. Are the paper's conclusions justified by its arguments and documentation?
6. Whether your comments to your classmate are written or oral, be supportive. Give the writer the kind of help you hope to get from your own peer reviewer.

You also can share your comments with classmates either through e-mail or through a course Web page. You can send drafts of your work to other students or exchange peer-review drafts directly online. Computer technology also allows you to extend your learning beyond the classroom. You can talk to students at other schools in chat rooms or e-mail questions to authors of course materials. Learning to work collaboratively will be of use when you leave school and enter a working environment in which these kinds of personal and digital interactions are common.

Communicating Online

You probably have already used the Web to access or work on class assignments. Your professor may post the course syllabus and assignments online. Some professors and students also use the Web as a means of expanding their academic experience. There are several ways of communicating online that you can use as educational tools. Online tools help you to gain control of course material, avoid dangerous pitfalls, make connections to relevant material, and understand the larger framework of your course. They allow you to communicate with scholars, archivists, and Webmasters in your field, find important and underexploited resources for your research, and broaden your knowledge of the theories surrounding a particular period or aspect of history. You will likely find e-mail, listservs, chat rooms, e-conferences, and e-seminars especially useful.

E-mail, Listservs, and Chat Rooms

The speed of e-mail interaction varies according to how quickly the participants initiate and respond to messages. **Listservs** (list servers) are a way of managing e-mail lists of people interested in a particular topic. Instead of allowing one-to-one or one-to-many communication—as with e-mail—listservs send out everyone's messages to everyone else on the list. Listservs are especially valuable in settings that emphasize group-oriented work. **Chat rooms** allow users to communicate with others who are in a specific "room." Your Internet service provider (ISP) may give you access to chat rooms. You may also find chat rooms by surfing for them on the Web. Chat-room communication may be either one-to-one or one-to-many; however, unless you are in a "private" chat room—just you and the recipient—your messages can be read by others. Chat rooms provide users with immediate communication, but unlike e-mail or listservs they do not provide users with any tangible record of the dialogue.

For educational purposes, you can use these tools to varying degrees. You may decide to pose a question to a classmate over e-mail or in a chat room: "What was Professor Smith's advice about reading this document?" You can work out difficult concepts in a chat room. For example, perhaps you are dealing with a complex topic. You know you need to understand the material because it forms the basis for future lessons. By communicating with others, you can work through that material and master it in much the same way as you would in a study group.

If you subscribe to a listserv for your class, you might post the following message:

> I understand Prof. Smith's discussion of the factors that led to an anticommunist belief/paranoia in the U.S. during the late 1940s and early 1950s. However, I'm confused about which groups expressed these fears. From the readings it appears that only the Republicans did; however, Prof. Smith's lecture leads me to believe that both Republicans and Democrats did. Can anyone help me with this point?

By posting this message, you are assessing what you know and what you don't know and trying to deepen your understanding. Your message may stimulate another student's thinking. A classmate might offer the following reply:

> I think that is exactly Prof. Smith's intention. As I understand it, both Republicans and Democrats expressed these fears; however, they employed different means to achieve the same ends. Because the Democrats' activities were less dramatic, the Republicans charged them with being "soft" on communism.

Responding gives the student an opportunity to think about the material, understand the connections, and see how the material works.

Despite the advantages of e-mail, listservs, and chat rooms, there are dangers as well. Most of this kind of communication is unmediated or unedited. This means that anyone can say anything at any time. Perhaps someone with whom you are communicating tells you that the Holocaust was a Hollywood creation. Although it is important to give credit to new theories, it is equally important to read electronic communication with a skeptical eye. If someone suggests something with which you are unfamiliar, it is perfectly acceptable to ask for references where you could find more information on that topic. The best advice is to know the individuals with whom you communicate, read messages critically, and don't be afraid to challenge someone if you have reason to believe that he or she is wrong.

The cooperative learning fostered through communicating over the Web is of great value. Too often at the undergraduate level students look at learning from a competitive rather than a cooperative viewpoint. Some students never study or work with others. They believe that if they do so they will lose their "edge." Historians, however, do not work in a vacuum; historical research relies on access to the discoveries, interpretations, and analyses of others. Seminar-type classes often rely on cooperative learning, but you can have a similar experience in any class by communicating with classmates and others using the Web. By sharing information, you are not losing any competitive advantage; you are increasing and solidifying your knowledge, pointing out errors, and sharing important findings.

EXERCISE
Communicating Online

Here is a self-study assignment to help you familiarize yourself with online communications.

a. Join one of the discussion groups listed in Appendix A (pp. 230–31).
b. Find an interesting topic, and read the recent messages so you know how the conversation has developed.
c. When you have something to contribute or a question to ask, post your message, following the instructions provided. As always, think and write clearly what you want to say.
d. If your message gets a thoughtful response, reenter the conversation by directly addressing the person who responded to you. If your message is challenged by someone on the list, don't be discouraged. Before responding, however, do some additional research and fact checking.

E-conferences and E-seminars

E-conferences and e-seminars are becoming important interactive means of scholarly discussion. Both make possible the online presentation, discussion, and criticism of scholarly papers; however, e-conferences present several papers and e-seminars deal with only one. You may find it difficult to locate these forums on the Web. Most are either sponsored by or affiliated with universities. If you do find one, check the participation requirements. Some are open only to scholars; others allow both students and scholars to participate.

There are important things to keep in mind when joining and participating in these online scholarly activities. Both assume a high level of knowledge and waste little time with introductions and background material. They assume that participants are thoroughly familiar with the topic of the conference or seminar and are able to read and write on a sophisticated level.

Web Communication and Advanced Research

Web communication can help students doing advanced course work to locate important resources. If you decide to tackle an obscure topic, you can use the Web to contact scholars who have done research in that area. If possible, contact more than one scholar so that you have more than one interpretation of the topic. The scholars, archivists, and Webmasters with whom you would communicate are busy individuals. When contacting them, introduce yourself, describe your research, and outline your reason for contacting them. Be sure that you are knowledgeable about your topic, that your contact can actually help you, and that you ask specific questions.

In communicating online, you are "talking" with others who can increase your understanding and whom you may be able to help as well. You will improve your grasp of the material about which you have questions. You will see the pitfalls to avoid by pointing out errors in other people's interpretations. This experience will give you insight into an important principle of the humanistic disciplines: your best work results from dialogue with other researchers. (For information about conducting research on the Web, see Chapter 4, pp. 93–103.)

How to Study for and Take Exams

When a test is announced, try to find out what kind of an exam it will be: essay, short answer, multiple choice, or a combination of those formats. Determine what topics will be covered and what portions of the reading material and lectures deal with those topics. If you have not done all of the necessary reading, do so immediately and record the important facts and interpretations as indicated in the section "How to Read a History Assignment" (pp. 19–25). If you missed any lectures, try to obtain lecture notes from someone who knows the rules of good note taking. Then gather together all the materials to be covered in the exam. Reread the parts of the texts that you underlined (or otherwise marked) as being important. Reread *all* of the relevant lecture notes, paying special attention to any points emphasized by the instructor. Sometimes it helps to do your rereading aloud. If an exam will cover visual materials — slides, films, maps — be sure to go over this information, even you have to watch a video a second time.

If the test is to be an **essay exam,** compose sample questions based on the important topics and themes in the readings and lectures. Many textbooks contain sample exam questions or topics for discussion at the end of each chapter. If you do not know how to answer any portion of the sample question, go over your study materials again and look for the information needed. If you are preparing for an **objective exam —** that is, one requiring short factual answers — pay special attention to the important facts (persons, places, events, changes) and key terms in your study materials. You must be precise in order to get credit for your answer. Make a list of outstanding people, events, and historical developments, and be sure that you can adequately identify them and explain their importance. Again, your textbook may help you by providing sample short-answer questions.

Take the time you need to prepare adequately. If tests make you nervous, keep on studying until you master your sample questions and until the material to be covered makes sense to you.

Objective and Short-Answer Exams

Objective exams call for short, factual answers. The three most common objective exams are (1) **short answer,** (2) **identification,** and (3) **multiple choice** or true/false. Read each question carefully, and don't jump to conclusions. Answer short-answer and identification questions briefly (there is usually a time and space limit) and directly. Don't put anything in your answer that wastes space or time. If you are asked to identify John F. Kennedy, don't mention how he was killed (unless that is part of the question); instead talk about some aspect of his presidency that was stressed in class or in course readings. When you have so little room to show what you know, answers that stray from the core of the subject are as bad as wrong answers.

Example of a Short-Answer Question

QUESTION   What were the motives that caused the European powers to explore Africa beginning in the late fifteenth century?

INCORRECT ANSWER   They wanted to dominate Africa and get all the gold for themselves. Columbus wanted to take slaves from Africa, but the Pope said it would start a war. But the war didn't start and the Europeans dominated Africa anyway because they were stronger.

CORRECT ANSWER   The wars between Christianity and Islam were an important factor. The Christian states wanted to weaken the hold of the Muslim religion on Africa and to convert the natives. They also hoped to break Muslim control of trade with Asia by finding a sea route around Africa.

(Check these two answers against the example of good note taking on pp. 39–40. The notes make clear why the second answer is satisfactory and the first one is not.)

Example of an Identification Question

QUESTION   Identify the "progressive" philosophy of historical interpretation.

INCORRECT ANSWER   Historian who believed that our country was always making progress because Americans were very hardworking people.

CORRECT ANSWER   The interpretation of history that holds that human beings and their condition are continually improving as each generation builds on the foundation laid by previous ones.

(See the section "Philosophies of History" in Chapter 1 on pp. 5–7 to find the basis for the correct answer.)

Example of a Multiple-Choice Question

The British monarch at the time of the American Revolution was:

    a. George II
    b. Charles I
    c. James II
    d. George III
    e. Henry I

If you look up the reign dates of these monarchs, you will discover that George III (who was king from 1760 to 1820) was the ruler of England at the time of the American Revolution.

Preparing for In-Class Essay Exams— Composing Sample Questions

Of course, the best preparation for an essay exam is to be given the question in advance. Some instructors do this (usually in the form of a **take-home essay exam**), but many give in-class essay exams and hand out in advance a number of possible topics or questions from which they will choose when making up the exam. (For more on take-home exams, see pp. 53–57.) If you face an essay exam without *any* questions presented in advance, the key to successful preparation is to come up with potential questions on your own.

As your instructor probably will tell you, the essay questions will deal with the major topics covered in the course so far. Using your textbooks, lecture notes, and other course materials, determine what these topics are. Then compose your own questions. For example, if the material to be covered in the exam is reasons for the decline of the Roman Empire, list the major reasons mentioned in the course work. Among them may be civil war, military insubordination, the cost of defending distant frontiers, declining agricultural output, "barbarian" invasion, heavy tax burdens on the peasantry, the growth of central bureaucracy, the decline of the Senate, the cult of the Emperor, the rise of Christianity, and the rise of Islam. The exam question is likely to focus on one or more of these explanations. Be prepared to write about *each* of these factors and how they relate to one another. If the course has covered the rise of industrialization in New England, study carefully the major social and technological changes and how people responded to them. Think about the aspects of industrialization that you might be asked about. One question might ask you to describe the ways in which factory production was different from the workshop production that it displaced. Other questions might be: "How did industrialization affect family life?" "What were the major technological innovations behind early industrialization?" "How did the rise of the textile industry affect the lives of young women?"

Don't prepare for an essay exam by composing questions that are too broad. If the class spent six weeks examining the decline of the Roman Empire, don't expect a broad question such as "Discuss the decline of the Roman Empire." Don't prepare questions that are too narrow either. For example, "Who owned the biggest textile mill in New England in the 1830s?" is a question for a short-answer or an identification exam.

Writing a Good In-Class Essay Exam

Even if you have prepared properly for an essay exam, you must stay calm enough to remember what you studied, you must understand the questions, you must answer them directly and fully, and you must not run out of time. None of this is easy, but here are a few pointers to follow until you gain the experience to overcome these problems.

Read over the exam slowly. Depending on the length and complexity of the questions asked, allot the proper amount of time to answer each question. Think about the central points you wish to make in your answer and create a brief outline of these points in the margin of the exam booklet. Directly address the questions asked. If the questions are very specific, for example, respond to them with the amount of detail required. Support the points you make with facts but avoid composing an answer that is merely a series of facts. Think about the questions asked in broad terms and pursue your central points. As you write, refer back to your outline and be careful not to repeat yourself; each sentence should add new material to your answer or advance its line of argument. Finally, try to leave a few minutes to proofread your answers.

The following guidelines summarize this advice.

Guidelines for Writing In-Class Essay Exams

1. When you are given the exam, don't panic. Read the entire exam slowly, including all of the instructions. Gauge the amount of time you will need to answer each question. Then choose the question you know most about to answer first.
2. Don't write the first thing that comes to mind. Read the question slowly, and be sure you understand it.
3. Determine how you will answer the question and the central points you wish to make.
4. Write these central points or even a full outline in the margin of the exam booklet. As you compose each sen-

tence of your answer, make sure that it relates to one of these points.

5. Model your answer on the question. Be as specific or general, as concrete or reflective, as the question suggests. Never allow your answer to wander away from the focus of the question. If the question asks you to "describe" or "trace" or "compare" or "explain," be sure that that is what you do.

6. Don't repeat yourself. Each sentence should add new material or advance a line of argument.

7. Where necessary, refer to the facts that support the points you are making. But the mere relation of a series of facts is not enough. You must also give evidence that you have thought about the question in broad terms.

8. Toward the end of your answer, you may wish to include your own opinion. This is fine, even desirable, but be sure that your answer as a whole supports this opinion.

9. If there is time, reread and correct an answer after it is finished. The pressure of an exam can often cause you to write sentences that are not clear.

Writing Take-Home Essay Exams

The first section of "How to Study for and Take Exams" focused on *preparing* for exams that you take in class. If necessary, refer back to that section because it complements this one. Here the emphasis is on take-home essay exams that you write outside of class. This kind of exam gives you the time to do your very best writing. The goal of such an exam is to demonstrate to your instructor that you understand the material needed to answer the question.

When writing take-home essay exam answers, all of the points made earlier in this chapter about clarity and continuity apply. A take-home essay exam question requires you to write an original essay of usually two to five pages. **Documentation** (**footnotes** and a **bibliography**) is not usually required. Of course, if your instructor asks for a specific length, topic, approach, or format, you need to follow those requirements even when they differ from the information provided here.

First, note the length requirements of the exam and the due date. Obviously, you will need more time to prepare a six-page essay answer than a three-page one. If your instructor allows you access to sources (which is common), you will need to review all course material that relates to the exam question. If you have not yet outlined or taken notes on this material, do so now. Focusing on the portion of the course material that relates to the question, make a list of the most important points. Try to find from two to six main points for each essay, depending on the length of the essay. Compose your answer by introducing and then supporting these points in logical order. Like all essays, your answer should have a clear, central **theme.** In this case, your theme is determined by the exam question. Be sure that your essay directly addresses the question. (See the section on writing in-class essay exams on pp. 51–53.)

The goal of any essay exam is to demonstrate (1) adequate knowledge of the subject, (2) clear thinking about the points covered, (3) clear and connected writing, and (4) clear understanding of the question. Read the following two answers to an exam question on Chinese history. Do they meet those four requirements?

> **QUESTION**   Explain the origins of the Chinese civil war of 1945–1949. How did the differing political programs of the two contenders affect the outcome of that conflict?

> **POOR ANSWER**   The Guo Mindang (Kuomintang) had a stronger army than the Communists, but the Communists won the civil war and took over the country. Their political program, communism, was liked by the peasants because they didn't own any land and paid high taxes.
>
> China was based on the Confucian system, which was very rigid and led to the Manchu dynasty being overthrown. The Chinese didn't like being dominated by foreigners, and Sun Zhongshan (Sun Yat-sen) founded the Guo Mindang to unite China. He believed in the Three People's Principles. At first he cooperated with the Chinese Communists, but later Jiang Jieshi (Chiang Kai-shek) tried to destroy communism because he was against it. Communism was not in favor of the wealthy people.
>
> The Communists wanted a revolution of the peasants and gave them land. They also killed the landlords. Jiang Jieshi worried more about the Communists than about the Japanese invasion. The Japanese looked to conquer China and make it a part of their empire. Jiang Jieshi wanted to fight the Communists first.
>
> After World War II the Chinese Communists attacked Manchuria and took over a lot of weapons. They fought the Guo Mindang army. The Guo Mindang army lost the battles, and Jiang Jieshi was chased to Taiwan, where he made a new government. The Communists set up their own country, and their capital was Beijing (Peking). That way the Communists won the Chinese civil war.

> **GOOD ANSWER**   The origins of the 1945–1949 civil war can be traced back to the rise of Chinese nationalism in the late nineteenth century. Out of the confusion of the Warlord period that followed the overthrow of the Manchu dynasty in 1911, two powerful nationalist movements arose—one reformist and the other revolutionary. The reformist movement was the Guo Mindang (Kuomintang), founded by Sun Zhongshan (Sun Yat-sen). It was based on a mixture of republican, Christian, and moderate socialist ideals and inspired by opposition to foreign domination. The revolutionary movement was that of the Chinese Communist Party (CCP), founded in 1921, whose goal was a communist society but whose immediate program

was to organize the working class to protect its interests and to work for the removal of foreign "imperialist" control.

Although these two movements shared certain immediate goals (suppression of the Warlords and resistance to foreign influence), they eventually fell out over such questions as land reform, relations with the Soviet Union, the role of the working class, and the internal structure of the Guo Mindang. (The CCP operated within the framework of the more powerful Guo Mindang during the 1920s.)

By the 1930s, when Jiang Jieshi (Chiang Kai-shek) succeeded Sun, the CCP was forced out of the Guo Mindang. By that time the CCP had turned to a program of peasant revolution inspired by Mao Zedong (Mao Tse-tung). A four-year military struggle (1930–1934) between the two movements for control of the peasantry of Jiangxi (Kiangsi) Province ended in the defeat but not destruction of the CCP.

The Japanese invasion of Manchuria (1931) and central China (1936–1938) helped salvage the fortunes of the CCP. By carrying out an active guerrilla resistance against the Japanese, in contrast to the more passive role of the Guo Mindang, which was saving its army for a future battle with the Communists, the CCP gained the leading position in the nationalist cause.

In the post–World War II period, the CCP's land reform program won strong peasant support, whereas the landlord-backed Guo Mindang was faced with runaway corruption and inflation, which eroded its middle-class following. The military struggle between 1945 and 1949 led to the defeat of the demoralized Guo Mindang army and the coming to power of the CCP.

Let's compare how well the two essays meet the requirements for a well-written answer.

1. *Adequate knowledge of the subject.* The writer of the poor answer fails to indicate adequate knowledge in several ways. The answer omits many important facts. It describes the political programs of the two contending parties in vague terms. It refers to the CCP only as the Chinese Communists, leaving the impression that they were a loose grouping of like-minded individuals rather than a strong, well-disciplined political organization. It does not even mention the name of the most famous leader of the CCP — Mao Zedong. Jiang Jieshi, the leader of the Guo Mindang, is mentioned, but there is no discussion of his political program or beliefs, other than that he was opposed to communism. Another serious defect is chronological confusion. The answer jumps back and forth between earlier and later periods, and no dates are given for major events.

The well-written answer illustrates good knowledge of the subject matter. The origins, philosophies, leaders, and relationship of the two contending parties are clearly described. This answer brings in related issues such as nationalism, Warlords, guerrilla warfare against Japan, corruption, and inflation, thus indicating knowledge of the historical **context** in which the Chinese civil war developed. The chronology is clear: events are mentioned in proper time sequence, and the dates of all major events are given.

2. *Clear thinking about the points covered.* The poor answer is not well organized. The paragraphs do not make separate points, and each succeeding paragraph does not further develop the theme of the essay. Paragraph one is a conclusion rather than an introduction. The second paragraph goes back to the founding of the Guo Mindang but, instead of discussing the origins of the hostility between it and the CCP, merely states that hostility came into existence. The third paragraph begins by introducing the CCP (though not by name). However, it does not expand on the CCP's programs and points of conflict with the Guo Mindang. Instead, it abruptly changes the focus of events and the time frame by introducing the Japanese invasion of China, which the last sentence of the paragraph only vaguely relates to the question. Instead of drawing conclusions about the causes of the Communist victory in the civil war, the last paragraph merely states that it occurred.

The well-written answer uses each paragraph to make a separate important point, and each succeeding paragraph further develops the theme of the essay. Paragraph one sets out the political programs of the two groups and the historical context in which the movements originated. The second paragraph explains the beginning of the conflict in the 1920s. Paragraph three discusses that conflict in relation to the Chinese peasantry during the early 1930s. The fourth paragraph relates the development of the conflict to the Japanese invasion of the late 1930s. The final paragraph summarizes the effects of the conflicts and of postwar developments on the outcome of the civil war.

3. *Clear and connected writing.* Many sentences in the poor answer are badly constructed: they are awkward, or what they say adds nothing to the answer. Some of the awkward phrases are "the Communists won the civil war and *took over* the country"; "communism was *liked by* the peasants"; "China was *based on* the Confucian system"; "communism was not *in favor* of the wealthy people"; "the Japanese *looked* to conquer China"; "the Communists *set up their own country.*" These phrases cause the sentences to be unclear, and they keep the student from getting his or her point across. The other major defect in sentence structure is repetitious or irrelevant sentences and phrases. These are "Jiang Jieshi (Chiang Kai-shek) tried to destroy communism *because he was against it*"; "they *fought the Guo Mindang army*"; "that way *the Communists won the Chinese civil war.*" The sentences of the well-written answer are clear, and each adds new material to the essay.

4. *Clear understanding of the question.* The poor answer does not deal with the central issue of the question—the political programs of the Guo Mindang and the CCP. It notes that the Guo Mindang was founded on the Three People's Principles, but it does not explain what these were. Of the CCP, it says that there was a belief in communism (which is obvious) and peasant revolution (which is vague). These are the only references to political programs in the entire answer! It is obvious that the writer of this answer failed to understand that the central focus of the question was on political philosophy.

The well-written answer is directed to the central issue of political programs and begins on that very point. The remainder of the answer makes clear the relationship of political programs to the origins and course of the Chinese civil war as called for in the first sentence of the question.

The Dangers of Plagiarism. A problem that sometimes arises with take-home exams is **plagiarism.** Your instructor may allow you to **paraphrase** the sources you use in preparing your essay. Be sure, however, that you write in your own words. If you use sentences from another source, you are plagiarizing whether you realize it or not. Most schools require instructors to penalize students severely for plagiarizing. This is a very serious matter. If you still have questions, turn *now* to the longer discussion of plagiarism and paraphrasing in Chapter 4 (pp. 113–15).

Studying history provides you with a variety of skills. Reading effectively, taking class notes, and understanding what you need to know for an exam are three primary skills. These prepare the way for more advanced goals: clear writing, adequate research, and the presentation of a well-prepared thesis. The book now turns your attention to these additional skills.

How to Write History Assignments: The Importance of Writing Skills

Why Clear Writing Is Important

The most important tasks in a history course often are the written assignments. You may be asked to write a short book review or a lengthy research paper. Whatever the writing assignment, you must take the time and care to make it your best work. Every instructor has had the experience of reading a poorly written paper from a student who did not take the trouble to do his or her best. If you hand in sloppy or thoughtless work, you will earn a poor grade and indicate that you are not aware of the importance of good writing. Writing is a task of great significance. You will be judged not only by your history instructor but also by everyone else who reads your words. Your writing skills tell the reader a lot about your ability to think clearly, whether you are writing a student paper or a proposal to your boss. As this chapter emphasizes, clear thinking is the source of clear writing. Two years after graduating, you may no longer remember the causes of World War I, but if you sharpened your writing skills in history assignments, you will have acquired a skill and an asset that will last a lifetime.

Clear writing accomplishes two important goals. First, it demonstrates that your thinking about a subject is logical. You cannot write clearly about something that you do not understand clearly. Second, it enables you to convey to your readers in a convincing way exactly what you want them to understand. Clear writing is persuasive.

The Components of Clear Writing

Think of your readers when you write. Tell your readers what you want them to know. Tell them this clearly, briefly, yet adequately.

Write Clear Sentences

Clear writing begins with clear sentences. A clear sentence leaves no doubt about the *subject* of the sentence. Consider the following examples. What are the subjects of these sentences?

EXAMPLES

On September 1, 1939, Germany was strong and Poland was weak, and so it attacked.

When Lindbergh landed his plane in Paris, everybody was very excited to see the first person to fly across the Atlantic Ocean by himself.

The subject of the first sentence, describing the outbreak of World War II, is unclear. The reader cannot tell if the subject is *Germany* or *Poland* and therefore cannot tell who attacked whom. In the second example, the subject, *Charles Lindbergh*, is removed from *fly*, the verb that describes his great feat; the reader must slog through an unclear and confusing sentence.

Now look at these revised sentences:

REVISED EXAMPLES

On September 1, 1939, Germany attacked Poland.

Charles Lindbergh made the first solo flight across the Atlantic Ocean.

The reader will know who (or what) the subject of the sentence is if that subject is placed as close as possible to the verb that describes what the subject is doing.

Do Not Clutter Sentences with Unnecessary Phrases

A phrase can add information to your sentence. But phrases that are used indiscriminately can obscure a sentence's meaning.

EXAMPLE   Lindbergh took thirty-three hours to make the first solo flight across the Atlantic Ocean.

Here a phrase has been added to the original clear sentence. It tells the reader how long the flight took. This added information does not affect the clarity of the sentence. But look what happens when several phrases are added.

EXAMPLE   Although his plane was loaded down with extra fuel, Lindbergh was still able to get off the muddy runway in New Jersey despite very bad weather that rainy morning in 1927 and the fact that several other people had been killed trying to become the first person to stay awake for the thirty-three hours it took to fly solo across the Atlantic Ocean.

In this sentence, Lindbergh's flight is surrounded by so many phrases that the main point of the sentence is lost. You should not attempt to make one sentence describe so many aspects of his first flight. If some facts are not necessary, leave them out. If they are necessary, make room for them by creating additional sentences. For example, if the weight of the fuel and the muddy runway are important but the weather conditions and the failed attempts by others are not, writing two sentences instead of one makes the additional points and makes them clearly.

REVISED EXAMPLE   Lindbergh's plane was so heavily loaded with fuel that it almost failed to get off the muddy runway in New Jersey. Once in the air, however, he was able to stay awake for the thirty-three hours it took to fly across the Atlantic.

Avoid Using the Passive Voice

The subject and verb are the core of any sentence. In the passive voice, the verb indicates that the subject is *receiving* rather than *performing* the action described by the verb.

EXAMPLE   A vaccination against smallpox was introduced by Edward Jenner in 1796.

A clear sentence usually uses the *active voice,* which shows the subject *initiating* rather than *receiving* an action (or thought).

REVISED EXAMPLE   In 1796, Edward Jenner introduced a vaccination against smallpox.

At times, however, the passive voice is acceptable, such as when you desire to emphasize the *receiver* of an action or thought. So although it is preferable to avoid the passive voice, you may find occasions in your writing to use it.

Use the Past Tense

When writing about historical events, use the past tense. The only exception occurs when you are referring to a specific written document or to an object (such as an old building or a work of art) that still exists. Use the present tense to describe them.

EXAMPLE   Thomas Jefferson *wrote* the draft of the Declaration of Independence.

Jefferson's action took place in the past, so it is correct to use the past tense when writing about the event. Because the Declaration of Independence is a written document that still exists, you should use the present tense to describe its content:

EXAMPLE   The Declaration of Independence *says* that "all men are created equal."

The effort to write clear sentences forces you to think about what your subject is doing and how many points about the subject's actions (or thoughts or feelings) you need to include. The result of this effort is a series of sentences that give the reader a clear understanding of what you have written.

Link Your Sentences

Another element of good writing is **continuity** — the *relationship* between words, sentences, or paragraphs as a writer moves from one point to the next. A new sentence (or paragraph) should say something *new* and *significant* about the **theme** of the paper. And a new sentence (or paragraph) should be connected to the sentences (or paragraphs) around it.

Sometimes a single sentence (or paragraph) cannot do both. Only a skilled writer can craft a sentence that advances the theme while also connecting with the surrounding sentences. Writers often separate these two tasks by means of a **linking sentence.** Such a sentence does not have to introduce new evidence about the theme. Its job is to tell the reader that the writer is shifting gears, moving from one point to a different but related one.

The middle sentence in the following example is a linking sentence.

EXAMPLE   Therefore, changes in printing technology made newspapers cheaper and more available. *But new technology alone does not explain rising readership.* As immigrants poured into the country from Europe, it was the new look of the newspaper, especially the use of large illustrations and photographs, that attracted these new "readers."

The linking sentence tells the reader that the paragraph (dealing with technological change) is to be followed by the introduction of a new point about the theme: how changes in the look of newspapers attracted new readers.

Linking sentences usually appear toward the end of a paragraph. Sometimes it is necessary to write an entire **linking paragraph** if the shift in focus is a major one or if you are moving from one section of a long essay to another (see pp. 62–63).

Write Clear and Coherent Paragraphs

A paragraph is a series of sentences about the same point. Each sentence in a paragraph needs to be clear, and each, as noted above, needs to add something to the theme or provide a link between sentences or paragraphs. Each paragraph also needs to be coherent— that is, to hold together. In a coherent paragraph, each sentence expands on the point being made. Look for places in your writing where you repeat yourself. When a sentence does not add anything significant to what you already said, leave it out. Also look for places where you begin to talk about a new and different point. It is there that you will need to begin a new paragraph.

Consider again the following sentences about Lindbergh's historic flight:

> **EXAMPLE**   Lindbergh's plane was so heavily loaded with fuel that it almost failed to get off the muddy runway in New Jersey. Once in the air, however, he was able to stay awake for the thirty-three hours it took to fly across the Atlantic.

Both sentences describe the famous flight. That is why they belong in the same paragraph. But suppose you are finished writing about the flight and want to talk about the wild celebration in Paris after his landing. This information probably belongs in a new paragraph.

> **EXAMPLE**   Once Lindbergh was on the ground, his plane was mobbed by excited Parisians who lifted him onto their shoulders.

The new paragraph would describe Lindbergh's reception in Paris until you decided to make a new point about him. If you wanted to describe the celebration for Lindbergh when he returned to New York, you would not add that to your paragraph about the events in Paris; you would start a new paragraph.

Of course, a paragraph can be short — three or four sentences — or long — seven or eight sentences. There is no rule about the correct number of sentences in a paragraph. The key to knowing when a paragraph is complete is to ask yourself: Am I moving on to a different point than the one I am making in this paragraph? If the answer is "yes," begin a new paragraph.

Link Your Paragraphs

Since each paragraph says something new, you must help the reader to see the *connection* between paragraphs. Disconnected paragraphs (like disconnected sentences) can leave the reader confused about what is coming next and why. Note the disconnection between the end of the paragraph about the flight and the sentence that begins a new paragraph in this example:

> **EXAMPLE**
> Once in the air, however, he was able to stay awake for the thirty-three hours it took to fly across the Atlantic.
>   In 1926, Lindbergh flew mail from Chicago to St. Louis.

Unless you say something in the new paragraph to explain why you are going back to the period before the famous flight, the reader will be confused and may think that you are too. If you have a good reason for going back in time in the new paragraph, make sure that the reader understands your reason.

REVISED EXAMPLE

Once in the air, however, he was able to stay awake for the thirty-three hours it took to fly across the Atlantic.

No one had expected the twenty-five-year-old Lindbergh to make it. Less than a year before the famous flight, he had been an inconspicuous pilot flying mail between Chicago and St. Louis.

By connecting your paragraphs, you let the reader understand why you are bringing up Lindbergh's earlier career. The addition of a linking sentence shows the reader why a new paragraph is necessary and what direction the writer is taking.

The following guidelines summarize this advice.

Guidelines for Clear Writing

1. Each sentence clearly names its subject.
2. Each sentence is clear about what the subject is doing (or saying, or feeling, etc.).
3. If you have several points to make about the subject, split them up into separate sentences.
4. Each sentence adds something to the thesis of the essay.
5. Each sentence is connected logically to the sentences around it.
6. Avoid the passive voice.
7. Use the past tense when writing about past historical events. Use the present tense only when writing about documents or objects (buildings, artwork, etc.) that still exist.
8. Each paragraph is clear about the point it is making.
9. When you get to a new point, start a new paragraph.
10. Prepare your reader for the transition from one paragraph to another with a phrase or sentence linking the two. (The link can be placed at the end of one paragraph or at the beginning of the next.)
11. Each paragraph is connected logically to the paragraphs around it.

Building an Essay

Clear and coherent paragraphs, held together by linking phrases or sentences, are the building blocks of essay writing. But clear and coherent paragraphs are just the foundation. To unify your points in an essay, your paper needs to have a beginning, a middle, and an end.

The Need for a Clear Beginning

The very first paragraph of an essay has a special task. In it, you should state briefly and clearly what you are going to write about. State your **theme** clearly and tell the reader briefly what central point or points you intend to make about it. This central point is your **thesis.** Conclude your opening paragraph with a statement about why your thesis is important. Generally you can accomplish all of this in one paragraph. However, if your paper is long or if your thesis is complex, you might need more than one opening paragraph.

Here is an example of a single, well-constructed opening paragraph.

EXAMPLE OF GOOD OPENING PARAGRAPH

This paper will explore the early history of the native peoples of New Mexico. It will describe their way of life before the arrival of European explorers in the sixteenth century. The paper will focus in particular on the evidence that over a thousand years ago many tribes living in this area had developed complex communities. Although European conquest destroyed most of these communities, there are still more than a dozen of them in New Mexico today.

The theme of this paper is "the early history of the native peoples of New Mexico." The thesis is that for a very long time these people have had complex communities. The opening paragraph accomplishes several important tasks:

- The first sentence announces the theme.
- The second and third sentences tell the reader the thesis that the paper will focus on.
- The final sentence prepares the reader for the conclusion of the paper and makes clear why the theme is worthy of study.

Now read another opening paragraph to the same paper and see if you can spot the problems in it.

EXAMPLE OF POOR OPENING PARAGRAPH

European conquerors took away the native peoples' way of life in New Mexico. Some of their villages were caves cut into hillsides; others were made of hardened clay with many rooms. They were happy for one thousand years, but all this came to an end. This paper will show you how they lived.

Instead of announcing the theme, the first sentence of this paragraph starts with the paper's *conclusion*. The reader does not know that the paper is about the way of life of the native peoples of New Mexico. The writer then jumps ahead and includes specific points about the kinds of houses in which they lived. The reader is left to guess that these dwellings are evidence of a complex civilization. All the reader is told about the ancient, native way of life is that the native peoples were "happy." The reader is given no idea of why the theme is important or how it will be presented. The writer's only way of telling the reader what the core of the paper will be about is vague: it will "show you how they lived." The writer should have included in the opening paragraph a thesis statement—in this instance saying that the native peoples of New Mexico had an ancient and complex way of life. The poor organization of the introductory paragraph leaves the reader uncertain of both the theme and the thesis.

Remember, your opening paragraph summarizes your thesis. If you change the organization or conclusions of your paper in an important way, be sure to rewrite the opening paragraph to reflect that change.

Creating a Writing Outline

Before you begin the actual writing of your paper, make a **writing outline** of the points that you intend to discuss. Your instructor may provide this outline, or you may have to create it yourself. This outline should reflect your research for the essay. You may have read one article or five articles, one book or five books. You may also have watched videos or researched on the **World Wide Web.** The information in those materials will provide the main points of your outline. Tailor your outline not only to your theme and thesis but also to the assigned length of your paper. If you include too many points in your outline, you will never fit them all in your paper. If you include too few, your paper will be short and probably weak.

Be aware that you may need to revise your outline during the research process. You may discover the need to add new points to your outline or to discard old ones. (For more on research and the outlining of papers, see Chapter 4.)

SAMPLE WRITING OUTLINE FOR A SHORT PAPER

Pueblo Culture:
The Ancient Roots of Modern New Mexico
1. The arrival of ancient peoples
2. Their way of life
   a. Architecture
   b. Agriculture
   c. Art
3. The Spanish conquest
4. Becoming part of Mexico
5. Becoming part of the United States
6. Pueblo villages today

(For examples of longer outlines see pp. 117–19 and 156–57.)

The Importance of Continuity

Just as important as clarity is **continuity.** Each paragraph should be connected to the paragraphs before and after it by **linking sentences.** Pay attention to the continuity of your essay. As you write each paragraph, ask yourself: "Does this paragraph follow from the preceding one?" "Does it add something significant to the theme of the paper?" "Do it and the following paragraphs move toward the thesis I announced in my opening paragraph?" Every time you begin a new paragraph, ask those questions. If you cannot see how the new paragraph connects with the one before it or if the content of the paragraph doesn't add anything to the theme, rewrite it so that it accomplishes these goals.

Writing a Conclusion

How do you know when to end your paper? If your instructor gives you a specific length, obviously you need to wrap up the paper once it reaches the limit allowed. But how do you know when you have written enough? You are ready to conclude your paper when you have covered all of the points in your *revised* writing outline.

How much space should you give to your **conclusion**? The overall length of your paper influences the length of your conclusion. For a short essay of five to seven pages, one to two concluding paragraphs are usually sufficient. A long essay of ten to twenty pages probably will require a concluding page. Some very long papers may need a concluding section of several pages.

What should your conclusion say? Your conclusion should summarize the main points of your essay. Take another look at your opening paragraphs. What did you tell the reader you intended to do? By the time you reach the concluding part of your paper, this job should have been accomplished. (If your paper has not yet accomplished this, you must ensure that your revision does.) Your conclusion is also a place to remind the reader of the significance of what he or she has read. Finally, the conclusion is the place where you can state your own opinion (unless your instructor has told you to be as objective as possible). As with your opening paragraph, it is often necessary to rewrite your conclusion after any significant revision of the body of your paper.

Revising Your Paper

The Rough Draft.   Even a skilled writer cannot produce a finished product from scratch. Good writing, in addition to following the guidelines in this chapter, is the product of revision. Think of writing as a multistage process. Whether you are sitting down to write a sentence, a paragraph, or an entire essay, what you are really doing is writing a **rough draft.** The goal of this rough draft is to present the most important information you have gathered (or been given) on the subject. Don't worry about writing style too much at this stage.

Organize your rough draft according to your writing outline. Keep in mind, though, that the writing process is not a rigid process. If your thoughts on your theme have changed, you may need to revise your writing outline before starting to write.

The Revised Draft. Next comes the crucial task of refining your thoughts and words to produce the revised draft. Remember, the longer the paper is, the more important the jobs of organization and revision are. To **revise** your paper, go over each page carefully, paragraph by paragraph, making sure that each conforms to the writing guidelines in this chapter. As you read each sentence and paragraph, ask yourself the following questions:

Is this sentence (paragraph) clear?

Have I put too many phrases in my sentences?

Have I made more than one main point in my paragraphs?

Does each of my sentences and paragraphs add something significant to my theme?

Is each sentence (and paragraph) connected to the sentences (and paragraphs) around it?

Do I need a linking sentence to make a transition clear?

Will my intended audience be able to follow what I am saying?

Rework each sentence and paragraph until it meets each of these tests. Then step away from your paper for a time (an hour, a day, or several days) to give yourself a fresh view of it when you return. For this final revision, pay special attention to organization on a broad scale. Ask yourself the following questions:

Does the introductory paragraph give an overall sense of the paper?

Does the introductory paragraph state my thesis clearly?

Do the paragraphs include all of the important information?

Does each paragraph make its contribution to advancing the topic and supporting the thesis?

Does the conclusion effectively summarize the main points I have made about my thesis?

If your revised draft meets these requirements, you are done writing. If there are still problems with clarity or continuity, go through your paper again carefully to find out what your paper lacks and to revise the weak sections. (For instructions on writing and revising long research papers, see Chapter 5.)

Proofreading Your Paper

The last step in preparing a writing assignment is **proofreading** the complete paper. Read your paper carefully, looking for misspellings, missing punctuation marks, typos, and layout issues (that is, how the text looks on the page). Read slowly to catch as many small errors as you can. It may be helpful to read the paper out loud. If you can, have a friend read the paper also. Your reader may spot something you missed. Even more important, your peer reviewer can tell you if something in your paper is confusing or not easily understood (for more on peer review, see p. 45).

Spell-checkers are a terrific help in avoiding typos and incorrect spellings, and you should always make use of them before turning in a paper. However, don't expect the spell-checker to catch every misspelled word. The spell-checker flags any word that it does not recognize, including correctly spelled words not in its electronic dictionary. It also will not catch misspelled words that it reads as other words. For example, if you write "him" when you mean to write "his," or "no" for "know," the spell-checker will not read it as a mistake. You must catch these kinds of errors yourself when you proofread your paper.

Grammar-checkers are even less reliable. When you use a grammar-checker, consider its advice as a suggestion for revision. If the grammar-checker questions the way you have said something, consider the advice given before deciding to make any changes to your original sentence, phrase, or word. Keep in mind that you, and not your computer, are the author of your paper.

You are done! It may have taken you a lot longer than you had expected. Some of the work may have been difficult and some tedious. For your effort, you should feel good about yourself even before you learn your grade. You have produced your best work. And with each paper to come, your "best" will get even better.

Preparing Specific Writing Assignments

Instructors give many kinds of writing assignments: among them are book reviews, papers that analyze historical arguments, and research papers. These papers range from a few pages in length to ten or twenty. This section helps you prepare some of the different kinds of writing assignments that you are likely to encounter in your history courses.

Writing Book Reviews

A **book review** is not usually a summary. Unless your instructor asks you to summarize a book's contents, devote most of your review to *analyzing* its contents. Determine its theme; then describe how the theme is presented and how well it is defended. Were you persuaded by the author's arguments? If it is part of the assignment, compare the book to other course materials. Be sure that your review makes it clear that you read and understood the book — or article, document, excerpt, or essay — and always provide the kind of analysis asked of you.

The following is an example of a book review of *Libraries through the Ages* by Fred Lerner (Continuum, 1999).

Sample Book Review

Jane Q. Student
History 100
February 14, 2003

Book Review of
Fred Lerner,
Libraries through the Ages (Continuum, 1999)

The thesis of this history of libraries around the world over the last 2,000 years is that libraries now have a greater impact on society than ever before and that the advent of the computer age is not likely to reverse that development. In the view of the author, libraries' current roles of preserving and dispensing information and of guiding users to what they need will sustain the modern public library in the information age. The author, Fred Lerner, holds degrees in history and in library science and is also the author of *The Story of Libraries.*

In tracing the development of the modern library, the author gives a clear and concise history of the collecting and use of books that followed the invention of writing by the Sumerians some 5,000 years ago. He begins with the earliest writing—characters that were pressed into clay tablets that later hardened. He then describes Egyptian papyrus rolls (rolls of paper made from the stems of papyrus plants) that were stored in jars and Jewish holy books that were written on animal skins.

The first true library was in the Greek colony of Alexandria (in Egypt). Here, possibly for the first time, the effort was made to bring together large numbers of manuscripts, organize them by subject, and make them available to scholars. Service to an elite of rulers, administrators, and scholars remained the role of the library until the nineteenth century.

Lerner then looks at libraries in the Roman Empire and in the early Christian church, when books were no longer rolls but individual, bound pages placed between hard covers. In medieval Europe, monasteries played a vital role in the preservation and duplication of manuscripts (handwritten books). This was the era of the private library owned by kings, aristocrats, bishops, and scholars.

Lerner turns next to an examination of the history of books and libraries in ancient China and India. In China, writing goes back more than 3,000 years (p. 40), and books were under the control of the state. The Chinese invented the modern form of paper, and Chinese scholars wrote down and then copied the classic works that sustained the role of the emperor. In the tenth century, the Chinese developed woodblock printing, making copying much easier. In India, Buddhist monasteries collected manuscripts that were usually written on palm leaves. Indian books were very unusual; according to Lerner, "The pages were pierced in the center and held together with string, then covered with wooden boards, which were often lacquered and brightly painted" (pp. 47–48).

A very important center of learning and writing, libraries developed in the Islamic world after the seventh century. By the year A.D. 1000, Muslim libraries had spread all the way from Spain to India. Many books were religious texts; others dealt with medicine, astronomy, geometry, and philosophy. Islamic emphasis on the words of God (in the Koran) led to rising literacy, and bookshops arose in nearly every major Arab city. Great Islamic libraries were erected. The largest, at the University of Córdoba in Spain, had 400,000 volumes (p. 60). Between the twelfth and fifteenth centuries, however, various invaders destroyed the great Islamic libraries.

In Europe, the copying of books was tremendously accelerated when, in the 1450s, Johannes Gutenberg used a printing press to mass-produce them. A printed book was not only easier to make than a manuscript but also more portable and afford-able, and its contents were uniform, enabling scholars to com-pare and discuss texts.

At the Vatican, the Catholic Church built a very large li-brary that still exists. Elsewhere in Europe, university libraries were established — although in this period, they served only professors and not students (p. 72).

In the early nineteenth century, a library was built in Washington, D.C., for the members of Congress. This is now the enormous Library of Congress. Large libraries were established in major U.S. cities and universities in the nineteenth century, and they were open many days a week and had large reading rooms for the public.

As literacy spread in the United States and Europe, public libraries were erected in cities and towns. At first, the libraries' stacks of books were closed, and patrons had to ask a librarian to get a specific book. By the mid-twentieth century, however, the stacks were open; readers could choose their own books and take them to a checkout librarian.

By the 1930s, public libraries were open to all, and each public school had its own library. The idea of serving the com-munity of readers became firmly established as the library's pri-mary role. This function went well beyond helping someone find a particular book. The "reference collection" of the average library held many hundreds of reference books. These atlases, encyclopedias, dictionaries, and other works held a great deal of factual information that readers needed to live in a complex, industrial society. Another part of the reference collection — bibliographies — helped readers find books and articles on dif-ferent topics. The reference librarian assisted the reader in using all of these works effectively. Another responsibility of the reference librarian was to assist the patron in navigating the huge card catalog, which had at least one card for *every* item in the library. Public and school libraries had established

themselves as places where access to all kinds of information
and knowledge was provided.

Because this new service role for libraries was well established before the age of digital technology, Lerner feels that libraries will not become museums of old knowledge. Instead,
their reference and service function will expand to include access to digital information. Just as we once needed the assistance of reference librarians to find everything from the meaning of a word to the location of a book, now we need them
to guide us through the maze of resources available via the
Internet.

Reviews can vary widely in content to accommodate the different
kinds of work they discuss. Still, a good review, like this one, includes
specific elements. The book under review is identified at the very beginning. Then the author's thesis (about the growing impact of libraries on society) is made clear, and the overall scope of the work
(the 2,000-year development of the public role of the library) is described. The author's qualifications are also mentioned in the introduction. The review then describes the stages in the development of
writing, books, and libraries and the many cultures that have contributed to the process. All of these historical developments are part of
the author's evidence for his thesis. The student reviewer does not assess the quality of the evidence, indicating that she has not become familiar enough with the subject to compare this work with others. If the
course for which she wrote the review included other information on
the history of libraries or on their impact on society, she probably
would be expected to make such a comparison. For this same reason,
the student closes with a summary of the book's conclusions rather
than with her own assessment.

If your instructor asks for a particular kind of review, you should follow those directions. You might be asked to include some of the evidence that argues against the theme and to assess the author's ability
to present that evidence fairly and respond to it effectively. Or you
might be asked to comment on the author's personal or academic
background and reasons for writing the book. This last point should
certainly be included if there is significant debate among historians
about the thesis of the book or if the book's preface or introduction
refers to such disagreements. With a book of this kind, your instructor
may ask you to comment on the debate and perhaps also ask you how
the book affects your views on the subject.

It is usually unwise to emphasize your personal opinion in a review unless your instructor asks you to do so. If you are asked to express it, don't write simply, "I liked the way the author defended women's rights." Instead say, "I was impressed by the author's use of many concrete examples of actions by women to dramatize their demand for the right to vote. The fact that one day they chained themselves to the White House fence made clear how strongly they felt about their cause." Show that your opinion is the result of serious thought about the arguments made in the book.

If your assignment is a review that is longer than a few pages, you might want to quote a sentence or phrase from the book to support a point you are making. But don't use too many quotations; fill your review with your own words rather than the author's words.

The following guidelines summarize this advice.

Guidelines for Writing a Book Review

1. At the top of the first page, put the name of the author, the title of the work, the publisher's name, and the date of publication.
2. State the author's theme and thesis.
3. Describe the evidence presented to support the thesis.
4. If appropriate, describe the author's background and reason for writing the book.
5. If possible, assess the arguments and evidence used. (Are they clear or unclear, strong or weak, convincing or unconvincing?)
6. If required, compare the work to related course materials. (Does it agree or disagree? Does it add a new perspective?)
7. If expected, close with your own assessment of the book's assumptions, arguments, and conclusions.

Writing Comparative Book Reviews

Not all review assignments are concerned with only one source. A comparative book review is more difficult than a review of only one book, because you must also be able to compare the content. You need to discover what the books have in common (consider theme, thesis, style, approaches to the subject, conclusions) and where they differ. The key to success in an essay of this type is to come up with a series of points of similarity or dissimilarity (or some of each) and to focus your essay on them. Don't spend too much time discussing each book separately. Build your essay around the connections between books. That is the purpose of a comparative book review.

Comparing Essays or Articles

If your assignment is to compare essays or articles rather than books, you probably will be expected to treat them in detail. The goals of this kind of assignment are the same as those for comparing books. What are the similarities or differences in the arguments presented? How do the authors make their points? What conclusions do they draw? Again, focus on comparing the works. Don't get bogged down with long descriptions of each one.

Comparing Primary Documents

Comparing documents is a difficult task, but many instructors use this kind of assignment to judge the depth of your knowledge and your interpretive ability. **Primary documents** provide the most direct contact we have with the past, and they are filled with facts and impressions about life in times and places often very different from our own (for more on primary documents, see Chapter 1, pp. 11–17). To understand them, we must know a good deal about the times and places they describe and, if possible, about the people who wrote them.

Consider the following assignment: You are given a series of letters written by U.S. soldiers fighting in Vietnam. Some of the letters talk about the heat and exhaustion of fighting in dense jungles or rice paddies. Some express deep hostility toward the enemy, but others contain no references to the enemy at all. Some letters are filled with questions about what is going on in the soldiers' families and hometowns and hardly even mention the war. The most surprising discovery is that a few letters mention the desire to be wounded (but not seriously) so that the letter writers can be sent home. To make sense of these letters, you need to know a lot about the ground war in Vietnam and the state of mind of the ground troops who fought there. The more you know about the historical event depicted in any set of primary documents, the more they will reveal to you.

Now you are given another group of Vietnam War letters. Unlike the first group written by front-line foot soldiers, these are from bomber pilots. Their war seems different. The pilots' letters don't complain about difficult living conditions. In fact, their lives on air bases or aircraft carriers seem fairly comfortable. They say that they rarely see their targets because they fly so high. Like some of the foot soldiers, the pilots do not talk about the enemy. But unlike some of the ground soldiers, none mentions wanting to get out of the war. In fact, the pilots' morale seems high.

If you are asked to compare the letters from these two groups of soldiers, you will be expected not only to notice the different things they write about but also to have some idea of *why* their letters are different. In this case, an understanding of the difference between the ground war and the air war and between the different types of people who fought in

each is needed. Interpreting and comparing primary documents requires you to go beneath their surface. You need to understand the historical **context,** or historical environment, that gave rise to them.

Writing Short Essays

Writing a short essay requires you to do some research and analysis.
You are assigned, or you may be expected to find on your own, the materials you need to prepare your essay. Many of the skills you need are
similar to those you will use in researching and writing a lengthy research paper of the kind described in Chapters 4 and 5.

You might be asked to take a position in a historical controversy and
to defend your position with historical evidence. You might be asked to
compare a group of readings and draw conclusions about the differences among them. Perhaps you will be asked to write about your own
life experience or that of an older relative and connect the story to important historical events. You might be asked to keep a journal in
which you will write regularly about your response to ideas and subjects
that arise in class discussion.

Some interpretive essays are similar to essay exams. Your instructor
gives you a list of topics to choose from. For example, in a course on
the history of journalism, you are asked to write an essay that includes a
variety of sources about the relationship between rising literacy and the
growth of newspaper circulation in the United States during the nineteenth century. If you study your sources closely you will discover that
your essay cannot take the easy route: the thesis that newspaper circulation increased because more people could read. If things were that
simple, your instructor would not have chosen the topic for this kind of
assignment.

As you dig into your research, you come across evidence that knowing how to read doesn't automatically give a person the desire (or the
money) to read a newspaper. You also learn from your sources that by
the late nineteenth century, illustrations took up a large part of a newspaper page. That meant that even people who knew very few words of
English might still enjoy "reading" a paper. The relationship between
literacy and readership is not a simple one — few things in history are.
Perhaps you will conclude from your research that rising literacy and
rising newspaper circulation reinforced one another, that neither was
the simple cause of the other.

How do you prepare for and execute an assignment like this one?
Here is some advice for preparing a short essay.

Documenting Your Essay. Some assignments of this type require
you to document (identify the sources of) the major facts and conclusions of your essay. Chapter 5 (pp. 130–41) presents examples of
citations to various kinds of sources (books, magazine articles, newspa-

pers, interviews, videos, etc.) You usually inform the reader about your sources in **footnotes** (at the bottom of the page) or **endnotes** (at the end of the essay). You may also need a **bibliography,** an alphabetical list of all the sources you used or consulted. The bibliography is placed at the end of your paper. See Chapter 5 (pp. 141–52) for advice on constructing a bibliography.

Organizing and Writing Your Essay.   If you choose your own topic for your essay, choose carefully. Ask your instructor if your choice is appropriate for the assignment and if it is clearly formulated. Make sure you have all the research materials you need to document your essay. Take careful notes from your research materials (see Chapter 4, pp. 109–12, on taking notes from your sources).

Then write a rough draft. Organize your essay so that it clearly introduces your theme. Then add paragraphs that pursue your theme, including all of the evidence you have gathered from your research to support that theme, utilizing clear, connected sentences that form clear and coherent paragraphs. Finally, write your conclusion, summarizing the main point or points you want to make. Briefly restate your theme, summarizing the most important evidence presented to support it. Proofread the essay for errors of grammar and spelling—even after you run the spell-checker.

The following guidelines summarize this advice.

Guidelines for Writing Short Essays

1. Choose a topic carefully. If you have questions about your choice, speak to your instructor.
2. Choose your research materials carefully so that they flesh out your theme.
3. Organize your paper by placing research notes in the right order.
4. Introduce your essay with a clear statement of your theme.
5. Link sentences and paragraphs so that each new point follows clearly from the one before it. This is your rough draft.
6. Read and revise your rough draft. Look for clarity, continuity, and evidence for your theme.
7. Write a conclusion—a brief restatement of your theme and a summary of the most important evidence presented to support it.
8. If the assignment requires them, include footnotes or endnotes and a bibliography.

---

9. Proofread your revised draft, looking for grammar and spelling mistakes.
10. Produce the final draft neatly, following all of the instructions given by your instructor.

A Note on Plagiarism: A Serious Offense

Whenever you prepare a written assignment while working from notes you have taken from books or other course materials, you must be careful how you use those notes. Otherwise, you run the risk of including in your paper sentences or extended phrases that you copied word for word from your sources. Even if you do this accidentally, you are guilty of **plagiarism.** Unless the phrases or sentences written by other authors are placed in quotation marks and their sources are identified in a **footnote** or **endnote,** you have committed a very serious breach of academic honesty. Plagiarism can lead to failing a course and even to suspension. Be sure to read the sections on avoiding plagiarism and on the art of paraphrasing in Chapter 4 (pp. 113–15).

CHAPTER 4

How to Research a History Topic

In introductory history courses, you may be asked to do historical research. In advanced courses, you certainly will be asked to write research papers. Whether you are preparing a short essay, a book review, a long class presentation, or a term paper, you will need to know how to gather all the necessary materials and how to organize and analyze your information. This chapter will survey sources of historical information and explain how to use these sources most profitably. The chapter also includes sections on how to choose a topic, how to develop a thesis, how to conduct research in your library and on the World Wide Web, how to record information, and how to organize your research.

What Is a Research Paper?

The assignment to write a **research paper** requires you to gather your own sources of information and draw your own conclusions. It is one of the most creative tasks you will do as a history student; the paper you write is uniquely your own. Because a lot of independent work is involved, research is often the most challenging history assignment. The skills you gain from this kind of a project (gathering, organizing, and interpreting evidence) are invaluable. Any professional or business career that you later pursue will call for one or more of these skills. In years to come, you may not remember the name of the secret research program that produced the atomic bomb during World War II (the Manhattan Project), about which you wrote a paper. But while you were engaged in the research *process* that produced the paper, you were strengthening important skills.

Five stages of research are involved in preparing your paper: (1) choosing a topic and developing a thesis, (2) finding the best sources of information, (3) determining what you need to record from these sources, (4) organizing your research, and (5) writing the research paper. The last step—actually writing the paper—is the subject of the next chapter. This chapter takes you through the first four steps.

What Should I Write About?
Choosing a Topic and Crafting a Thesis

Some instructors assign a specific **topic** for research, but most set out a range of possible topics and leave the choice to you. Choose your topic carefully. You will become bored if you have to spend weeks searching out and reading information about a subject that does not interest you. Try to select a topic about which you are genuinely curious. No matter what subject, person, or event you are interested in, it has a history. Every subject can be studied backward in time because every event was caused by events that preceded it. A history research project can be created out of almost anything. Perhaps in the neighborhood where you grew up there was a very old building and you always wondered when it was built and what it was used for. Finding out what the neighborhood was like when that building was new can be an exciting search.

An ideal topic is not only one about which you are curious but one about which you already know something. Perhaps you read a book about Socrates and want to know more about why he was condemned to death. Perhaps you saw a movie about the Depression and want to know what it was like to live through it. Instructors are eager to help students who show a real interest in a topic. Your instructor can assist you in selecting a topic related to your interests that also suits the particular course you are taking.

Moving from a Topic to a Theme

A **theme** is more narrow than a topic. A *topic* is the general subject: the influence of Islam on the kingdom of Mali; the philosophy of Martin Luther King Jr. A *theme* is some important aspect of the topic that you wish to investigate. For a paper on King, you may want to show that his "I Have a Dream" speech at the Lincoln Memorial in 1963 expressed several elements of his religious beliefs. In that case, your theme is the connection between the speech and King's religious development. This connection will be the central point of your paper, and making that connection will direct your research and writing. Without a theme, you will not have a clear idea of which sources of information to investigate, what to take from them, or how to organize your paper.

The transition from a broad topic to a narrower theme is not always easy. The key is to find an aspect of your topic that can serve as the core of your paper, that fits the sources available to you, and that can be satisfactorily researched in the time available to complete the assignment. A topic such as the Spanish conquest of the Aztec Empire can produce both workable and unwieldy themes. The theme "the correspondence of Hernán Cortés and King Ferdinand" may be feasible if it is confined to letters from Cortés about the conquest of the Aztecs. The trouble here is access to sources. Unless this correspondence is available in your library or on the **World Wide Web,** you will not have the research material to explore this theme. In contrast, the theme "the factors that enabled the Spanish to defeat the Aztecs" is workable because you should have no difficulty in finding enough material on this subject.

Even if resources are available, make sure that your theme is not too broad. For a topic such as European exploration of Africa, you might come up with the theme "exploration of the Congo River." However, dozens of such explorations were made over many years, so this is not a proper theme—it is actually a topic. If you begin to research "exploration of the Congo River," you will soon discover that there are too many sources and that you do not have time (or space in your paper) to do them justice.

Narrowing Your Theme

Formulating a theme that is narrow enough yet not too narrow is tricky. When narrowing a theme, it is often useful to compose questions about your topic. If your topic is Native Americans of the western United States, ask yourself a question you would like to know the answer to. Maybe some aspect of Native American life, such as the thoughts of medicine men or the conflict between a particular tribe and European settlers, has aroused your curiosity. You might ask yourself: "What did medicine men believe?" or "How did the Indians defend their lands?" These questions might yield themes such as "the practice of magic among the Cheyenne," or "efforts of the Nez Perce to protect their native lands in Oregon." For a topic about Canadian frontier communities in the nineteenth century, ask yourself what specific things you would like to know about them. Was the coming of the railroad of great importance to them? This might lead you to the theme "the Canadian Pacific Railroad comes to Winnipeg, Manitoba." Although composing questions is usually helpful in arriving at themes, be careful that the questions you ask are not too broad ("Why did the Roman Empire fall?"). Questions also can be too narrow ("Who was the first person to sign the Declaration of Independence?") or too unimportant ("Why are Ping-Pong tables green?").

If you know very little about your topic, then it is wise to learn more before you attempt to narrow it and produce a good theme. If your topic is the Mexican Revolution of 1910, check a brief history of the subject in a good historical dictionary or **encyclopedia** (for example, the *Encyclopaedia Britannica* or the *Encyclopedia of Latin America*). The description of the Mexican Revolution in these works will likely mention its principal leaders—Francisco Madero, Pancho Villa, Emiliano Zapata, and Venustiano Carranza. Perhaps your interest will then be triggered by the recollection of stories concerning Villa's daring raid on the U.S. border town of Columbus, New Mexico, in 1916 and how the U.S. Army under General John Pershing marched into Mexico to capture Villa—but never did. Or perhaps you have seen the Hollywood movie *Viva Zapata,* which tells the story (not very accurately) of the peasant leader Emiliano Zapata and his fight to preserve the lands of the Indian villages in his native state of Morelos. If you have ever seen photographs of Zapata, you know his piercing eyes and look of determination.

If your interest in the Mexican Revolution is now focusing on Villa or Zapata, you should next turn to a biographical dictionary. Here you will discover that Villa's real name was Doroteo Arango and that he was a cattle thief as well as a brilliant military commander. Zapata, you will learn, led a peasant guerrilla army whose aim was to recapture village land seized by the owners of expanding sugar plantations. To flesh out a paper on Villa's military career or Zapata's land reform program (some elements of which Mexican peasants are still struggling to achieve today), turn to the **subject bibliographies** in Appendix A (pp. 192–209), to the reference section of your library, or to an online reference source such as *Encyclopaedia Britannica* online. These tools will lead you to individual historical works on the Mexican Revolution, and from the book and article titles (and the descriptions of their contents if they are annotated) you will be able to identify those that may contain information on the theme you are considering.

Moving from a Theme to a Thesis

Your **thesis** is a specific point or argument that you intend to make about your theme. Crafting a thesis is the last step in the narrowing process that takes you from a general topic to a more narrow theme and finally to a specific thesis. Your thesis is not a description of your theme; it is a statement of the central argument or claim you intend to make about your theme. It should reflect your conclusions and be based on your analysis of the sources you consulted. For example, "European imperialism in Africa" is a topic; "Belgian rule over the territory of the Congo" is a theme; and "the brutality of Belgian rule over the Congo" is a thesis.

It is usually not necessary to finalize a thesis until you complete your research, unless your instructor says to do so earlier. Just as you need to have knowledge of your topic in order to create your theme, so you must wait until you have conducted research on your theme before you can decide which particular aspect of the theme will be your thesis. (See "Why Your Paper Needs a Thesis," pp. 121–22.)

Creating a Research Outline

A **research outline** is different from the outline you will create when you actually write your paper (see the section on preparing a **writing outline** on pp. 116–19). A research outline helps you to investigate your theme in an organized way. It tells you which parts of your research should come first. Here is a sample research outline for investigating the topic of agrarian reform in the Mexican Revolution, which, after preliminary research, led to the theme "the land reform program of Emiliano Zapata." It also includes an *estimate* (shown in italics) of the time needed for each step.

RESEARCH OUTLINE

Task #1: [Background] Gain a general knowledge of the Mexican Revolution from a good encyclopedia, textbook, or Web site. *Approximately 2–3 hours over 1 day.*

Task #2: [Background] Learn about land reform *before* the revolution. An encyclopedia or a general history of Mexico in the nineteenth century. *Approximately 2–3 hours over 1 day.*

Task #3: [Information about Zapata] Life in Ananecquilco, Morelos (village and state where Zapata grew up). A biography of Zapata and a book or articles examining changes in village life in Morelos in the decades before 1910. *Approximately 6–9 hours over 3 days.*

Task #4: [Information about land reform] Books, articles, and documents (including online resources) about how the villagers lost their lands before 1910. *Approximately 6–9 hours over 3 days.*

Task #5: [Zapata's role in the effort to regain village lands] Sources that examine Zapata's early career as a village leader. *Approximately 6–9 hours over 3 days.*

Task #6: [The period of the revolution, 1910–1920] Sources examining the role of Zapata and his followers in the revolution. *Approximately 8–12 hours over 4 days.*

Task #7: [Specific land reform programs] Books (maybe old ones available online or in your library on microfilm or microfiche) that contain quotations from or copies of the actual proposals made by Zapata. *Approximately 4–6 hours over 2 days.*

Task #8: [The fate of the programs] Read about the final years of the revolution and of the fate of Zapata (assassinated in 1919). *Approximately 4–6 hours over 2 days.*

Not all research outlines can be this specific. The time frame, in particular, is only an estimation. It contains nineteen days of research and assumes that you spend about two or three hours each day conducting research and reading. Your particular assignment may require more or less time, depending on the length of your paper and the importance given to it by your instructor. (Remember this is only the time needed for *research*. Writing your paper will, of course, take additional time.) Moreover, no outline can be followed exactly. Your own research may move back and forth among the tasks (especially the later ones) on a given day in the library. While you are gathering material on Zapata's early life, you may come across a book or a Web site about his land program.

The information you find in the library and on the World Wide Web will not be neatly divided into the tasks you have laid out. The reason for organizing your research in a formal way, even if the actual process turns out to be much messier, is to give yourself a sense of direction that you otherwise would lack. If you don't know what kinds of sources to look for first, which to read first, and which to read later, you may try to take notes on specific land reform proposals before you even know who Zapata was or how long the revolution lasted. Even if you cannot actually follow an outline like the one opposite, just making the outline and having it in mind as you do your research will help you. In short, don't begin serious research until you have a clear idea of what you will be looking for. You may change directions (even change your theme) after some background reading, and you can always adjust your outline. It is better to have a research outline that you change than no outline at all.

After conducting preliminary research to decide which aspects of your topic interest you most, narrowing your topic to a manageable theme, and creating a research outline to direct your research, you are ready to seek out sources of information. Your **library catalog** and the materials (print and digital) listed in Appendix A should enable you to create a list of potential sources. The next step, of course, is to find these sources. They may be in print form on the shelves of your library, they may be in microprint form (**microfilm** and **microfiche**), or they may be in electronic form such as CD-ROM databases or Web-based documents. To find these sources, you will first have to learn how to conduct research in your library and on the Web.

Conducting Research

Exploring Your Library's Resources

A college library can be an intimidating place. Don't begin your research until you are familiar with it. Take a library tour to find where and how different library resources are housed. Never hesitate to ask a librarian about the organization of the library. For example, you should know where the **library stacks**[1] are — the shelves where bound books and journals are stored. You should also be able to find such areas as the section where **reference books** (encyclopedias, dictionaries, **atlases,** etc.) are shelved and the microprint section (microfilms and microfiche).

Once you have a sense of the place, sit yourself down at one of the **on-line catalogs.** Become familiar with the library's **home page.** It should tell you how to search for different kinds of material. Explore the home page carefully so that you don't overlook major portions of the material available to you. For example, the home page should link you to a list of the library's electronic databases. (For a description and list of electronic databases, see Appendix A, pp. 212–14.) It is often possible to jump from the home page to the **World Wide Web.** But finding information on the Web can be tricky, so it is best to begin your search in your library. (For help on conducting research online, see pp. 93–103.)

Creating a Research Bibliography

As you begin to discover useful materials in your library, make sure to copy down *exactly and fully* all of the information on each item. Your goal is to compile a **research bibliography,** a list of the sources that you think will give you the information you need to describe your theme and to document the facts you use to support it. When you finally write your paper, you may decide not to use some of these items. At this stage of your research, however, cast your net broadly. (For more on creating a bibliography, see Chapter 5, pp. 141–52.)

Using the Library Catalog

The main catalog is the most important pathway into the materials you need to know about to conduct your research. To get what you want out of the catalog, you need to know the rules for searching its contents. You can search for books in the online catalog by author, title, or subject. The catalog will have a screen or menu that tells you which commands begin an author search, a title search, a subject search, or a keyword search.

Searching the Catalog by Author and Title. Author and title searches are usually simple as long as you know the proper commands and spell the names or titles correctly. If you enter the author name "Chakspeere, William" (instead of "Shakespeare, William") you will not get very far. The spelling of ancient and foreign names is especially tricky. Check the spelling before you begin your search. If you still are uncertain, ask the reference librarian. Title searches also pose a few

---

[1] Some library stacks are open to students; others are not. If possible, wander around the stacks of your college library so that you know what the inside of the library looks like.

dangers. Again, spelling is crucial. In addition, titles that *begin* with "A" or "The" can confuse the computer. The catalog's rules for title searching usually tell you which words in titles can cause trouble. Finally, be sure to get all of the words of the title just right.

Although author and title searches are fairly straightforward, they require you to know in advance what person or book you are looking for. This is often not possible, especially when you are beginning your research. For the most part, you will need to discover which books by which authors are related to your theme. To do this, you must search the online catalog by subject. This is a little more difficult. Unless you enter the right words, the computer will not list the materials you really need.

Searching the Catalog by Subject or Keyword. Online catalogs allow you to search their contents by subject or by keyword or both. Though similar, subject and keyword searches are not the same. In a library catalog, a **subject heading** is a term (or terms) that the library profession has chosen to describe the contents of the material listed under that heading. A **keyword,** in contrast, is a term that *you* choose because it seems to describe the kinds of sources that you think you need.[2] This discussion first takes up subject headings; an examination of keywords follows.

SUBJECT HEADINGS

If you want to search by subject heading in the most complete way, go to the official set of headings compiled by the Library of Congress. These headings are printed in the volumes *Library of Congress Subject Headings,* usually kept in the reference section of the library or near the computer terminals. The online catalog will use these headings in its own internal organization. Another way to discover the best subject headings is to look up a book that you already know about (by author or title), and when you get it on the screen, go to "long" or "full" display. This display tells you more than the author, title, and location; you get full publication data as well as the subject heading or headings under which the book is listed in the catalog. Other books on your theme may be listed under this heading, so you can use this heading to find them. Because no two computer catalogs are exactly alike, finding out how to use subject headings may require the help of a librarian. Don't be shy; a librarian's assistance can save you a great deal of time.

KEYWORDS

Another way of searching the computer catalog is by keyword. Most catalogs enable you to search in this way. Instead of trying to figure out which subject your topic is under, you ask the computer to search its records of books and other materials for certain words.

---

[2]An example of a subject heading is "Textile industry—Massachusetts—Lowell—History—19th Century." A keyword in the same topic area might be "women textile workers."

Suppose your topic is women workers in early industrial America and you have narrowed it to the theme "women workers in the Lowell, Massachusetts, textile mills, 1820–1850." Your keywords are the nouns in your theme—"women," "workers," "Lowell," "textile mills." Don't search by using any of these words by themselves, for they are too general and will generate a long list of sources, most of which will not be related to your theme. Entering the word "women," for example, will get you everything in the library that has anything to do with the topic of women. Most computers allow you to do complex keyword searches that combine several key words. You can ask the computer, for example, to find records that mention "women" *and* "workers" or, better yet, "women workers" *and* "textile mills." (Placing the word "and" between your keywords narrows the search accordingly.) The rules for keyword searching are often described in the Help menu on the computer. Again, if you need assistance with keyword searches, ask for it. Using the wrong keywords will get you a lot of material that you cannot use. Even the precise keyword can turn up unrelated items. The keyword "textile mills" may give you a useful title such as *The Textile Mills of Lowell, Massachusetts,* but it might also give you *Textile Mills in Japan during World War II.* Notice that time period is crucial in a history search. A search for "history" *and* "textile mills" or "history" *and* "women workers" should cut out most studies that are about recent developments.[3]

Don't sit at the computer monitor for long stretches trying to find that one subject heading or keyword that will give you everything you want. Once your searches have turned up a number of promising titles, print out or write down (preferably on note cards) *all* of the information on the screen that you will need for your **bibliography** (see pp. 141–52) as well as the **call number** of each book. The call number indicates a book's location in the library stacks (see the section on locating materials and using call numbers on p. 92). You will probably discover that many of the books you listed have call numbers that begin with the same letters or numbers. When you get to the stacks, don't look only for the specific books you found in your computer search; look at *all* of the books on nearby shelves as well. You will likely find additional works related to your theme.

A word of caution about using an electronic catalog: You cannot find what is not there. Not everything in the library may be cataloged. The electronic catalog may list only material received by the library after a certain date. Some libraries have not yet put all of their holdings online. Ask the librarian for the starting date of the catalog. An-

---

[3]The spelling of place-names can make keyword searches difficult—especially place-names that have changed over time. Persia became Iran; New Spain became Mexico; Siam became Thailand. Know the proper name of the place you are looking for *during the period you are focusing on.* Geographical subdivisions present problems as well. Umbria is a region of Italy; if you did not know this, you might not be able to search for it effectively. Always learn the larger geographical or political unit of which your own subject is a part.

other problem is that some electronic catalogs may list material that is not in your library but in one very far away. Be sure to find out whether the material you want is on campus. Getting material from a distant library can take time. The process in which your library borrows a book from another library is called **interlibrary loan.** Don't wait until it is too late to find out that a book you really need has to be borrowed from another library.

EXERCISE
Finding a Book in Your Library

Here is a self-study assignment to help you determine whether you have mastered the basic research skill of finding a book in your library.

a. Choose a research theme and then two or three keywords that relate to that theme.
b. Conduct a catalog search using your chosen keywords.
c. Scan the list of books generated in response to your search, and select several of the most promising-sounding titles.
d. Find these books on the library shelves, and determine how, if at all, they address your theme. If none of the books is useful, return to the online catalog and refine your search terms. Continue refining your search until the list of items returned is manageable in size and contains several titles that turn out to be useful.

Searching for Articles in Journals, Magazines, and Newspapers. Students often search for books but skip over other valuable sources. Some computer catalogs don't even include what librarians call "nonbook" items. If, for example, you want to find journal or newspaper articles related to your theme, you need to know where to look for them. Usually nonbook items are listed in databases contained either on **CD-ROMs** or on the Web (for more on the World Wide Web, see pp. 93–103). Like the online catalog, databases are searchable by title, keyword, and author (the most useful history databases are described in Appendix A, pp. 212–14).

Periodical articles are important nonbook sources of information. This category of publication includes **journals** (which contain articles for students and scholars) and *magazines* and *newspapers* (which contain articles for the general reading public but can sometimes be helpful to students). Web-based or CD-ROM databases can give you access to a large number of journal articles. Others can be found in your library stacks or on microfilm or microfiche.

JOURNALS

Journals are the best periodical sources for history research. Articles in journals may contain important information related to your topic. For the theme "women workers in the Lowell, Massachusetts, textile mills, 1820–1850," you could gain useful information from the article "Letters of a Lowell Mill Girl and Friends," published in the journal *Labor History* in 1976. How would you find out about this article and whether you can get a copy of it? In this case you need an **index** (electronic or printed) that lists journal articles by author, title, and subject.

The journal indexes accessible in your library may be part of the library's main computer catalog or may be housed in separate databases. Most libraries also have printed copies of journal indexes. Journal indexes are also available on the World Wide Web. Your library probably has indexes such as *America: History and Life* and *Historical Abstracts,* which list articles in scholarly journals. Check the subject index under "women workers," "textile mills," and "Lowell, Massachusetts." In this way, you should be able to find any journal articles related to your theme. What you are doing is searching for journal articles in the same way you searched for books—by subject or keyword. Of course, if you already know the author or title of the article you want, those are also search options. For a list of journal indexes for history, see pages 213–14.

An important advantage in searching for journal articles, especially on a computer, is that the indexes are often annotated—that is, they contain brief descriptions (called **abstracts**) of the contents of each article. The annotations can help you to decide whether to read an article. Some databases allow you to print out an entire article in your library even if the library does not have the journal in its print collection. In this way, a student at a small library can obtain articles without requesting an interlibrary loan. Before you print out a copy of an article, however, make sure that the title and annotation really sound promising. Your library may charge for such a service. Even if it is free, there is the danger that you will be tempted to print the article mainly because doing so is easier than going into the stacks to look for articles that you cannot print out. Seek out the articles that are most relevant for your theme, not simply those that are easiest to come by.

One final problem in searching for articles in databases or on the Web is that they usually only include articles that were published recently. Databases are huge but not infinite. One of their limitations is that they only hold material published *after a certain date.* (Another less common problem is that they may *stop* at a certain date.) It is important to know the **date range** of a database. If a database has only material less than ten years old, you cannot find in it sources published or created longer ago. In history research, the date range of a database is important to know; it can tell you what is *not* there and save you a lot of searching time.

Many academic journals have their own printed indexes. For example, all of the articles in the *Canadian Historical Review* will be printed in the volume *Index to the Canadian Historical Review*. Printed indexes to specific journals are kept in the stacks next to the bound volumes of the journal. Once you have looked at general journal indexes (ones that cover many journals), you will probably discover that several articles related to your topic come from a small number of journals. If this is the case, it is wise to go into the stacks and seek out the indexes to these journals. Returning to the theme "women workers in the Lowell, Massachusetts, textile mills, 1820–1850," you may have discovered that the journal *Labor History* has several articles that sound promising. If this is the case, look through the index to that journal. You will probably find other useful articles there.

Another, and quicker, way to find journal articles related to your theme is by looking at the documentation in the books and articles that you have *already* found. The **footnotes** (or **endnotes**) in these sources will mention the books and articles that the author relied on, and many of them will also be relevant to your theme. From the footnotes or endnotes, copy down the titles of any articles (and books) that seem relevant to your theme. In fact, whenever you find a good source, check its note and bibliography against the sources you already have, and add any promising items to your **research bibliography.** Be sure, as always, to copy down *all* of the relevant information for your own notes and bibliography. (See the section on documenting your paper in Chapter 5, pp. 127–52.)

MAGAZINES AND NEWSPAPERS

Current issues of popular magazines (Such as *People, Time,* and *National Geographic*) and newspapers rarely contain serious historical studies. However, if your library has printed or electronic copies of magazines and newspapers from the period of your theme, these can be valuable sources. For example, the *Lowell Courier* from the 1830s may very well have *contemporary* articles on women workers in the textile mills. This is a valuable source because it is also a **primary source** (see the section on primary and **secondary sources** of evidence in Chapter 1, pp. 11–15). Old issues of magazines and newspapers may be available in your library (usually on microfiche or microfilm) and can be very helpful. When you search for newspapers or magazines in your library's catalog, be sure to note the span of years that are included. If a particular magazine was published in the 1830s and 1840s, it may be useful in a research paper on early textile mills. However, your library may not have issues going back that far. If your library does not have the newspaper or magazine you are looking for, try to find it on the Web.

Research in Primary Sources

One of the most interesting aspects of historical research is to read what someone who was part of a historical event or period felt and thought about the experience. The diary of a young woman crossing the West by wagon train, a newspaper article describing Babe Ruth hitting a home run, the minutes of a private meeting between President John F. Kennedy and his advisers during the Cuban missile crisis, a recording of Bessie Smith singing the blues—each of these is as close to history as you can get and helps you to imagine what the past was like for those who lived it. If at all possible, include primary material in your research.

If a history **archive** (a place such as a museum or historical society or a Web site where primary sources are stored and collected) has primary materials related to your theme, be sure to include some of them in your research. If your topic is less than fifty years in the past, you may be able to *interview* someone who lived through it. You can't get any closer to history than that!

Most college libraries have copies of primary materials—on microfilm, on microfiche, or in electronic databases. The World Wide Web is by far the best source for primary documents. Entire sites are dedicated to placing historical documents on the Web so that anyone, anywhere, can read and copy them. It is likely that the Web will become the principal resource for primary documents of all kinds — print, visual, and sound. (For a list of some of these sites, see Appendix A, pp. 216–29.)

One final point about primary documents: You need to have read a lot about your theme in order to understand them. You won't know why the faces of the Italian family look so bewildered in the old photograph of immigrants arriving in America if you haven't learned about the mixture of confusion, fear, and excitement that was part of coming to the United States in the late nineteenth or early twentieth centuries. You won't know why the letters of Thomas Jefferson on the subject of slavery sound so uncertain unless you know about the battle going on in his mind about the place of Africans in a republic. Use primary sources if you can, but save them until you are acquainted with your theme.

Reference Sources

Reference material is available in two places: (1) your library's section of printed reference works and electronic databases and (2) the World Wide Web. Each year, more and more reference works (such as the *Encyclopaedia Britannica* at britannica.com) that once existed only in print form are beginning to appear on the Web. To discover the reference sources that will give you background information and lead you to more detailed information on your theme, be sure to make use of both kinds of resources.

A useful printed reference book or database may be just a few steps away from where you are sitting in your library. For printed bound works, ask for the reference section. You will find there hundreds of books (thousands in a large library) — dictionaries, encyclopedias, atlases, periodical and magazine indexes, and specialized **subject bibliographies.** In general, these works can help you define your terms; gather background information on a topic; and locate specific facts, dates, and biographical or statistical details. They also serve as starting points for locating additional materials. Each reference work has its own way of organizing its contents. Just as you need to learn how to conduct a Web search, so you need to learn the organizational schemes of various reference works. An explanation is usually found at the beginning of each work. If you are having trouble with a printed reference source, ask the librarian for help.

There are two places to look for electronic reference sources: databases in your library and databases on the World Wide Web. Your library most likely has a number of CD-ROM databases that are useful reference tools. Be sure to ask which databases are accessible in the library. Some of these databases can also be found on the Web; your library may have contracted for direct access to them. To find databases on the Web, ask your librarian and also see the list of digital sources in Appendix A; it begins on page 212.

Subject Bibliographies. The most useful reference sources are subject bibliographies. They are available in printed form in the reference section of your library, in database form on CD-ROM, also in your library, and, of course, on the Web. (You will find a large number of printed and electronic subject bibliographies listed in Appendix A.) Subject bibliographies list all kinds of research material by subject. Of course, not all of the works listed in these bibliographies will be available to you either in your library or on the Web. Still, they are the best place to begin your research for the sources you will need to explore your theme. If your theme is the use of chemical weapons in the Vietnam War, the print subject bibliography *The Wars in Vietnam, Cambodia, and Laos, 1945–1982: A Bibliographical Guide* may lead you to many relevant sources. If your theme is the diplomacy of the Vietnam War, the Web site *Documents Related to the Vietnam War* (mtholyoke.edu/acad/intrel/vietnam.htm) may be a good place to find useful material.

There is no one path to the best sources. Printed and electronic works have their own strengths and weaknesses. On the one hand, Web sites may be organized so that you can search their contents in the same way you search an online catalog. This is a very useful tool. On the other hand, a Web site can move and not leave a forwarding address, but a printed volume will always be on the shelf—unless someone else is using it.

Locating Library Materials and Using Call Numbers

After completing your search of the subject bibliographies, you will have a list of materials that you want to look at. If some of these are not in your library, you may be able to find them on the Web or borrow them from another library. A librarian will have to assist you in the latter task. If the materials are in your own library, the **call number** will lead you to them.

If the library stacks are open to students, pay attention to signs on the walls and at the ends of rows of shelves that tell where a particular group of call numbers is to be found. Almost all online catalogs will tell you whether a book has been taken out by someone else. If it has not been checked out and you still can't find it on the shelf, go back to the catalog and verify the call number. An error of even one number in a call number can make your search all but impossible. Always be sure to copy call numbers letter by letter and number by number exactly as they appear in the catalog. If the number is correct, and you still can't find the book, ask the librarian to help you locate it.

Browsing the Library Shelves.   Most of the call numbers on the list you have created will be in groups. They will begin with similar letters and numbers. All of the books with similar call numbers will be near one another on the library's shelves. As a result, when you get to the place in the stacks where one book is located, it will be surrounded by other books with very similar call numbers. Because the system of filing books by call number is related to subject matter, nearby books may also be on your list. Just as important, nearby books that are not on your list may be just as close to your topic as those that are. Read the titles of the books near to the one you are seeking. If the titles seem promising, add them to your list.

Locating Other Historical Materials

The easiest way to go beyond the resources of your library is, of course, via the World Wide Web. However, if you are fortunate, your topic will be one on which special historical materials are available at a nearby special collections library, a museum, a historical society, the archives of an institution or corporation, or the film and audiotape libraries of television and radio studios (see the section on research in primary sources earlier in this chapter).

Older members of your community or your own family also can be sources of historical information. People who have been leaders in local and national affairs have personal knowledge of important historical events. Perhaps you could prepare a series of questions concerning past events in which they were participants. You can write to these individuals or perhaps speak with them. They may also have personal papers they would permit you to see. This kind of historical research is exciting and satisfying, and it may enable you to use primary historical material that no other historian has uncovered.

As already mentioned, older adults are good sources of historical material. They can tell of their years in another country or describe the America in which they grew up. They may not have been important historical figures, but they reflect the experiences of countless others and are thus the stuff of which history is made. Their recollections of how they felt and of what they and others did and said when, for example, women won the right to vote, Lindbergh flew across the Atlantic, World War II ended, or the Berlin Wall came down are priceless pieces of the historical puzzle. (See also "How to Research Your Family History" in Appendix B, pp. 233–35.)

Conducting Research on the World Wide Web

Many of the computer terminals in your library and probably your own computer are connected to the **World Wide Web.** On the Web you can search for information stored in millions of computers around the world. If you know how to explore the Web, you can add a world of information to the materials available on the shelves of your school library.

Web searching offers numerous advantages. The material available is immense. If you know the correct electronic path, you can reach what you are looking for in seconds. The variety is almost endless as well: books, journal articles, magazines, newspapers, primary documents, photographs, audio and video files, and so on.

Another advantage of Web searching is that you can communicate with people as well as with computers. E-mail, newsgroups, and discussion groups put you in touch with other Web users who are communicating with one another. There are many history-oriented newsgroups where you can post messages, ask questions, and join conversations on history topics of interest to you. See "Electronic Discussion Lists in History" in Appendix A (pp. 230–31).

Because the pool of information is so huge, you need to use a variety of search tools to navigate the Web. Knowing how to use these tools will save you a great deal of time and help ensure that you come up with the most relevant and valuable material.

Using Subject Indexes and Directories

Subject indexes and directories are long lists of Web-based information sources that are arranged hierarchically by subject. They start with the broadest subject and narrow the choices offered on the screen until you reach a subject area that is close to your theme. (At present, Yahoo! is one of the most extensive and popular directories.) For example, if you are searching for information on women textile workers in Massachusetts, you will need to begin with the first screen of the subject index containing very broad categories such as "science," "business," or "literature." You would choose the category "history," if it is available. From the history page, you would narrow your search by making links to "U.S. history," then to "19th century," then to a choice such as "labor history" or perhaps "women's history," and finally to any additional links that seem to head toward "Massachusetts" or "textile mills." If you can find either of these last two categories, all of the sources listed at that point should be very close to your theme. Unless the list is very long, check each one for historical material relevant to your theme.

The key to searching a **subject index** or **directory** is to choose the most promising **link** (or links) at each stage of the search. If you seem to be getting off track—for instance, heading toward "famous Massachusetts women" or "the art of textiles"—press the Back button and try a different route. One of the most useful aspects of indexes and directories is that most links are clearly labeled so that you have a good idea of the kinds of sites you are heading toward.

Here is another example. For the theme "public education in Japan, 1900–1930," don't click on the choice "Asian history" if the more specific choice "Japanese history" is on the same page. Don't choose "current educational outcomes in Japan" rather than "Western influences on Japanese education before World War II." Remember, the index or directory may not give you easy choices; don't expect it to have a category that fits your theme exactly. The challenge is choosing the category that best matches your theme. As noted above, if the category you choose leads you away from your theme, go back and try another.

When you reach a Web site that seems to fit your topic (or, better yet, your theme), your next task is to search the site to see if it has relevant research material. Even a site with a promising title such as "Why Japan Is Number One in Education" may contain only comparisons of students' test scores from the 1990s, clearly not the kind of material you need. In many instances, you cannot determine the usefulness of a site until you have explored it. However, if a few minutes of exploration make it clear that the site is not relevant (for instance, it is about faculty exchange programs at Japanese universities), retrace your steps and take a different route through the directory.

Other dangers lurk in cyberspace. Each day more commercial sites are added to the Web and more commercial messages are *built into* existing Web sites. In the traditional library, you do not have to worry about an ad for an online bookseller popping up as you open the pages of a book. Numerous and distracting advertisements on a Web site usually mean that its purpose is commercial rather than educational. Still, there are some exceptions, and the best advice is to ignore the ads and focus on the text or graphics in the main frame of the page.

Another difficulty with Web searching is that some sites are available only to subscribers. This means that access to a site or to a portion of its content is controlled. If the site is not a free one, you will have access to it only if your library has a license to use it. In a predigital library you needed a library card to borrow a book, but looking at a book was free. Unfortunately, parts of the Web are not free. Still, do not be discouraged. An enormous amount of useful material on the Web is free and accessible. The main challenge is finding it.

The last difficulty in using the Web has already been introduced — determining the *quality* of the information on a Web site. You may be delighted to come across an essay on "modern Japanese education" only to discover that it was written by a Japanese high school student. If you have any doubts about the *quality* of the information you have downloaded or printed out, show it to your instructor. See also "Evaluating Web-Based Sources" later in this chapter.

Using Search Engines

Search engines are search tools more powerful than indexes or directories but also less precise, making search skills even more crucial. The main difficulty with search engines is that they search by word or group of words, not by subject. To search with a search engine, you type a word or phrase into the search box (say, "women textile workers"), and the engine scans millions of Web pages for these words, looking especially for pages in which the words you are searching for occur more than once or appear close together on the page. (Lycos, AltaVista, and Google are search engines that you may be familiar with.) The result, even for a fairly specific search phrase such as "women textile workers," could be hundreds (perhaps thousands) of pages that match one or more of the search words. The search engine will list all of the sites where these words appear. The list usually begins with the ones that best fit the search terms.

Each search engine searches and displays its results a little differently. If you have a choice of engines, it is best to ask the reference librarian which is best for the kind of search you are making. Unlike the search results from subject indexes and directories, the list of sites that the search engine brings to your screen will have only a brief description to indicate its possible relevance to your topic. This means that you will need to click on a lot of sites to see whether they are useful. Once at a site, if you follow one of its links, you may discover yourself in a strange place (such as "fashions in women's clothing" because clothes are made from textiles). You will then have to backtrack to your list of sites to try another one. As you click on promising sites, you may come up against the most frustrating part of Web searching: dead or moved links. If you are lucky, you will get a message that tells you where the new link is. If not, you will get an error message indicating that the site you were looking for cannot be found. Then back you must go to the long list of sites your search engine came up with. As noted before, search engines cover many more Web sites than directories do, but they are not as specific in what they give you. To avoid being handed thousands of sites by your search engine, type in a search term that is as specific as possible.

There are other obstacles to overcome when searching for useful research material on the Web. First of all, each search engine explores only a small portion of the Web. Moreover, each works differently, and you have to know the strengths and weaknesses of the one you are using. Sometimes you need to use more than one (or use a meta-engine that combines the searching of several engines) to find what you are looking for. Don't expect to type the name of your theme in the search line and then sit back to harvest all the information you need. If you ask an engine to search for the topic "education in Japan," it will dump onto your screen every site it finds that has Web pages related to Japan or to education. This could be a *very* long list. Buried within it might be a site useful to research on the history of Japanese education, but it might take you days to find it. For serious research, it is almost always advisable to use *advanced* search techniques. These techniques are usually explained on the **home page** or on the Help pages of the search engine. Be sure to read about them before you begin your search.

With advanced search techniques, you ask the engine to look for certain words and not for others, or for words in a special order, or for words that appear together on the same Web page. For example, an advanced search for information on the theme "public education in Japan, 1900–1930" might look like this: "public education" AND Japan AND history. The quotes around "public education" tell the search engine to look for Web pages that have *both* words together; the "ands" between the three segments of your search term tell the engine to return *only* those pages that mention *all three* terms. Again, be sure to take the time to learn these and other advanced search techniques. They will direct your search more specifically toward the Web pages that are closest to what you are looking for and will save you a great deal of time. Advanced search rules vary from engine to engine, so be sure to follow the particular ones that are built into the search engine you are using.

One type of search engine is relatively easy to navigate. This is a **periodical database.** The engine searches only the data stored on a CD-ROM or on one site on the Web. Of course, you must choose a periodical database that contains a large number of history journals. (*America: History and Life* and *Historical Abstracts* have already been mentioned.) Not all periodical databases will be available to you. Some are free, but you can use others only if your library has a license. Some databases contain only the title and date of the article and the name of the journal; you will have to get a copy on your own from your library or from the Web in order to read it. Other databases are **full-text databases,** which let you read the entire article or print it out for later reading. The reference librarian can help you pick the best periodical database for your theme. Searching in periodical databases should be part of any serious research effort.

EXERCISE

Finding an Article in a Periodical Database

Here is a self-study assignment to help you determine whether you have mastered the basic research skill of using a periodical database to find an article.

a. Determine the content and range of your chosen database (that is, which periodicals it contains and for what years).

b. Choose a research theme and then two or three keywords that relate to that theme.

c. Conduct a database search using your chosen keywords.

d. Scan the list of articles generated in response to your search. If an **abstract** (or brief description) accompanies the article, be sure to read it.

e. Check your list of promising articles against the full-text versions of the articles to see how many actually focus on your theme.

f. If your keywords generate too many articles or if the articles do not seem relevant, refine your search terms. Continue refining your search until the list of articles returned is manageable in number and contains several titles that turn out to be useful.

Whenever you come across a Web site that has useful information, be sure to make an electronic **bookmark** so that you can get back to the site directly the next time you need it. Each site on the Web is identified by a **URL** (Uniform Resource Locator). Your bookmark will store the URL. Electronic bookmarking is much better than trying to remember a long URL or even writing it down, as you will also be sure to find the site later. If you make the slightest mistake when typing a URL in the search box of the **Web browser** (for example, by leaving out a "." or a "/"), the result will be an error or a site that is useless to you.

Despite the problems inherent in conducting searches on the Web, you should always search for information on your theme using subject indexes and directories as well as search engines. In a few years, the two types of searches are likely to be combined. Some search engines already have directories within them. (For example, Yahoo! is both an engine and a directory.)

One final caution about the Web concerns the quality and reliability of what you find there. When you have finally tracked down the article (or document, picture, video, or other resource) you have been searching for and have downloaded it or printed it, you may discover that what your hard work has brought you is junk. Printed materials, the books and journals on the library's shelves, are written, for the most part, by people who know their subjects well, who had their work accepted by publishers that first submitted the manuscripts to other scholars and writers, and later to editors and proofreaders. In contrast, *anyone* can "publish" on the Web. There is much excellent and serious material available on the Web (especially **primary sources** in print, audio, and visual form), and some of it may be helpful in your research. But nothing separates the good stuff from the bad, the serious from the silly. Web searching is less organized and less reliable than searching your library's online catalog. Be prepared to get some very strange and often unrelated material, and in huge quantity. If you find something on the Web that you want to use in your research but you question its reliability, ask your instructor what he or she thinks of it. See also the section "Evaluating Web-Based Sources" later in this chapter.

Using Web material in your written work raises the question of how to document it—that is, how to record in your paper the exact place on the Web where you found the material and when. For help with this problem, see the sections on documenting Internet sources on pages 140–41 and 151–52.

As with all material that you might use in written assignments, you must not *plagiarize* from Web sources. You must not use the words of an Internet document as if they were your own. Be sure to put any text that you download or print from the Internet into your own words or to quote it appropriately. For more discussion of **plagiarism,** see pages 113–15.

Although for major research projects you cannot (and should not) do all of your research on the Web, it is important to become familiar with it. In a few years the Web is likely to be the principal avenue for finding just about anything or anyone. Just as computer literacy has become essential for living in a modern information environment, so Web literacy will be essential for finding your way around that environment.

Example of a Web Search Using Keywords

Here is an example of the steps one student took in a keyword search using a search engine. Of course, no *description* of a Web search is as useful as actually conducting your own search. Until you acquire a sense of what words are best for your topic and what links are most promising, don't be a timid surfer. Try one set of terms and then another to see how different the results are. Likewise, you may find it useful to try different search engines because each will yield slightly different (sometimes vastly different) search results. If a particular link is not a good one, press the Back button and try another. Most searches require testing a number of links before you find a good one. Once you find a good site, be sure to explore it and its links to other sites and bookmark it for future reference.

Due to the dynamic nature of the Web, a search you conduct one week using a particular search engine and set of keywords may yield different results the next week. If you try to duplicate the example below, you will likely get somewhat different results. Nevertheless, good search techniques are discussed throughout this section. Because of the changeable nature of the Web, be sure to carefully document your sources (see Chapter 5, pp. 127–52).

Using a Search Engine to Look for Scholarly Information on the Theme "Women Textile Workers in Lowell, Massachusetts, 1820–1850." To begin a search, you need to be familiar with the program in the computer you are using that searches the Web—its **browser.** The first page of the browser is usually the "default" search engine or gives you the option of selecting one. A student researching the history of women textile workers in Lowell, Massachusetts, from 1820 to 1850 began her search by using the default engine, which was Metacrawler. Metacrawler is a search engine that *combines* the search results of several different engines. If you have the option, it is often helpful to begin your search with such a meta-engine. (One *disadvantage* of a meta-engine is that it may not return the same list of sites on a second search *even if you use the same search terms.*)

The student's first, and most important, decision was the set of keywords she chose for the engine to search for. At the top of the screen, in the empty search box, she typed the following set of terms: +women +labor +history (see Figure 4.1). The plus signs between the words *on this search engine* tell the engine to look for Web pages that include *all* of those words but not necessarily in that order. (Note that she also accomplished this goal by clicking on the "all" circle under the search box.) Always look at any links next to the search box that explain the way the engine will read your keywords. Sometimes this means linking to an "advanced" search page. Engines may vary greatly in the meaning they give to the symbols and words (such as +, −, AND, NOT, ALL, ANY) that connect your keywords. Finally, as any Web searcher knows, keywords that are too broad (for example, "women" or "labor") will return thousands of sites, and keywords that are too narrow (such as "Lowell textile mill workers") might return only a few.

After the student typed in her keywords, she pressed the Search button. Her search yielded approximately seventy possible sites to investigate. Figure 4.2 shows some of these sites. Each item on the list has a brief description of the site as well as its Web address or URL. Clicking on the link will bring you to the Web site—if the link is a "live" one. Sometimes, however, some of the sites retrieved by a search engine will have moved to a new Web address, and the link will give you an error message. This message may tell you where the site moved to, but sometimes you reach a dead end. In that case, try another site.

Once you have a list of sites, you need to determine which ones are most likely to have information about your theme. Look at Figure 4.2 to see whether you can find the most promising sites. In this case, the student chose to explore the links "Sources in US Women's Labor History" (1) and "About—Women's History: Work and Labor" (7). She chose them because their titles and descriptions indicated that they might lead to a wide choice of sites on women's history. She chose to ignore the link "Living the Legacy: Women's Rights" (3) because the

FIGURE 4.1 Example of a Search Box with Keywords
Here is the Metacrawler search box as the student researcher saw it. Note the keywords used and the plus signs between them. The student selected "all," telling the search engine to look for Web pages that include all of these terms. Reprinted with the express permission of InfoSpace, Inc. All rights reserved.

1. Sources in US Women's Labor History—SOURCES IN US WOMEN'S LABOR HISTORY.
   This is a finding guide for research materials on the history of American women and labor at . . .
   http://www.nyu.edu/library/bobst/research/tam/women/cover.html

2. A Curriculum of United States Labor History for Teachers
   . . . Integrating Labor History into Effective Teaching of the Period. Have students interview women relatives to learn more about the contribution of women labor . . .
   http://www.kentlaw.edu/ilhs/curricul.htm

3. Living the Legacy: Women's Rights
   Contains resources commemorating the 150th anniversary of the first women's rights convention, held in Seneca Falls, NY, in June 1848.
   http://www.legacy98.org

4. AFSCME LaborLinks—Women's Labor History
   American Federation of State, County and Municipal Employees presents this directory of materials on the history of women in the workplace.
   http://www.afscme.org

5. H-Labor Discussion Network
   . . . It also recognizes that teaching the history of workers entails maintaining some knowledge of working people and . . . , H-LABOR/UNION WOMEN: Forging Feminism . . .
   http://www.h-net.msu.edu/~labor

6. Labor Site.com—Women in the Workplace: A History
   Looks back at the history of the roles of women in labor reform movements and labor unions. Includes photographs.
   http://www.thelaborsite.com/women1.cfm

7. About—Women's History: Work and Labor
   Provides access to articles and study resources focused on women in the workplace, definitions of women's work, and women's role and status in labor unions.
   http://womenshistory.about.com/cs/work

8. Working Heroes—Men and Women Who Shaped America's Labor Movement
   . . . Working Heroes—Men and Women Who Shaped America's Labor Movement, . . . background information supplied by Dorothy Sue Cobble, professor of History and Labor . . .
   http://www.aflcio.org/aboutaflcio/history/history/bios.cfm

9. The United States Department of Labor Home Page, Secretary of Labor Elaine L. Chao
   The U.S. Department of Labor is charged with preparing the American workforce for new and better jobs. DOL is responsible for the administration and enforcement of over 180 federal statutes.
   http://www.dol.gov

FIGURE 4.2 Search Results
Here is a partial list of the search results generated by the keywords "+women +labor +history" entered in the search box for the search engine Metacrawler. Note the brief description that follows each potential site.

description made it clear that it was about the 150th anniversary of the Seneca Falls convention. If neither of the two promising sites worked out, she might search for a site that seemed to deal with *all* aspects of women's history (not just labor history); a larger site might include links that were close to her topic.

Figure 4.3 shows a page of the second site the student researcher chose to review. She is clearly getting closer to her theme since one of the links here covers the Lowell mill girls. Of the sites in this list, several are directly on her topic. The other sites probably have some material but don't look as promising as the two specifically about the mill girls.

On one of the sites shown in Figure 4.3, the student found a letter from a mill girl (a primary document); on another, good background material on working conditions. Both sources were the kinds that belong in a research paper. Not all searches will go so smoothly. If the sites you end up with have no serious historical material or if they lead away from your theme, press the Back button and try another link. If most of the sites in your list are off the theme, you need to change one or more of your keywords. There is no one correct search term or one correct path through the links. Be prepared for dead ends, but don't give up. Each Web search will sharpen your skills at choosing keywords and identifying promising links. These skills soon will be as necessary as knowing how to read a road map or use a telephone directory.

Lowell Mill Girls

Women's work: Young women left the farm and went to work in the mills of Lowell, Massachusetts, six days a week, twelve or more hours a day.

Lowell History
From the Lowell National Historical Park comes this history of the 19th century textile mill history.

Lowell Mill Girls
Harriet Hanson Robinson writes of her experience as one of the factory workers in the Lowell textile mills, 1832-1848.

Mill Girls
A short history of the Lowell Mill Girls, from the Lowell National Historical Park's web site. Includes reproduction of contemporary newspaper mention.

FIGURE 4.3   Lowell Mill Girls Links
This is a page reached from "About—Women's History: Work and Labor," the seventh link shown in Figure 4.2. All of these links are clearly related to the student's paper theme and are therefore excellent potential sources.

EXERCISE
Conducting Internet Searches

Here is a self-study assignment to help you determine whether you have mastered the basic research skill of conducting an Internet search.

  a. Select a search engine, a research theme, and an initial set of two or three keywords that relate to that theme.
  b. Conduct a Web search using your chosen keywords.
  c. Scan the list of sites generated in response to your search. If your keywords generate too many sites or the sites do not seem relevant to your theme, refine your search terms. If your keywords generate too few sites, broaden or rework your set of keywords.
  d. Continue refining your search until the list of sites returned is manageable in number, probably 10 to 30 sites.
  e. Expore each site briefly, looking for research-type material that is close to your theme.
  f. Bookmark any promising sites, and later examine these sites in detail.

Mining Information from Your Sources

Once you have a source in hand—be it book, Web site download, or journal article—you need to find out whether it contains the kind of information on your **theme** that you are looking for. If you chose wisely, the source should be relevant to your theme. Examine it closely to determine which parts are most useful. A book on Charles de Gaulle that you intend to use in your paper on "the Free French forces in World War II" may turn out to cover only his later period as president of France. A Web download with the promising title "The Impact of World War II on France" may turn out to deal with the German occupation of France and not the Free French forces.

A source needs to be written for a scholarly audience. If the journal article you printed out from a **periodical database** is written for a high school reader, it is not likely to be of value to you. The same is true for a source that is meant to entertain rather than inform, like a video of the 1956 World Series, unless, of course, your topic is baseball history.

The absence of **footnotes** and a **bibliography** in a printed source—unless it is a primary document—usually indicates that it is not meant for serious research. There is no substitute for the close examination of a source before you decide to use it in your research.

Another potential problem of any source (printed, electronic, visual, or audio) is the **bias** of the author or creator. In the world of books, for example, a history of World War I by a French author is likely to have a different viewpoint from one written by a German author, especially if the books were written close to the time of the war. It is very important for you to understand the point of view from which a book was written. Many historical events and their interpretation are the centers of profound controversy. It is almost impossible for a historian to investigate one of these controversial areas without being affected by his or her own biases. A particular attitude toward a topic is not necessarily bad, however. Historical problems are immensely complex, and without a sense of which things are important, the historian will not be able to choose from among those facts that can give some clear meaning to the larger questions involved. In any event, it is important for you to become familiar with the biases of the authors you read so that you will not unknowingly accept their viewpoints. If you agree with an author's bias, it is natural that you will favor his or her work in your research. But unless you understand the biases of the authors you read, and your own as well, you will not know why you agree with some authors more than with others. Furthermore, you won't be able to make a logical presentation in your research paper of various points of view.

Evaluating Print Sources

In addition to the problem of bias, you will need to evaluate other aspects of printed works so that you can use them effectively. Always begin by looking at the table of contents. A quick look will show you how broadly the topic is covered and will let you know if all or only parts of the work deal with your theme.

If the book has a preface, read it. In it the author may explain why he or she wrote the book and identify the intended audience. The audience is a good indicator of whether a source will be useful. For instance, a book written for high schoolers will likely be too low level.

Print sources may also contain an **introduction,** sometimes instead of a preface, sometimes following it. In the introduction, the author usually explains the background of the book and the kinds of questions it addresses, and perhaps mentions some of the conclusions. The introduction will give you an overview of the topics discussed and can help you evaluate the usefulness of a work. You should also read the concluding chapter or section of the work to see whether the author addressed aspects of the topic that you will need for your paper. It will also tell you something about the author's bias.

Consider the date of publication. Is the book a new or an old work? Does that fact matter to your research? The older a book is, the less it will reflect recent scholarship. Nevertheless, an old book may be a classic or may be a primary document useful to your research.

Take a look at the bibliography. Here the author lists all the sources he or she examined when preparing the text. Do these indicate background material that is relevant to your topic? Do they seem to be serious sources? Are they the kind that you should use in your research? If so, the book may be valuable. Indeed, the bibliography may be a source of other books on your theme.

Next, consider the body of the work. This, of course, is the heart of the book itself. Once you have decided that it is a serious and useful source, you must read it with comprehension. You need to note whether it is a primary or a secondary source. If it is a **primary source**, you must place it in its historical context. If it is a **secondary source**, you should note whether it is based on primary sources or only on other secondary sources. Finally, you must grasp the author's theme, **thesis**, and conclusions. Your notes on these subjects will determine your ability to use the book effectively in your own paper.

Guidelines for Evaluating Print Sources

1. What information is given about the author? Is the author a scholarly writer and an expert on your theme?
2. Read the table of contents, preface, and other introductory materials. Take a look at the conclusion or any concluding chapters. These sections will give you an overview of the subject matter of the work. Do all or only parts of the work deal with your theme? Who is the intended audience? Is the work written for historians or for a general audience? Is the level appropriate for your research?
3. What is the date of publication? If the book is old, it will not reflect recent scholarship. Does this fact matter to your research? Remember that older works may be classic works or primary sources that are valuable to your research.
4. Is the work a primary or secondary source? If it is a secondary source, does it use primary sources as evidence? You may find it useful to consult the primary sources directly.
5. Consider the bibliography. Do the sources listed indicate serious works that are relevant to your theme? You may find it helpful to consult directly other sources listed in the bibliography.

Evaluating Web-Based Sources

If you have downloaded or printed out text from the Web, many of the guidelines for evaluating printed sources apply. This is especially true for the issue of bias. Web documents, however, have some special characteristics.

The quality of a Web site is determined by the quality of the material on it. A well-maintained, regularly updated university, library, museum, or government site usually contains reliable information. However, not all material linked to a site has been evaluated by the Webmaster—the person who maintains the site. Often a site has links that lead to less serious sites. Make sure that any site you get material from is as serious as the site through which you found it. If you go offsite, know the kind of territory into which you have moved. (You will need the **URL** of the new site to document your source.)

The currency of a site can tell you much about its possible relevance. A site that hasn't been updated in a long time will not contain very recent materials. It will also likely contain dead links. Determining the date of a Web document can be difficult. Some authors place this date, or the latest "update of the document," in a prominent location. But sometimes the date cannot be found. Do some exploring, but if you cannot tell the date a document was created, note that fact so that if you use the document you can alert your reader to the problem. (Because your documentation of a Web-based source includes the date on which you retrieved it, you should not lead the reader to assume that the retrieval date and the creation date are the same.)

Web documents, just like printed works, may be primary or secondary sources. This distinction is usually, but not always, made clear. A Web document can be a copy of a primary document, or it may be a new primary document created by its author for the Web without the use of other sources. Many Web documents, however, are secondary sources placed on the Web to make the information they contain widely available. These documents should have all of the hallmarks of a printed secondary source: author, date of publication, footnotes, and bibliography. If you cannot tell who the author of a document is or whether a source is primary or secondary, you should hesitate to use the document in your research. If you do use it, explain the problems about its source to your reader.

When citing Web sources, you will need to record page numbers, but sometimes page numbers on a Web document can be confusing. If a printed document has been reformatted to fit the needs of the Web, the original page numbers may be lost. At other times, the "pages" of an electronic document are different from the pages of the original, but the latter appear in the Web version. It is best to record the original page numbers for your research.

Another difficulty with Web documents is that they can be removed from the site where you found them. A well-maintained site should be a stable site, one where things don't disappear without notice. But be aware of such a possibility. The content of some Web sites regularly changes, usually to make way for newer content. This should not be a serious problem with historical sources on the Web, but be sure to note the date on which you took something from the Web.

Evaluating the quality of sources on the Web is more difficult than evaluating printed sources because the Web has millions of potential authors. That is one of its strengths. But for researchers, it can also be one of its weaknesses. If you are sure to do your Web research in stable, scholarly sites, the problems noted here will be greatly reduced. Here are some questions that you should ask of any Web site that you are reviewing.

Guidelines for Evaluating Web Sites

1. Who or what is the sponsor of the site? This information should be indicated in the URL and somewhere on the **home page.** Is the sponsor a university or public library or an individual who created the site as a hobby? If a Web site is an individual's site, what information is posted about the author and the author's credentials?

2. Does the sponsor of the site have a bias that has influenced the kind of material on the site? Are various views expressed on the site?

3. What is the intended audience for the site? Are its contents meant to serve students, faculty, or other professionals? Is it designed for research? Is it filled with commercial links and advertisements or links to sites that are concerned with entertainment rather than research?

4. Does the site contain links to historical sources? Can you get (download or print out) from it the kind of material you would find in a good library? The best sites are often those that give you access to sources in libraries or archives.

5. How current is the site? Has it been kept up to date? (Look for this information on the home page.) A site that has not been updated since, say, 2000, may not have important recent material. Are most of the links live? A site with many dead links has not been well maintained.

6. If the site seems promising, are the materials there relevant to your theme? Does the material on the site include the information you need to document it in your work? Does the information support or go against the material you have already uncovered? If it is very different from what your research has already uncovered, pay special attention to the preceding guidelines.

7. If you have any questions about the relevance or reliability of a site, check with your instructor.

EXERCISE
Evaluating a Web Site

Here is a self-study assignment to help you determine whether you have mastered the basic research skill of evaluating a Web site.

    a. Choose a Web site that you have used recently or are planning to use for an upcoming assignment.

    b. Examine the Web site as a whole. Try to identify its sponsor and the author of any substantive text or visual materials on the site itself. Try to determine whether the site is well maintained.

    c. If you follow any link from this site, evaluate the linked site using the same criteria. Determine the quality and ultimate usefulness of both sites for your research.

How to Read Your Sources

Reading scholarly books, journal articles, and Web documents may seem easy, but you may have problems unless you have had experience in reading serious historical studies. Some of the vocabulary may be new to you. A work on the French Revolution will contain such words as "Jacobin," "Thermidor," and "Girondin." A study of the atom bomb will talk about implosion and fission and such places as Tinian and Eniwetok. It is best to keep a good dictionary handy. Another problem will be the academic or scholarly style of writing often found in specialized works. Read difficult sentences slowly, and look up any words unfamiliar to you. As you become familiar with your topic, you will learn the meanings of the terms used by scholars. The way to get through the complex prose and vocabulary is to have a good command of English grammar and familiarity with the subject being discussed. Ease into your topic by reading the least specialized works first.

As you become familiar with the style and terminology used in a work, your main task will be to understand the points the author is trying to establish. In particular, you will need to know the author's thesis. All good works of history do more than lay out a series of historical events and then combine them to tell an understandable story of what occurred. Good historians want to prove a point, to show that a series of historical events means one thing rather than another.

A history of the rise of Adolf Hitler won't merely tell you that the National Socialist Party, which he led, increased the number of its representatives in the German Reichstag (parliament) from 12 to 107 in the election of 1930. It will attempt to describe the conditions that led to such an outcome and to explain the impact of the election on later events. Perhaps the author will discuss unemployment, German nationalism, the cartelization of German industry, the Treaty of Versailles, the growth of the German Communist Party, anti-Semitism, the structure of the German family, the philosophy of Nietzsche, or the insecurity of the lower middle class. The author will probably deal with some of these subjects more extensively than others, and will attempt to show how the emphasized factors offer a better explanation of the subject than any other factors. Although almost all historians will agree on the number of National Socialist members of the 1930 Reichstag, each will construct the causes and effects of that fact in different ways—sometimes in *very* different ways.

If you wish to understand a particular author's interpretation of an event, you must know how the author arrived at that interpretation and what significance he or she believes it to have. Only a careful reading of the entire work and close attention to its main arguments can give you such knowledge. Remember, history works are a selection of certain facts and interpretations constructed to explain a particular writer's understanding of a historical subject. If your own research relies heavily on a particular book, you will need to know its thesis and bias.

How to Take Notes from Your Sources

The first rule in note taking is to know in advance what you are looking for. In order to avoid either taking note after note that you will never need or failing to note things that you will, you should have a clear understanding of your theme and the kind of evidence you are seeking. This is especially difficult at the outset of your research when your understanding of your theme is still somewhat vague. It is thus important to define the scope and content of your research, as well as a preliminary thesis, as quickly as possible; otherwise, your research and note taking will wander, and valuable time will be lost.

As you go through a source, you will find portions that you will want to refer to in your own research paper. You will want to note the author's general idea or perhaps even record the actual words used. Although overreliance on quotations can be a weakness, if you feel that a quote is necessary, be careful to copy the words exactly. Be sure that the meaning of the words you quote is clear and that you have not altered the author's point by quoting it out of **context.**

Suppose you wish to use a quotation to show that Robert E. Lee was a good military strategist. A quotation such as "Lee was more admired by the average soldier than any other commanding officer" does not make that point because it refers to Lee's popularity, not his generalship. Moreover, if the next sentence in the book you are quoting from is "However, his strategic decisions were not usually equal to those of

Union army commanders," then you actually altered the author's point by ignoring the original context. Make sure you understand an author's meaning before you use a quotation. Be sure not to overquote. Do not quote more material than is necessary to convey the desired point clearly and accurately. Finally, never quote something simply because you find it difficult to express in your own words. You will have to compose the idea in your own words when you write your paper, and it is best to think about the meaning of your research material now.

The most important points made by an author usually cannot be summed up in easily quotable form. When you want to record general arguments and conclusions, it is best to write your own **paraphrase** or summary of particular points. Suppose the author has spent several pages relating the decline in trade between Spain and Mexico to the Wars of Mexican Independence. You may want to summarize the findings by noting that the author feels that the diminishing economic tie between colony and mother country was one of the major factors leading to Mexican independence. If you wish to note the evidence itself, you may want to paraphrase the author's description of the decline in trade with several sentences of your own that include the main factors of this decline.

Whether you are quoting an author's exact words or summarizing a general point, the guidelines of note taking are the same. As you read, it is best to have a pile of 4-by-6 or 5-by-8 index cards beside you. On your first or **source card,** write the author's name, the book title, and the page number or numbers. If the source is from your school library, the source card also contains the library call number. If you are taking notes on a journal or newspaper article, record such information as date, volume number, section, and page number. Exact page numbers are essential because you will need them when you write your footnotes. Although your *first* card for each source must have all of the information you will need to create a footnote, an endnote, or an entry in your bibliography, *subsequent* cards need only the author's last name, a shortened version of the title, the page number, and a subject heading about the note (see Figure 4.4). If a quote or paraphrase covers more than one page from your source, be sure to make that fact clear on your note card. Also, it is advisable to place each paraphrase or quotation on a separate card so that you can arrange cards by subject when you prepare your paper. Placing a brief subject heading in the corner of each card will make such arrangement easier.

If you are quoting, be sure to use quotation marks and to copy the quotation word for word. If you are quoting something that the author has quoted, you must be sure to point this out when you use the material and to identify the original source. Be sure to include in your note an introduction to the quoted material in your own words, stating who said it (if someone other than the author) and in what context. This will ensure that you use the quoted material properly in your paper.

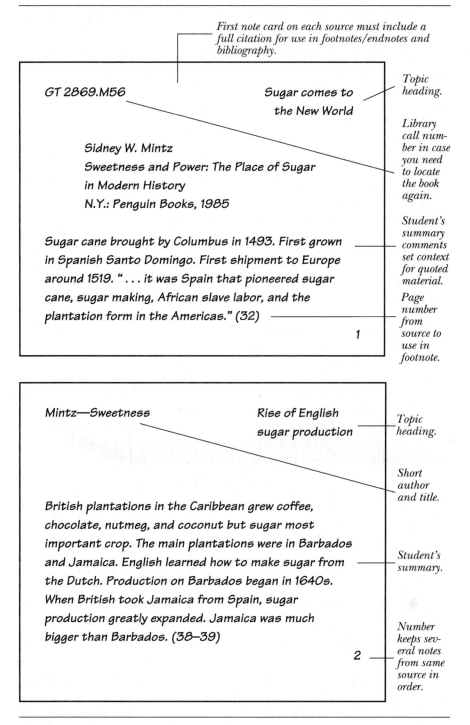

First note card on each source must include a full citation for use in footnotes/endnotes and bibliography.

GT 2869.M56 — Sugar comes to the New World — *Topic heading.*

Library call number in case you need to locate the book again.

Sidney W. Mintz
Sweetness and Power: The Place of Sugar
in Modern History
N.Y.: Penguin Books, 1985

Student's summary comments set context for quoted material.

Sugar cane brought by Columbus in 1493. First grown
in Spanish Santo Domingo. First shipment to Europe
around 1519. " . . . it was Spain that pioneered sugar
cane, sugar making, African slave labor, and the
plantation form in the Americas." (32)

Page number from source to use in footnote.

1

Mintz—Sweetness — Rise of English sugar production — *Topic heading.*

Short author and title.

British plantations in the Caribbean grew coffee,
chocolate, nutmeg, and coconut but sugar most
important crop. The main plantations were in Barbados
and Jamaica. English learned how to make sugar from
the Dutch. Production on Barbados began in 1640s.
When British took Jamaica from Spain, sugar
production greatly expanded. Jamaica was much
bigger than Barbados. (38–39)

Student's summary.

Number keeps several notes from same source in order.

2

FIGURE 4.4   Sample Note Cards

If a quotation is very long and if some parts of it relate to matters other than the subject you are referring to, you may omit portions of the original quote and indicate the omission by inserting **ellipses**— three periods (. . .)—in the quoted material. If the portion omitted is the end of a sentence, insert four periods—three to indicate omission and the fourth to indicate the end of the original sentence. In this case, the closing quotation mark follows the fourth period. Suppose the quotation reads "Feudalism, despite later idealizations of it, was maintained by an oppressive social order." You may want to omit "despite later idealizations of it" and quote the sentence as "Feudalism . . . was maintained by an oppressive social order."

Never omit anything from a quotation if doing so would change the original author's meaning. If the sentence quoted above had read "Feudalism in its later stages in Moravia was maintained by an oppressive social order," the entire sentence would have to be quoted; otherwise, its meaning would be seriously altered.

To give a clearer sense of what note taking involves, there are two sample note cards in Figure 4.4 on page 111. The top card is a first (source) card and the bottom a later card for the same work.

Taking Notes on a Computer. If you can bring your sources to your computer or, better yet, bring your laptop computer to your sources, you have another note-taking option. You can use **word processing** to create your notes, and the computer can organize them. For example, you can code your notes and the files you put them in with a term or terms that will allow you to bring them together by using the Search function of your word processing program. Be sure you know your program very well, especially if it does not have special tools for creating and organizing notes. Even a simple program can be useful if you create a series of folders for the major aspects of your paper and type your notes into files within those folders. Be sure to name each file with a word or two that refers to its content. In this way, if you later change the organization of your paper, you will have a clue as to which files need to be moved to new folders. Also, when you begin to write your paper, be careful to save these text files and folders under names that cannot be confused with the names you created for your notes. Someday almost all research notes will be made in this way. If you are fortunate enough to have the hardware and software, learn how to use them to their fullest potential.

Photocopying and Downloading Sources from the Web

It is possible to print out source material that you find on **CD-ROMs** or the Web. And you can take a book or article from the library shelf over to the copy machine. Whenever you come across a source of modest length (such as an article) that you feel may be very important to your research, photocopying it or downloading and printing it may be preferable to note taking because it will save time. But don't fool yourself. At some point you will have to read and take notes on all those copied pages or downloaded or printed-out computer files. Don't copy or print out anything without reading enough of it to know that it contains material central to your theme.

Avoiding Plagiarism

The only thing worse than misquoting your sources is plagiarizing them. Because of your inexperience with your theme, it may be tempting to use the sophisticated language of the trained historians you are reading. In most cases, their expertise enables them to make their points clearly, and it is easy to fall into the dangerous habit of using their words instead of your own. Remember that your instructor is also a historian and can tell the difference between the language of someone who has spent years researching a topic and that of the average history student. Second, and more important, thinking is learning. If you substitute the simple task of copying for the more difficult but rewarding one of thinking about something and then expressing it in your own words, you are doing yourself a disservice. Finally, **plagiarism** is **cheating** and is a very serious violation of college rules. The penalty can be severe, sometimes leading to expulsion.

When taking notes, *never* copy the author's words unless you intend to quote them in your paper. In that case, be sure to put very clear quotation marks on your note card at the beginning and end of each word-for-word passage. In all other instances, summarize the author's ideas and information *in your own words*. Of course, proper names, dates, statistics, and other very specific facts need to be recorded exactly as they appear in the material you are using. Even here, you must be careful. If the source says: "George Washington, a great patriot, a great general and our greatest president, was born in 1732," you can put the date of his birth in your paper without quotation marks, but you cannot say he was "a great patriot, a great general and our greatest president" *or anything very close to this* without plagiarizing.

There will always be some resemblance between the points that you make in your paper and those that are in your research sources. This is even necessary if you are to correctly interpret your sources. *However, all the words in your paper (except for documented quotations) must be your own.*

The Computer and Plagiarism

The increasing use of computers in note taking and writing intensifies the difficulty of avoiding plagiarism. If you enter your research notes directly into a computer (rather than using note cards), be sure to put your notes into files that are different from the files that you are using for

drafts of your paper. Never cut and paste words from a source into any draft of your paper. In your note files, clearly distinguish between quoted and paraphrased material by enclosing the former in quotation marks. It is also wise to change the color or the font of quoted material so that you can never confuse it with your own words.

The computer revolution has also created a new temptation—downloading an entire paper from the Internet. People trying to make money and students overwhelmed by the task of conducting independent research and writing come together at Web sites where thousands of papers are available. Submitting such work as if it were your own is dishonest and foolish. Software that allows you to search the Internet for plagiarized papers can be used by your instructor to search for the source of "your" paper. Don't play this dangerous game. It has serious consequences.

The Art of Paraphrasing

To help you avoid plagiarism, here is a passage from J. Joseph Hutchmaker and Warren I. Sussman, eds., *Wilson's Diplomacy: An International Symposium* (Cambridge, Mass.: Schenckman, 1973), 13, followed by two paraphrasings. Paraphrase A constitutes plagiarism; paraphrase B does not. The subject is the diplomacy of Woodrow Wilson. Here is the original text:

> Wilson took personal responsibility for the conduct of the important diplomacy of the United States chiefly because he believed that it was wise, right, and necessary for him to do so. Believing as he did that the people had temporarily vested their sovereignty in foreign affairs in him, he could not delegate responsibility in this field to any individual. His scholarly training and self-disciplined habits of work made him so much more efficient than his advisors that he must have thought that the most economical way of doing important diplomatic business was for him to do it himself. Experience in dealing with subordinates who sometimes tried to defeat his purposes also led him to conclude that it was the safest method, for he, and not his subordinates, bore the responsibility to the American people and to history for the consequences of his policies.

> **PARAPHRASE A**   <u>Wilson took personal responsibility</u> for conducting diplomacy because he believed it was right <u>for him to do so</u>. Believing that the <u>people had vested their sovereignty in foreign affairs in him,</u> he couldn't delegate this responsibility. <u>His scholarly training and self-discipline made him more efficient than his advisors</u>. He thought that <u>the most economical way of doing important</u> business was to <u>do it himself. Experience in dealing with subordinates who sometimes tried to defeat his purposes led him to conclude that it was the safest method</u> because he <u>bore responsibility to the American people for the consequences.</u>[4]

---

[4]Underlined phrases are the same as the words of the source. Their use constitutes plagiarism.

PARAPHRASE B Wilson felt personally responsible for major diplomacy because he believed that the voters had entrusted him with such matters. He was more capable than his advisors in this area. He, and not his advisors, was responsible to the people.

Paraphrase A is too close to the original. Rather than recording the main points of the passage, it repeats much of the text word for word. Not only is it time-consuming to take such lengthy notes, but the unacknowledged use of the author's wording constitutes plagiarism. Paraphrase B records only the principal point of the passage—that Wilson decided major foreign policy issues on his own because he felt personally responsible to the people in such matters. It does not copy phrases from the original text. This type of note taking saves time, avoids plagiarism, and still conveys the central idea of the passage.

Paraphrasing that reduces your readings to their essential points and uses your own words is not easy to do at first. But by mastering this technique, you will avoid plagiarism and produce a finished paper that is truly yours.

Guidelines for Avoiding Plagiarism

1. When taking notes from sources, do not use the exact words of the source; instead, paraphrase to summarize source material. If you enter research notes directly into a computer, be sure to put your notes in a file separate from the file you are using for draft versions of your paper.
2. When you intend to quote from a source, be sure to place quotation marks around the exact phrase, sentence, or passage you intend to use and to identify its source. If you enter these selections directly into a computer, change the color or font of the quotation to avoid confusion with your own words.
3. When writing your paper, be certain to acknowledge your sources and to correctly document quoted material.

Plagiarism and Group Work

Working with other students can be an enjoyable and rewarding experience. Still, group work can lead to forms of plagiarism different from those arising from individual research. If the work of your team is evaluated as a whole, each member of the group is responsible to see to it that no part of the group's work has been taken improperly from research sources. Do not let the fact that your work is a group product lessen your concern for this vital matter.

Organizing Your Research

During the process of research you are aided by your **research outline** (see pp. 82–83), which helps you to determine what sources to seek first and when to read them. When your reading is finished (or almost finished), it is time to arrange all those notes and note cards so that you can create a paper out of them. It is time to prepare a **writing outline.** Take a good look at your note cards and especially at the headings that you placed in the corners of the cards. It is from among these headings that you should find the major parts of your theme. If you have created computer files, be guided by the file names.

Preparing a Writing Outline

Suppose your topic is the conflict between Israel and its Arab neighbors, and you have narrowed it to the theme "origins of the 1947 partition of Palestine." Several major points should have appeared in your reading and should be reflected in your notes and in the headings on your note cards. The claims of three parties (Arab, Jewish, and British) were no doubt mentioned in many of your readings. As a result, you should have notes concerning Arab nationalism, Zionism, and British colonial policy. These three perspectives are natural sections of your paper, each with a place in the writing outline. The shifting state of opinion within the United Nations (the body that would vote on the partition of Palestine) and the role of the United States (the most important power outside the region) should have appeared in your research and in your notes as well. This suggests two more possible sections for your paper. If your notes reflect what your research uncovered about your theme, you should have more notes, say, on the British decision to withdraw from Palestine than you do, say, on the Balfour Declaration of 1917. That declaration should be *mentioned* in your paper, but the British decision to withdraw is much closer to your theme and thus deserves a section rather than a mention. That is why, as noted above, British colonial policy should be an important part of your writing outline. Be guided by your notes. If your research has been broad and thorough and your notes contain material closely related to your theme, you will end up with more notes on some points than others.

Once you have a general plan for the *parts* of your paper, the next question is: In what *order* should you include them in your paper? Suppose your theme is "the impact of the Great Depression on African Americans." You may decide to deal with the theme chronologically and separate your paper into sections dealing with the period before 1929, Herbert Hoover's administration, and the New Deal. Or perhaps you want to cover the subject topically, setting up separate sections on African American reactions to economic discrimination, the National Association for the Advancement of Colored People, the U.S. Communist Party, organized labor, and New Deal legislation. Or perhaps you will want to consider the ideas of important African American leaders and writers of the day, setting up sections dealing with E. Franklin Frazier, Richard Wright, Ralph Bunche, W. E. B. Du Bois, A. Philip Randolph, Langston Hughes, Zora Neale Hurston, and Claude McKay.

A paper that has a **chronological organization** begins with events that predate those that are the main focus of the paper. It then moves, step by step, through stages that group together spans of time. These spans may be in years, decades, or—for a very broad theme—centuries. Each time span is later than the one preceding it, and spans generally do not overlap. Time spans do not have to be the same length. It is best to use larger time units when discussing events that occurred long before the main events covered in the paper and to use smaller units when covering the period closest to the main events. A different rule applies to the length of each *section* of the paper: those portions dealing with periods removed from central events should be briefer than those portions close in time to such events.

A common problem with chronological organization is determining how far back in time to begin. Do you start ten or a hundred years before the time of the main events of the paper? A similar problem is determining where to stop. Do you stop with the main events themselves, or do you add short sections covering later periods as well? There is no hard-and-fast rule, but it is wise not to cover too much ground. Don't start too long before or end too long after the principal events of your topic. A paper covering a long period of time can be very unwieldy and is best handled by another form of organization.

A **topical organization** is suited for more general themes—those that deal with ideas, social systems, or other complex phenomena that involve a mixture of political, social, economic, cultural, and intellectual backgrounds. In this form of organization, the task is not so much to build a historical sequence leading up to a particular event, but to weave a fabric composed of the many separate lines of historical development that form the background to the main theme.

In some cases, the same theme can be organized either topically or chronologically. To give you an idea of how the same theme might be organized by each method, here are sample outlines showing each one. The student's research dealt with the topic of the United States and Vietnam and was narrowed to the theme "how did the United States become involved in the war in Vietnam?"

CHRONOLOGICAL ORGANIZATION

Japanese invasion of Indochina turns U.S. attention to the area. (1940–1941)

U.S. policy toward Southeast Asia in World War II (1942–1945)

Strategy against Japan
Aid for anti-Japanese guerrillas in Vietnam
The U.S. military and the Viet Minh

U.S. attitude toward the return of French control (1945–1949)
Defeat of Japan
Creation of a government by the Viet Minh under Ho Chi Minh
Tensions between U.S. and French goals in Vietnam

Impact of the Cold War (1949–1954)
The "fall" of China and its impact on U.S. policy
Need for French involvement in NATO
War in Korea and the "containment" of communism

Geneva Conference and the creation of the Republic of South Vietnam
(1954–1960)
France defeated by the Viet Minh
The Geneva Conference
The roles in the conference of France, China, the Soviet Union, and the
United States

The United States and the government of Ngo Dinh Diem
The failure of reform efforts in the South
The rise of insurgency in the South
Aid from the North

United States defends the South from "aggression" from the North (1960–1963)
The role of U.S. advisers
Instability in the government of South Vietnam
The overthrow of Diem's government

Growing U.S. military involvement to prevent the defeat of the Saigon government
(1963–1968)
U.S. ground troops sent to Vietnam
The escalation of the air war

Conclusion (1968–)
Military stalemate in Vietnam
Growing domestic opposition to the war
The decision to withdraw from Vietnam
The lessons to be learned

Note that the sections are in almost perfect chronological order. Don't
expect to write your paper in fixed time compartments, however.
There are bound to be sections that run into each other. In fact, to tie
your paper together, some overlap between sections is necessary. (See
"Your Writing Outline" in Chapter 5, pp. 122–23.)

TOPICAL ORGANIZATION

Anticommunism in America
The Red Scare after World War I
The New Deal and the debate over American "socialism"
The cultural bases of anticommunism

The Cold War and resurgence of anticommunism in the United States

The Soviet Union as a threat to the American "way of life"
The "loss" of China—the domestic political debate
Stalemate in Korea—the domestic political debate

U.S. interests in Southeast Asia
Strategic positions and economic investments
The "domino theory"

Debate over U.S. involvement in Vietnam
The debate within the U.S. government
The debate in Congress
The debate in the universities

Conclusion
The forces that drew the United States into Vietnam
Contemporary judgments about U.S. involvement in Vietnam

The topically organized paper covers some of the same ground as the chronologically organized one. Nevertheless, the topical organization leads to a different paper. In the final analysis, the outline that you create will reflect the nature of your interest in your theme, the kind of research materials you have uncovered, and the way they have influenced your thinking. (For another example of organizing a paper, see the outline on pp. 156–57 for the sample student paper.)

Organizing Your Notes

The note cards or computer files and the kinds of information they contain have helped you to create a writing outline (at least a tentative one) for your paper. Now that the outline is done, go back to your notes and decide which section of the paper they are most relevant to. For example, the notes concerning the impact of the Korean War on U.S. involvement in Vietnam, which you took from a book about the Cold War in Asia, should become the basis for the section in the chronologically organized paper named "War in Korea and the 'Containment' of Communism," or the section in the topically organized paper named "Stalemate in Korea—The Domestic Political Debate." Mark each group of notes (usually in the upper right-hand corner) with the name of the section of the outline to which they are most directly related (see "How to Take Notes from Your Sources," pp. 109–12). Some groups of notes will not neatly fit in just one section; in that case, mark two or more section headings in the corner. If you cannot find any place in your outline where certain notes go, then something is wrong. Either don't use this group of notes, because they are not dealt with in the outline, or change the outline to accommodate them.

Make sure that you have enough information on each section of your outline to do it justice. If, looking at your notes, you see a mismatch between a section of the outline and the notes needed to support it, you must alter or eliminate that section or, more likely, reread the relevant sources and take notes more directly connected with the point you want to cover in your outline. Notes and outlines are rarely in perfect harmony at the outset. Be sure you have the notes you need. Don't wait until the paper is half written to discover that an important part lacks the kind of documentation it should have.

Budgeting Your Research Time

If you are writing a fifteen- to thirty-page paper, expect to read about a dozen sources. This is not a firm figure, of course, and your teacher and the subject you choose are the best guides to the proper amount of research. If you read too few sources, your work will be shallow and perhaps unsatisfactory. If you read too many, you will not complete your work in the allotted time. It is best to make a tentative bibliography early in your research and discuss its adequacy in terms of topicality, authoritativeness, and length with your instructor. In addition, discuss with your teacher the outline for your paper.

If you have never written a long research paper before, you may be unsure about how much time to allow for each aspect of your research and writing. Only experience will tell you how best to budget your time for your particular work habits, but here are some general rules.

For a paper of fifteen to thirty pages due at the end of a fifteen-week semester, you should allow approximately one to two weeks for choosing a topic and theme, preparing a tentative bibliography, and familiarizing yourself with the general contours of your theme; about seven to eight weeks for reading the available research materials and taking notes from them; about another week for thinking and talking about what you have read and organizing your notes; and about two to four weeks for writing and typing the preliminary and final drafts. If your term is much shorter than fifteen weeks, or if your assignment must be finished before the end of the semester, you will need to shorten your budget accordingly. Remember that by the end of the term, exams will dominate your attention, and a paper due in the final week of classes is best finished at least a week before that time so as not to conflict with studying for finals.

How to Write
a Research Paper

Preparing to Write

Why Your Paper Needs a Thesis

Before you begin to write, you need to have narrowed your **topic** to a **theme,** to have fully researched that theme, and to have organized your research according to your **writing outline** (see pp. 116–19.) Now comes the final step—narrowing your theme to a **thesis** and stating that thesis clearly in the **introduction** to your paper. A thesis is that aspect of your theme that you wish to make the central argument of your paper. To put it another way, your thesis is the specific point, question, or argument about your theme around which you will organize your paper. For example, "the Japanese attack on Pearl Harbor" is a theme. The process of narrowing this theme into a thesis might begin by examining the *reasons* for the success of the attack. This might lead to the thesis "why the United States was unprepared for the Japanese attack on Pearl Harbor." An introduction to such a paper might be as follows:

> This paper will examine several factors that led to the success of the Japanese attack on Pearl Harbor. It will discuss the strength of Japan and its policy in the Pacific. It will also discuss how the issue of Japanese control of China increased tensions between Japan and the United States. Its principal point will be that, despite years of growing tensions between the two countries, the United States was militarily unprepared for the Japanese attack.

Just as narrowing your theme makes clear the kind of research you need, so stating your thesis at the beginning of your paper will orient the direction of your writing. At each stage of the writing process, be

121

sure that you are sticking to your theme and that you are pursuing your central argument or thesis. If your instructor does not require a formal thesis statement, then substitute for it a narrowed-down statement of your theme, one that makes clear to the reader what specific points about the theme you intend to make.

As you prepare to write, keep the limitations of your thesis and of your research in mind. Be sure to confine your writing to these limits. Avoid the temptation to go beyond your thesis except to provide your reader with necessary background information. Let your thesis guide your paper. Don't attempt to record in your paper *everything* on which you took notes. Just because you read something doesn't mean that it belongs in your paper. Look carefully at your writing outline. It should have excluded peripheral material that turned up in your notes. As you write, ask yourself, "Does what I am writing belong in my paper? Is it part of my outline?" If the material isn't in your outline, then don't write about it. (Or, if necessary, change your outline to include it.) Most importantly, ask yourself if what you are writing supports (or lays the basis for later support of) your thesis. Finally, ask yourself, "Does what I am saying belong in *this* part of my paper, or should it be in some other part?" Be sure that your notes are organized according to your outline; otherwise, you will be putting material in the wrong place, and your paper will not be logically developed.

Your Writing Outline

By the time you begin to write, your writing outline may look different than it did when you first put it together. There is nothing wrong with that. The effort to match research to your outline usually leads either to further research (if you don't have documentation for part of the outline) or to expansion of the outline (if you find important documentation for a relevant point that was not originally included). If you discover that your sources make an important point that you had not intended to cover, you must make room for it in your outline so that it appears in your paper. Another reason for changing an outline is finding material that differs strongly with one of the points you had intended to make. Always make room in your paper for **counterevidence**—points made by authors that disagree with part (or all) of your thesis. Having done so, be sure to explain why you believe the evidence in support of your thesis is stronger. You should not claim that your ideas are the *only* correct ones. You should show, however, that there is solid evidence for your interpretation.

If you have not already done so, review your notes now and arrange them according to the section of your outline (and the section of your paper) to which they most directly refer. Now, finally, you are prepared to write. The goal of your writing should be to (1) state your thesis clearly and briefly, (2) describe it in a series of well-documented parts, and (3) draw clear and brief conclusions concerning what you have said about your thesis.

Writing the Text

Chapter 3 discusses the importance of writing skills. As you prepare your paper, you may find it helpful to review the material in Chapter 3 (see pp. 58–68) on the components of clear writing and building an essay.

The Rough Draft

Your first draft will change, perhaps many times, so don't worry too much about the exact wording when you write it. Your introductory paragraph (or two) will certainly have to be rewritten after the **rough draft** is done, but it is still a good place to start. By setting out in your introduction the points that you wish to make in the paper, you will make it easier to confine your writing to statements that develop your thesis. For example, a paper on the independence of Texas that concerns the theme "the role of Sam Houston in Texas's independence" needs to focus tightly on Houston's role. Moreover, if your thesis is that Houston's actions were vital to the success of Texas independence, you need to state this in your introduction. By doing so, you will make clear to the reader that this is your goal. You will keep yourself on track. Of course, other people will appear in your paper (the Mexican general Antonio López de Santa Anna, for example), but a clear focus on Houston and his leadership role in your draft introduction will keep you from writing a long section of your paper on Santa Anna or having too much to say about the defense of the Alamo (Houston was not there). Although these subjects should be mentioned in your paper, only the parts that directly bear on the issue of Houston's leadership should be included. Always use the test of relevance to the thesis as you write your paper.

How long should each section of your paper be? There is no correct length, of course, but each section should be long enough to make the point you want to cover in it. As you write the rough draft of each section, keep in mind the information you want to include. Develop each section from the notes that support it, but don't feel obliged to use all of these notes. When you have made the point you intended to make— stop. In addition, you need to write a connecting sentence—either at the end of one section or at the beginning of the next—that introduces the next point you intend to make. Now you are prepared to repeat the process in the next section of your paper, and in the next, until you reach your conclusion.

Keep the overall length of the paper in mind as well. If your paper is limited to twenty-five pages and your outline has seven points to it, don't start out with a section ten pages long. Of course, sections may be of unequal length; some points are more important than others or take more space to document. Here is a very general guide: for a paper of twenty-five to thirty pages, it is best to have no more than six to eight sections. You will need at least two, and perhaps as many as four pages, to make the points you wish to cover in each section. You also need to leave a few pages at the beginning for your introduction and a few pages at the end for your conclusion. Footnotes or endnotes and your bibliography are not usually counted as part of page length. It is best to clarify this point with your instructor. Keep your overall limit in mind; otherwise, you can end up with too many (or too few) pages.

The last section of your paper is, of course, the **conclusion.** It is usually wise *not* to include it in your rough draft. If you change your paper in subsequent drafts, your conclusion will then need a complete rewriting. Still, it is worth pointing out here that the goal of your conclusion is to summarize briefly the points you have made concerning your thesis. In the paper about Sam Houston's leadership, for example, you would briefly refer to the evidence, both positive and negative, that you presented about his leadership and why you concluded that it was vital to Texas's independence.

Clear Writing: A Matter of Continuity

As you write the rough draft of each section, keep in mind the information you wish to include and the points you wish to make. If your theme is "German aid to the forces of General Franco in the Spanish civil war," then the section that deals with the reasons behind the German support might begin by briefly describing the circumstances surrounding Franco's appeal to Hitler in 1936. The main body of the section would explain in some detail Hitler's reasons for giving aid (for example, strategic and economic considerations, ideological and diplomatic factors) and would conclude by relating these reasons to the subject of later sections, such as the actual aid given and its effect on the course of the war. Your principal concerns as you construct each section of your paper should be: Does this section follow logically from the one preceding it; does it adequately support and develop the theme and thesis; and does it establish the necessary background for the section that follows?

As each section mirrors the overall structure of the paper by containing an introduction, a main body, and a transition to the next section, so each paragraph of which the section is composed contains a similar structure. A well-constructed paragraph begins with a sentence that introduces the information to be developed and concludes with a sentence that leads to the next paragraph. If each paragraph is developed in this way, and if sentences explaining the relationship between paragraphs are included where necessary, then the paper as a whole becomes a tightly knit series of related statements rather than a random group of facts that do not seem to move in any clear direction. The key to tight construction is for each sentence to have two components: it must be related to the one preceding it, and it must continue the development of the thesis to which it is related.

The best way to ensure that there are no gaps in logic between your sentences is to construct each paragraph from the viewpoint of the average person who might read your paper. Very often, a disconnected set of sentences may seem clear to you because as you write them you unconsciously fill in the gaps with your own knowledge. Your reader most likely does not have this knowledge and has to depend entirely on the words you write. If these are not enough to make your point clearly, you must be more explicit. Refer back to Chapter 3 for detailed help on writing.

Quotations: When and How to Use Them

Good general rules are: don't quote too often, don't quote too much, and rely on your own words unless there is a good reason for quoting those of your source. Unless it is necessary to use the *very same* words found in a source to make a point that is crucial to your thesis, don't use a quotation. However, if your source says something highly controversial, you may want to make it clear to the reader that you have not misinterpreted it. In this case a direct quotation may be useful. If you do quote, be sure to include enough of the original statement to make its meaning clear. Don't make a quote any longer than is necessary. Finally, enclose quoted words in quotation marks. (A common error is forgetting one set of quotation marks.)

Quotation Form. In most cases a paraphrase or summary of your source, properly footnoted, is sufficient. If you need to quote, however, the following guidelines will help.

If a quotation is brief, taking up no more than two or three lines of your paper, then it should be written as a part of your text and enclosed in quotation marks. Introduce the quotation by clearly identifying the speaker. The reader will always want to know who is speaking and in what context. Don't say: *The strikers were "a dangerous mob."* Say: *According to D. H. Dyson, the plant manager, the strikers were "a dangerous mob."* If you do not wish to quote a whole statement, it is necessary to insert **ellipses** (three periods ". . .") wherever words have been omitted.

SHORT QUOTATION EXAMPLE The early settlers were not hostile to the Native Americans. As pointed out by the Claxton *Banner* in 1836: "Our Sioux neighbors, despite their fierce reputation, are a friendly and peaceable people."[1]

SHORT QUOTATION EXAMPLE WITH OMISSION   As pointed out by the Claxton *Banner* in 1836: "Our Sioux neighbors . . . are a friendly and peaceable people."[1]

If your quotation is very long, it must be set off from the sentences that precede and follow it. It should be indented ten or more spaces and appear in single-spaced type. Do not put quotation marks around a long quote. Even though you are quoting, indenting a quote makes this fact clear to the reader.

LONG QUOTATION EXAMPLE   The early settlers were not hostile to the Native Americans. As pointed out by the Claxton *Banner* in 1836:

> Our Sioux neighbors, despite their fierce reputation, are a friendly and peaceable people. No livestock have been disturbed, and the outermost cabins are unmolested. We trust in God that our two peoples may live in harmony in this territory.[1]

Remember that all quotations must be footnoted.

A problem that many students face is being sure that quotations actually support the point being made. For example, the first quotation below does *not* support the point that the early settlers got along with the Native Americans; the second quotation does support the thesis.

IMPROPER QUOTATION EXAMPLE   The early settlers were not hostile to the Native Americans. As pointed out by the Claxton *Banner* in 1836: "Our Sioux neighbors are peaceable but only when they are penned up in closely guarded reservations."

PROPER QUOTATION EXAMPLE   The early settlers were not hostile to the Native Americans. As pointed out by the Claxton *Banner* in 1836: "We have always respected our Sioux neighbors. There has never been warfare between us."

Incorporating Visual Materials into Your Paper

Ask your instructor about the usefulness of visual material. Be sure to find out if the space taken up by visuals will be counted as part of the assigned length of the paper or if it will be an addition to this limit. If visuals are acceptable, you should try to find ways to include them. Illustrating important points in your paper with visual material such as maps, charts, tables, drawings, and photographs can strengthen your arguments. Some points—the way something looks, a very important fact of comparison of number (as in a chart)—can best be made by *showing* your reader a picture of it.

Computers have made it easier to integrate visuals into your text. You can create your own charts and tables on your computer or download drawings and photographs to illustrate an important point about your theme. Be sure not to "pad" your paper with visuals, however. Ask your instructor about the quantity that is appropriate.

You can place the visuals on or near the page with the text they illustrate, or you can put all visual material at the end of the paper in an **appendix.** If you use an appendix, you need to place a note in the text that directs your reader to the page where the corresponding image is located—for example, "See Figure 3.2 on page 14." If your visuals are within the body of the paper, make sure that they are cleanly separated (perhaps by a top and bottom line) from the surrounding text. Even more important is formatting them so that they end up where you want them when your paper is printed out. Each visual, regardless of its position (within text or in an appendix), should have a title above or below it that tells readers what it refers to. Finally, except for visuals that you create, be sure to note at the bottom of each where you found it. Doing this is as necessary as documenting printed sources with footnotes or endnotes.

For a paper about the importance of Sam Houston's leadership to the success of Texas independence, a variety of visuals are relevant. You could use a map showing his army's successful, strategic retreat before a large Mexican army in 1836. You could create a bar graph comparing the size of the two armies. Or you could use a dramatic painting of Houston at the Battle of San Jacinto, where a Texas army under his command defeated a much larger Mexican army and in capturing its commander, López de Santa Anna, who was also the president of Mexico, effectively gained independence for Texas. Each of the visuals would illustrate some aspect of Houston's leadership—that is, each would support the thesis that his leadership was important to achieving Texas independence.

Be sure that any visual you use will reproduce clearly. More importantly, be sure that the visual is accurate and that it illustrates and supports your thesis. Your map of the retreat of Houston's army must get the place-names and the movement of the armies correct. Your graph must be calibrated accurately. The painting of Houston at San Jacinto that you choose, however dramatized its subject, should be based on evidence in your paper that Houston's generalship at the battle was excellent. For example, the picture may show Houston at the battle, when in fact, he was well behind the battle lines. A visual may seem "real" simply because it looks that way. Don't treat visuals as facts until you examine them as carefully as you would any important point made in your paper. (Be sure to document any visuals. See footnote and endnote documentation models on pages 138–39.)

Documenting Your Paper:
Citing Your Sources

Documentation tells your reader where the material in your paper comes from. Documentation usually takes the form of **footnotes** or **endnotes,** but it can also include illustrations, diagrams, photographs, or any special material that you place in your paper to support your thesis.

When and How to Use Footnotes and Endnotes

Footnotes are forms of documentation that appear at the bottom of the page; endnotes appear at the end of the paper. (A sample endnote page can be found on p. 174.) They include the same information. If your instructor has no preference, you can choose to put your documentation in either place, but you must be consistent throughout the paper. You must number your notes consecutively. (When **proofreading,** be sure that the number in the text matches the number of the note.) As both footnotes and endnotes have the same form, the following discussion that describes how to write them will, for convenience, use the word "footnotes" to refer to both types.

If you quote from or closely summarize your research sources, you must tell your reader where the original information can be found. In this way, the reader can check the accuracy of your quotes and statements, judge the **bias** and credibility of your sources, or carry out research of his or her own. On occasion, you may also want to use footnotes to make comments that qualify or supplement statements in your paper. These are called "explanatory" footnotes.

The question that troubles students the most is: Which of the statements that I make in my paper need footnotes? There are only a few hard-and-fast rules to guide you. However, three types of statements *must* be footnoted: (1) direct quotations, (2) controversial facts or opinions, and (3) statements that directly support the main points made in your paper. Another group of statements — those that summarize important points from your sources — should be footnoted and *must* be if they are used to sustain an important part of your argument. Finally, statistics are almost always footnoted.

Some clarification concerning controversial points and support for main points may be helpful. Controversial facts or opinions are those on which your sources disagree or which will surprise your reader. Suppose, in your paper on the "treatment of slaves on Mississippi plantations," you write that some slaveowners were kind to their slaves. This statement may surprise the reader and thus must be footnoted. Researching "European discoverers of America," you find that all sources agree that Vikings visited the New World long before Columbus. However, if most people believe that Columbus was the first European to see the New World, then it is necessary to show the reader the source of your information with a footnote. Finally, statements of fact or opinion that directly support main points should be footnoted. If your theme concerns the Protestant Reformation, and you treat nationalism as a major factor in the break with Catholicism, then your references in the text to nationalist forces should be footnoted. If you treat the wealth of the Catholic Church as a very minor factor, then your brief references to that need *not* be footnoted.

The number of footnotes to use is another thorny problem. As a rule of thumb, if your paper has quite a few pages without any footnotes, you are probably not documenting as much as you should. If you are writing five or more footnotes per page, you may be overdoing it.

One final point about what to footnote. Using a footnote does not give you permission to plagiarize. If the words in your paper are the same, *or very nearly the same,* as those in your source, you have commited **plagiarism** even if you include a footnote. (For more on plagiarism, see Chapter 4, pp. 113–15.) You should not use sentences or even phrases from your research sources. Your ideas may come from your sources, but the words must be your own. Only words in quotation marks should be copied word-for-word from a source.

Directory to Footnote/Endnote Documentation Models

How to Write Footnotes and Endnotes

When a footnote or endnote is necessary, place a number at the end of the sentence that contains the information to be documented. Occasionally, you may want to footnote or endnote two different things in the same sentence. In this case, place each number right after the word or phrase that you want to reference in the notes. Some writers place the number at the end of a paragraph rather than at the end of a sentence, but this is proper only if the note refers to the material in the paragraph as a whole. If you are documenting specific facts or quotations, the number should appear right after the facts or quoted material. If you are documenting a general idea or opinion, place the number at the end of the paragraph or paragraphs that discuss it. All footnote or endnote numbers in the text should be in superscript—that is, a half-line above the line of the type. The number should not be put in parentheses and should be inserted after any punctuation (except a dash).

Footnotes are placed at the bottom of the page to which they refer. Endnotes are gathered together in numerical order and placed after the text of the paper, and this page (or pages) should be headed "Endnotes." The first line of an endnote is indented five spaces; the other lines begin at the left margin. (See the endnote examples in the sample research paper on pp. 174–76.) Both footnotes and endnotes are single-spaced. Remember to use only footnotes or only endnotes in the same work.

Footnote or Endnote Form.   The following examples of footnotes and endnotes show the different forms required for citing different types of sources. These forms are drawn from *The Chicago Manual of Style,* Fifteenth Edition (Chicago: University of Chicago Press, 2003).

Books

1. BASIC FORMAT FOR A BOOK (FIRST REFERENCE)

The first time you refer to a book, include the author's full name, followed by a comma; the book title in full (including subtitle after a colon), italicized or underlined; publication information enclosed in parentheses—place of publication (followed by a colon), name of publisher (followed by a comma), date of publication; and page number(s) cited (followed by a period).

1. Robert Darnton, *George Washington's False Teeth: An Unconventional Guide to the Eighteenth Century* (New York: Norton, 2003), 64.

2. BOOK (SECOND REFERENCE)

If a footnote or endnote directly follows a previous note to the same source, you may use "Ibid." (short for the Latin *ibidem,* meaning "in the same place") to indicate the source, followed by a comma and a page reference.

2. Ibid., 62.

A second or later reference to a source that does not immediately follow a previous citation to the same source need only use the author's last name and the page number.

3. Darnton, 102.

If, however, you cite more than one book (or article, etc.) by the same author, any second or later reference must include a shortened form of the title in order to make clear to the reader which of the works you are citing.

4. Darnton, *George Washington's False Teeth*, 68.

Some book notes are more complex. If a book has several authors, a translator or editor, or multiple editors, or if a book was published in several volumes or editions, then the footnote or endnote has to include such information as in the following examples.

3. TWO OR THREE AUTHORS

When there are two authors, both names are listed, in the order in which they appear on the title page.

5. Catherine Clinton and Christine A. Lunadini, *The Columbia Guide to Women in the Nineteenth Century* (New York: Columbia University Press, 2000), 48.

If there are three authors, include all three names separated by commas, in the order in which they appear on the title page.

6. Ronald Inden, Jonathan Walters, and Daud Ali, *Querying the Medieval: Texts and the History of Practices in South Asia* (New York: Oxford University Press, 2000), 22.

4. FOUR OR MORE AUTHORS

If there are more than three authors, the footnote or endnote includes the name of the author listed first on the title page followed by "and others" or by "et al." (from the Latin, meaning "and others").

7. James A. Henretta and others, *America's History*, 5th ed. (Boston: Bedford/St. Martin's, 2003), 226.

5. CORPORATE AUTHOR

When writing a note for a source with corporate authorship, use the name of the corporation or agency as the author's name.

8. Congressional Quarterly, *Congressional Quarterly's Guide to Congress*, 5th ed., vol. 2 (Washington, DC: Congressional Quarterly, 2000), 122.

6. BOOK BY AN UNKNOWN AUTHOR

If the author of a work is unknown or is listed as "Anonymous" on the title page, skip the listing of the author in your footnote or endnote and begin the reference with the title of the work.

> 9. *Through Our Enemies' Eyes: Osama Bin Laden, Radical Islam and the Future of America* (Washington, DC: Brassey's, 2002), 134.

If a work is anonymously written but has a known editor, you may treat the book as an edited volume (see section 9).

7. TRANSLATED BOOK

When a work has been translated, put the name of the translator after the title of the work, preceded by the notation "trans."

> 10. Mahatma Gandhi, *An Autobiography: Or the Story of My Experiments with Truth,* 2nd ed., trans. Mahadev Desai (Ahmedabad: Navajivan Press, 1956), 74.

If a work has been translated and edited by the same person, follow the title of the work with the notation "trans. and ed."

> 11. Giovanni Boccaccio, *Famous Women,* trans. and ed. Virginia Brown (Cambridge: Harvard University Press, 2001), 37.

8. BOOK WITH ONE OR MORE EDITORS

If a work has both an author and an editor, keep the author's name at the beginning of the reference and put the name of the editor after the title, preceded by the notation of "ed." (for either a single editor or multiple editors).

> 12. George Fox, *The Journal,* ed. Nigel Smith (New York: Penguin Books, 1998), 44.

In an edited work without an author, the editor's name, followed by "ed.," appears where the author's name normally would.

> 13. T. Douglas Price, ed., *Europe's First Farmers* (Chicago: University of Chicago Press, 2000).

In a work with multiple editors and no author, use the same format as for multiple authors, but follow the names with "eds."

> 14. G. W. Bowersock, Peter Brown, and Oleg Grabar, eds., *Interpreting Late Antiquity: Essays on the Postclassical World* (Cambridge: Harvard University Press, Belknap Press, 2001).

For four or more editors, write only the first name followed by "and others" or "et al." to indicate the other editors and conclude with "eds."

15. Esther Breitenbach and others, eds., *The Changing Politics of Gender Equality in Britain* (New York: Palgrave, 2002).

9. SELECTION IN AN EDITED WORK

If you are using only a part (chapter, essay, document, etc.) of a larger edited work, begin the note with the name of the author of the part used, followed by the title of the selection, the title of the volume, the name of the editor, and publication information.

16. Paul R. Jones, "The Two Field System," in *Europe's First Farmers,* ed. T. Douglas Price (Chicago: University of Chicago Press, 2000), 26.

10. EDITION OTHER THAN THE FIRST

If you are using a later edition of a work, the edition is placed after the title. Use "2nd ed." for a second edition, "3rd ed." for a third edition, "4th ed." for a fourth edition, and so on.

17. Eugene F. Rice Jr. and Anthony Grafton, *The Foundations of Early Modern Europe 1460–1559,* 2nd ed. (New York: Norton, 1994), 108.

For a revised edition, use "rev. ed."

18. Cornel West, *Race Matters,* rev. ed. (Boston: Beacon Press, 2001), 52.

11. MULTIVOLUME WORK

If there is more than one volume to the work and the volumes all have the same name, then put the volume number after the title.

19. Fernand Braudel, *The Mediterranean and the Mediterranean World in the Age of Philip II,* vol. 1, trans. Sian Reynolds (Berkeley: University of California Press, 1996), 46.

If, however, there is more than one volume to the work and each volume has its own title, then the volume title and the number of the specific volume used come first, followed by the general title and the publication information.

20. Robert A. Caro, *Master of the Senate,* vol. 3, *The Years of Lyndon Johnson* (New York: Knopf, 2002), 85.

12. ENCYCLOPEDIA OR DICTIONARY

With well-known reference books, facts of publication are usually omitted. However, you must cite the edition if it is not the first. When a work is arranged alphabetically, the item is preceded by "s.v." (short for the Latin *sub verbo,* meaning "under the word").

21. *The Columbia Dictionary of Quotations,* s.v. "Lincoln, Gettysburg Address."

If an encyclopedia tells you the author of the entry, then list the author at the end of your footnote or endnote.

22. *Handbook of American Women's History,* 2nd ed., s.v. "Willard, Frances E. (1839–1898)" by Anita M. Weber.

Periodicals

13. JOURNAL ARTICLE (FIRST REFERENCE)

The first reference to an article should include the author's full name followed by a comma; the title of the article followed by a comma, all in quotation marks; the title of the journal, italicized or underlined; the volume number of the journal; the year of the volume in parentheses, followed by a colon; and the page number(s) cited, followed by a period. The reference should look like this example:

23. Monique Scheer, "From Majesty to Mystery: Change in the Meanings of Black Madonnas from the Sixteenth to the Nineteenth Centuries," *American Historical Review* 107 (2002): 1416.

14. JOURNAL ARTICLE (SECOND REFERENCE)

If a footnote or endnote directly follows a previous note to the same article, you may use "Ibid." to indicate the source, followed by a comma and a page reference:

24. Ibid., 1423.

A second and later reference to the same article that does not immediately follow a previous citation to the same source need use only the author's last name and the page number.

25. Scheer, 1421.

If, however, you cite more than one work by the same author, any second or later reference must include a shortened form of the title in order to make clear to the reader which of the works you are citing. This is true even if one work is a book and the other is an article.

26. Scheer, "From Majesty to Mystery," 1420.

15. ARTICLE IN A JOURNAL PAGINATED BY VOLUME

Journals often have multiple issues per year, generally denoting each year by a volume number and then specifying individual issues within that volume. Sometimes the journal carries over the numbering system throughout the year (that is, throughout the several issues of a volume). If a journal paginates by volume, there is no need to identify the issue number in your citation.

> 27. E. Lawrence Abel, "And the Generals Sang," *Civil War Times* 39 (2000): 45.

16. ARTICLE IN A JOURNAL PAGINATED BY ISSUE

If a journal paginates by issue (that is, every issue begins with page 1), then it is necessary to include both volume and issue numbers (indicated by "no.") so that the reader can easily find your reference. If a journal paginates by issue but does not have issue numbers, then include the season or month of the issue before the year in the parentheses.

> 28. Daniel Horodsky, "How U.S. Merchant Marines Fared during WWII," *Insight on the News* 16, no. 1 (2000): 46.

17. ARTICLE IN A MAGAZINE

Reference to a popular magazine (rather than a scholarly journal) requires author, title of article, title of magazine, date, but no volume number or page number.

> 29. Patricia J. Williams, "Remembering in Black and White," *Nation,* February 28, 2000.

18. ARTICLE IN A NEWSPAPER

Reference to a newspaper article requires day, month, and year (and edition if more than one) as well as author, title, name of paper, section (if appropriate), and page. If the newspaper has sections, mark the section with "sec." and the page number with "p." If the newspaper does not have sections, there is no need to use "p." to indicate the page.

> 30. Steven R. Weisman, "South Korea, Once a Solid Ally, Now Poses Problems for the U.S.," *New York Times,* January 2, 2003, sec. A, p. 1.

19. ARTICLE BY AN UNKNOWN AUTHOR

If the magazine or newspaper article has no author, the citation begins with the name of the article.

> 31. "Australia's Aborigines: A Dispute over Mistake Creek," *Economist,* December 14–20, 2002, 37.

20. EDITORIAL

The editorial page of a newspaper generally has pieces written by the editorial board of the paper as well as by contributing writers. If the authorship of an editorial is given, then cite the editorial as an article in a newspaper. If, however, there is no authorship given and the piece is an editorial, write "Editorial" in the space normally reserved for an author's name.

> 32. Editorial, "The Price of Guessing Right," *Wall Street Journal,* December 27, 2002, sec. A, p. 10.

21. LETTER TO THE EDITOR

For a letter to the editor in a newspaper or journal, put the author's name first, then "letter to the editor" (without quotation marks), then the name of the publication, date, and page number. If the letter appears in a scholarly journal, then the volume, date, and page number should appear as in the journal article format.

> 33. Paul J. Herr, letter to the editor, *Foreign Affairs* 79, no. 2 (2000): 180.

If the letter appears in a newspaper or popular magazine, then the date and page number should appear as in the magazine or newspaper format.

> 34. Eric Chivian, letter to the editor, *Boston Globe,* January 21, 2003, sec. A, p. 10.

22. BOOK OR FILM REVIEW

A reference for a book or film review should include the author of the review, the name of the review article, the title of the work being reviewed, the name of the author or director of the reviewed work, the journal or newspaper in which the review appears, the date, and the page number. Like the format for letters to the editor, the format for volume, date, and page varies according to whether the citation is to a scholarly journal or a popular magazine or newspaper. The following example cites a scholarly journal:

> 35. Wulf Kansteiner, "Mad History Disease Contained? Postmodern Excess Management Advice from the UK," review of *In Defense of History,* by Richard Evans, *History and Theory* 39 (2000): 221.

Other Sources

23. MATERIAL FROM AN INFORMATION SERVICE OR DATABASE

When citing an information service or database, list the service, agency, or corporation responsible for collecting the information as the author, the name of the article or survey (if applicable) in quotation marks, the name of the database (if applicable) italicized or underlined, followed by any Web site reference.

36. United Nations Population Division, "World Population Prospects: The 2000 Revision," *United Nations Population Information Network,* http://www.un.org/popin.

24. GOVERNMENT PUBLICATION

The format for a government publication is like that for a corporate author. Use the standard model for a book, but put the name of the government agency in place of the name of an author.

37. U.S. Department of State, *Arab-Israeli Dispute, 1964–1967,* vol. 18 of the Lyndon B. Johnson series of *Foreign Relations of the United States* (Washington, DC: GPO, 2000), 25.

25. PAMPHLET

Treat a pamphlet like the first reference to a book in your footnotes or endnotes.

38. Pat Nyhan and Helen Epstein, *Kenya's Unfinished Democracy: A Human Rights Agenda for the New Government* (Washington, DC: Human Rights Watch, 2002).

26. DISSERTATION

When citing a dissertation in footnotes or endnotes, list the author of the dissertation, the title in quotation marks; then in parentheses put "PhD diss." followed by the university at which the dissertation was written, and the date, all separated by commas. Finally, outside the parentheses, list the page number.

39. Nadja Durbach, "Disease by Law: Anti-Vaccination in Victorian England, 1853–1907" (PhD diss., Johns Hopkins University, 2001), 69.

27. ABSTRACT OF A DISSERTATION

To cite a dissertation abstract, list the work as you would a dissertation, but indicate where the abstract was found, including volume number and date, if applicable, before the page number.

40. David Charles Engerman, "America, Russia and the Romance of Economic Development" (PhD diss., University of California, Berkeley, 1999), abstract in *America since 1607* 678 (1999): 308t.

28. POEM

If a poem is included in a published anthology, cite it in the same way that you would cite a selection in an edited work.

41. Jacopo Sadoleto, "The Poem of Jacobus Sadoletus on the Statue of Laocoon," in *The Gazer's Spirit: Poems Speaking to Silent Works of Art,* ed. John Hollander, trans. H. S. Wilkinson (Chicago: University of Chicago Press, 1995), 97.

If a poem was published in a popular magazine or newspaper, the citation should be modeled on the form for articles in magazines or newspapers.

42. John Updike, "To a Well-Connected Mouse," *New Yorker,* January 6, 2003, 30.

29. COMPUTER SOFTWARE

To cite a software program, list the name of the software, the version used, the publisher, and the location of the publisher. Do not separate the version from the name of the software.

43. U.S. History: The American West CD-ROM Ver. Windows NT, Fogware Publishing, San Jose.

30. FILM OR VIDEOCASSETTE

The citation for a film or videocassette starts with the title (italicized or underlined) followed by the type of medium (videocassette, DVD, etc.), the name of the director (preceded by "directed by"), and the publication information (enclosed in parentheses).

44. *In the Barracks,* videocassette, directed by Hellmut Kirst (New York: The Scholar's Bookshelf, 1999).

31. MUSICAL SCORE

To cite a musical score, list the composer, the title of the piece, the name of the editor ("ed.") or arranger ("arr."), if applicable, and the publication information. If the score is part of a series, list the volume number and title of the series after the title of the score.

45. Luciano Berio, *Alternatim: per clarinetto, viola e orchestra* (Vienna: Universal Edition, 2001).

32. SOUND RECORDING

A footnote or endnote for a sound recording varies depending on whether the recording is of a musical composition or a speech or reading. For the performance of a musical composition, list the name of the composer, the title of the piece, the performers, the recording company, the number of the recording, and the type of medium (compact disc, audiocassette, etc.).

46. Bernard Rands, *Le Tambourin, Suites 1 and 2,* Philadelphia Orchestra, New World Records 80392, compact disc.

If the recording is of a speech or reading, list the speaker, the title of the recording, the publication information, and the type of medium.

47. Martin Luther King Jr., *Martin Luther King at Zion Hill* (Los Angeles: Duotone Records, 1962), audiocassette.

33. PHOTOGRAPH OR ILLUSTRATION

If you found a photograph or illustration in a printed work, the format for citing it is similar to that of a selection of an edited work.

48. Alexis Preller, "Hieratic Women," in *A History of Art,* ed. Sir Lawrence Gowing, rev. ed. (Ann Arbor: Borders Press, 2002), 973.

If the artist is unknown, begin with the title or description of the work.

49. "A Chavin hammered gold plaque," in *A History of Art,* ed. Sir Lawrence Gowing, rev. ed. (Ann Arbor: Borders Press, 2002), 479.

If you are not using a printed work as the source, then you must indicate where the work can be found, whether in a museum, archive, private collection, or building. It may be tricky to determine whether you are citing an original work or a photograph of the work; for example, an archive service might own the rights to a photograph of an ancient sculpture, but the sculpture itself is found in a museum. If you are citing the photograph, you will need to reference the archive service, but if you are citing the sculpture, you should indicate the museum's location.

In your citation of an unpublished image, be sure to include the name of the artist or photographer (if known), the title of the work, the type of medium, the date of creation, and where the work can be found.

50. Ansel Adams, *The Golden Gate before the Bridge, San Francisco, California,* gelatin silver print, 1980, National Gallery of Art, Washington, DC.

34. SLIDE

A citation for slides should include the compiler of the collection, the title of the collection, the name of the editor (if any), the publication information, and the indication that the medium is "slides."

51. Elizabeth Hammer, *The Arts of Korea: A Resource for Educators,* ed. Judith G. Smith (New York: Metropolitan Museum of Art, 2002), slides.

35. LECTURE OR PUBLIC ADDRESS

If a lecture or public address has been published, then use the published source as your reference and follow the appropriate footnote/endnote citation. However, if the lecture or public address has not been published, then you should list the speaker, the title of the speech, the location, and the date.

52. Eva Bremner, "From Heldenkaiser to Hausvater: Wilhelm I. as the King of Christmas" (paper presented at Young Scholars Forum: "Gender, Power, Religion: Forces in Cultural History" at the German Historical Institute, Washington, DC, March 31, 2001).

36. INTERVIEW OR ORAL HISTORY

When an interview has been published, you should cite it by listing the person interviewed, the title of the interview, the name of the interviewer, the publication, date, and page number.

53. Herman J. Viola, "Viola Records the View of the American Indian," interview by Stephen Goode, *Insight on the News,* January 3, 2000, 37.

If you are citing an unpublished interview or oral history, you should include the name of the speaker, the interviewer, the location of the interview or history, the date, and, if the interview is kept in an archive, the location of the transcript or recording, if any.

54. William Coleman, interviewed by the House Select Committee on Assassinations investigators, Washington, DC, August 2, 1978, http:// history-matters.com/archive/jfk/hsca/unpub_testimony/contents.htm.

Internet Resources

37. WEB SITE

Books and journals are kept in libraries and thus are available for a reader to find even if they have gone out of print. In contrast, the Internet is a quickly changing medium in which Web sites may unexpectedly disappear. If the same source is both in print and on the Internet, you should cite its printed form. However, if you wish to reference something that is available only via the Internet, begin with the author's name or, if none is listed, the name of the organization that is claiming responsibility for the material. Then put the title of the piece in quotes. Give the URL and then add, in parentheses, the date on which you accessed the Web site if the site is likely to have frequent substantive updates or if the material is particularly time sensitive (for example, legal material). Otherwise, do not include an access date.

55. Richard Hooker, "The Idea of America," http://www.wsu.edu :8000/~ dee/AMERICA/ (accessed January 14, 2003).

38. E-MAIL MESSAGE

It is courteous to ask the sender of an e-mail message that you wish to reference for permission to cite it before you do so, because the contents of the message may not have been intended for publication. In the citation, give the author of the e-mail, the subject header, and the date on which it was sent. Denote that the source is a personal e-mail, but do not include the author's e-mail address.

56. Lynn Temple, "Re: Question about the Bedford flag," personal e-mail message, March 26, 2003.

39. LISTSERV MESSAGE

The format for citing a listserv message is like that for an e-mail message, except that you should put the e-mail address of the listserv after the date on which the message was sent. There is no need to indicate in the citation that this was a listserv message.

57. Liz Ten Dyke, "South Asians in 19th century USA," listerv message, January 17, 2003, h-world@h-net.msu.edu.

40. NEWSGROUP MESSAGE

A newsgroup citation is similar to that of a listserv or e-mail message, except that you should include the location of the newsgroup.

58. Domenico Rosa, "Vietnam's Women of War," newsgroup message, January 19, 2003, soc.history.war.vietnam.

41. SYNCHRONOUS COMMUNICATION

Synchronous communications over the Internet should be cited by listing the author of the message or the sponsor of the group, then the title of the group (if any) or the indication that this was an instant message, the date on which the group or sponsor was created (if applicable and known), the URL for accessing the group or messenger, and the date on which the communication occurred. A difficulty in citing this kind of material is that the author of a message may use a pseudonym. If you know that the name is a pseudonym, you may put "(pseud.)" after the name.

59. Absolute MUSH, absolute.spod.org:6250 (January 9, 2003).

Organizing a Bibliography

A bibliography is an alphabetical listing of the sources you used when writing your paper. It must include *all* of the sources that appear in your footnotes or endnotes. However, do not include all of the sources you looked at in the course of your research. If your bibliography is long, you might separate it into several categories, such as primary sources and documents, books, articles, and nonprinted sources (tables, pictures, Internet pages, etc.). Each list is alphabetized according to the last name of the author. If a work has no author (or editor or translator), alphabetize it according to the first word (except for "A," "An," "The") of the title.

Begin each entry at the left margin and indent any additional lines five spaces. Each item in a bibliography is single-spaced. Use double-spacing between items. If a work has more than one author, alphabetize according to the last name of the first author mentioned on the title page of the book or article. That name should be followed by the names of all of the other authors listed with first names first. (See the sample bibliography for the research paper on pp. 177–78.)

Bibliographic Form The following examples of bibliography entries show the different forms required for citing different kinds of sources. These forms are drawn from *The Chicago Manual of Style,* Fifteenth Edition.

Books

1. BASIC FORMAT FOR A BOOK

A bibliographic reference for a book refers to the book as a whole. An entry in a bibliography for a book should include the author, last name first, followed by a period; the full title of the work (including any subtitle after a colon), italicized or underlined, followed by a period; the place of publication, followed by a colon; the name of the publisher, followed by a comma; and the date of publication, followed by a period. (If there is a "Jr.," "Sr.," or numeral after the author's name, put it after the first name, preceded by a comma, as in: Mansfield, Harvey C., Jr.) The reference should look like this example:

Darnton, Robert. *George Washington's False Teeth: An Unconventional Guide to the Eighteenth Century.* New York: Norton, 2003.

2. MULTIPLE WORKS BY THE SAME AUTHOR

If you include more than one source by the same author, use three hyphens or dashes instead of repeating the name. List the works in alphabetical order by title.

Darnton, Robert. *George Washington's False Teeth: An Unconventional Guide to the Eighteenth Century.* New York: Norton, 2003.

———. *The Great Cat Massacre and Other Episodes in French Cultural History.* New York: Vintage Books, 1995.

3. TWO OR THREE AUTHORS

Bibliographic format is the same for books with two or three authors except that the names of the second (and third) authors are not inverted. Put a comma after both the last and first name of the first author listed, and place the authors in the order in which they appear on the title page.

Inden, Ronald, Jonathan Walters, and Daud Ali. *Querying the Medieval: Texts and the History of Practices in South Asia.* New York: Oxford University Press, 2000.

4. FOUR OR MORE AUTHORS

If there are more than three authors, the reference usually includes the names of all of the authors.

Henretta, James A., David Brody, Lynn Dumenil, and Susan Ware. *America's History.* 5th ed. Boston: Bedford/St. Martin's, 2003.

5. CORPORATE AUTHOR

If the author of the work you are citing is a corporation rather than a person, you should put the corporate name in the space for the author.

Congressional Quarterly. *Congressional Quarterly's Guide to Congress.* 5th ed.
Vol. 2. Washington, DC: Congressional Quarterly, 2000.

6. BOOK BY AN UNKNOWN AUTHOR

If the author of a work is unknown or is listed as "Anonymous" on
the title page, skip the listing of the author and begin the reference
with the title of the work.

*Through Our Enemies' Eyes: Osama Bin Laden, Radical Islam and the Future
of America.* Washington, DC: Brassey's, 2002.

If a work is anonymously written but has a known editor, you may
treat the book as an edited volume.

7. TRANSLATED BOOK

In a bibliography, the name of the translator appears after the title
and is introduced with "Translated by" and finished with a period.

Gandhi, Mahatma. *An Autobiography: Or the Story of My Experiments with
Truth.* 2nd ed. Translated by Mahadev Desai. Ahmedabad: Navajivan
Press, 1956.

If a work has been edited and translated by the same person, indicate this in the reference.

Boccaccio, Giovanni. *Famous Women.* Translated and edited by Virginia
Brown. Cambridge: Harvard University Press, 2001.

8. BOOK WITH ONE OR MORE EDITORS

If a work has both an author and an editor, keep the author's name
at the beginning of the reference and put the editor's (or editors')
name(s) after the title, preceded by the notation of "Edited by" and
concluding with a period.

Fox, George. *The Journal.* Edited by Nigel Smith. New York: Penguin Books,
1998.

In an edited work without an author, the editor's name, followed by
"ed.," appears (last name first) where the author's name normally
would.

Price, T. Douglas, ed. *Europe's First Farmers.* Chicago: University of Chicago
Press, 2000.

In a work with multiple editors and no author, use the same format
as for multiple authors but follow the names with "eds." (Only the first
name listed should be in inverted order—last name first.)

Bowersock, G. W., Peter Brown, and Oleg Grabar, eds. *Interpreting Late Antiquity: Essays on the Postclassical World.* Cambridge: Harvard University Press, Belknap Press, 2001.

For four or more editors, write only the first name followed by "and others" or "et al." to indicate the other editors, and conclude with "eds."

Breitenbach, Esther, and others, eds. *The Changing Politics of Gender Equality in Britain.* New York: Palgrave, 2002.

9. SELECTION IN AN EDITED WORK

A reference for a selection (chapter, essay, document, etc.) of a larger edited work, begins with the name of the author, followed by the title of the selection in quotation marks, the name of the entire work, the name of the editors, and standard publication information. The names of the author, selection, work, and editor(s) should all be followed with periods.

Jones, Paul R. "The Two Field System." In *Europe's First Farmers,* edited by T. Douglas Price. Chicago: University of Chicago Press, 2000.

10. EDITION OTHER THAN THE FIRST

If you are using a later edition of a work, the edition number is placed after the title and followed with a period. Use "2nd ed." for a second edition, "3rd ed." for a third edition, "4th ed." for a fourth edition, and so on.

Rice, Eugene F., Jr., and Anthony Grafton. *The Foundations of Early Modern Europe 1460–1559.* 2nd ed. New York: Norton, 1994.

For a revised edition, use "Rev. ed."

West, Cornel. *Race Matters.* Rev. ed. Boston: Beacon Press, 2001.

11. MULTIVOLUME WORK

If you are citing one volume of a multivolume work and the volumes all have the same title, then put the volume number after the title.

Braudel, Fernand. *The Mediterranean and the Mediterranean World in the Age of Philip II.* Vol. 1, translated by Sian Reynolds. Berkeley: University of California Press, 1996.

If, however, the volume has its own title, then the volume title and the number of the specific volume used comes first, followed by the general title and the publication information.

Caro, Robert A. *Master of the Senate.* Vol. 3, *The Years of Lyndon Johnson.* New York: Knopf, 2002.

When your bibliographic reference is to all of the volumes of a work, then you should note the number of volumes within the citation.

Schama, Simon. *A History of Britain.* 2 vols. New York: Hyperion Talk Miramax, 2000–2001.

12. ENCYCLOPEDIA OR DICTIONARY

Reference works are generally not cited in bibliographies.

Periodicals

13. JOURNAL ARTICLE

An entry in a bibliography for a scholarly journal article should include the author, last name first, followed by a period; the title of the article followed by a period, all in quotation marks; the title of the journal, italicized or underlined; the volume number of the journal and, in parentheses, the year of the volume, followed by a colon; and the pages on which the article begins and ends, followed by a period.

Scheer, Monique. "From Majesty to Mystery: Change in the Meanings of
Black Madonnas from the Sixteenth to the Nineteenth Centuries."
American Historical Review 107 (2002): 1412–1440.

14. ARTICLE IN A JOURNAL PAGINATED BY VOLUME

Journals often have multiple issues per year, generally denoting each year by a volume number and then specifying individual issues within that volume. Sometimes the journal carries over the numbering system throughout the year (that is, throughout the several issues of the volume). If the journal paginates by volume, there is no need to identify the issue number in your citation.

Abel, E. Lawrence. "And the Generals Sang." *Civil War Times* 39 (2000):
45–50.

15. ARTICLE IN A JOURNAL PAGINATED BY ISSUE

If a journal paginates by issue (that is, every issue begins with page 1), then it is necessary to include the volume and issue numbers (the latter indicated by "no.") so that the reader can easily find your reference. If a journal paginates by issue but does not have issue numbers, then include the season or month of the issue before the year in the parentheses.

Horodsky, Daniel. "How U.S. Merchant Marines Fared during WWII."
Insight on the News 16, no. 1 (2000): 46–49.

16. ARTICLE IN A MAGAZINE

Reference to a popular magazine requires author, title of article, title of magazine, and date, but no volume number or page number. Remember, the pages encompassing the entire article are listed in the bibliographic entry, but the specific page or pages are cited in a footnote or endnote.

Williams, Patricia J. "Remembering in Black and White." *Nation,* February
28, 2000, 9–11.

17. ARTICLE IN A NEWSPAPER

Individual articles from daily papers are not usually listed in a bibliography. Instead, the newspaper should be listed along with the years cited.

New York Times, 1999–2003.

18. ARTICLE BY AN UNKNOWN AUTHOR

If a magazine or newspaper article has no listed author, then the citation begins with the name of the article.

"Australia's Aborigines: A Dispute over Mistake Creek." *Economist,* December
14–20, 2002, 37.

19. EDITORIAL

Because newspapers are not generally cited in bibliographies, any newspaper editorial cited may be referenced in the bibliography simply with the name of the newspaper and the year(s) of publication. If, however, you are citing an editorial in a magazine, then the format varies by whether or not an author is listed. If one is, follow the format for a magazine article. If no authorship is given and the piece is an editorial, write "Editorial" in the space normally reserved for an author's name.

Editorial. "TRB from Washington: A Century of Insight." *New Republic,*
January 3, 2000, 17.

20. LETTER TO THE EDITOR

Because newspapers are not generally cited in bibliographies, any letter to the editor in a newspaper may be referenced in the bibliography simply with the name of the newspaper and the year(s) of publication. For a letter to an editor in a magazine or journal, put the author's name first, then "Letter to the editor" (without quotation marks), then the name of the publication, date, and page number. If the letter appears in a scholarly journal, then the volume, date, and page number should appear as in the journal article format.

Herr, Paul J. Letter to the editor. *Foreign Affairs* 79, no. 2 (2000): 180.

If the letter appears in a magazine, then the date and page number should appear as in the magazine format.

Burnett, Christina D. Letter to the editor. *Harper's Magazine,* November
2002, 4.

21. BOOK OR FILM REVIEW

A reference for a book or film review should include the author of the review, the name of the review article, the title of the work being reviewed, the name of the author or director of the reviewed work, the journal or newspaper in which the review appears, the date, and the page numbers. As with the format for letters to the editor, the format for volume, date, and page varies according to whether the citation is to a scholarly journal or a popular magazine. The following example cites a scholarly journal:

> Kansteiner, Wulf. "Mad History Disease Contained? Postmodern Excess Management Advice from the UK." Review of *In Defense of History,* by Richard Evans. *History and Theory* 39 (2000): 218–229.

Other Sources

22. MATERIAL FROM AN INFORMATION SERVICE OR DATABASE

When citing an information service or database, list the service, agency, or corporation responsible for collecting the information as the author, then the name of the article or survey (if applicable) in quotation marks, then the name of the database (if applicable) italicized or underlined, followed by any Web site reference. This is almost identical to the footnote/endnote method of citing a database, except for the indentation and the substitution of periods for commas.

> United Nations Population Division. "World Population Prospects: The 2000 Revision." *United Nations Population Information Network.* http://www .un.org/popin.

23. GOVERNMENT PUBLICATION

The format for a government publication is like that for a corporate author. Use the standard model for a book, but put the name of the government agency in place of the name of an author.

> U.S. Department of State. *Arab-Israeli Dispute, 1964–1967.* Vol. 18, Lyndon B. Johnson series of *Foreign Relations of the United States.* Washington, DC: GPO, 2000.

24. PAMPHLET

In a bibliography, a pamphlet is cited in the same format as a book.

> Nyhan, Pat, and Helen Epstein. *Kenya's Unfinished Democracy: A Human Rights Agenda for the New Government.* Washington, DC: Human Rights Watch, 2002.

25. DISSERTATION

When citing a dissertation in a bibliography, put the author of the dissertation first, followed by the title in quotation marks. Then list "PhD diss.," the university at which the dissertation was written, and the date, all separated by commas.

Durbach, Nadja. "Disease by Law: Anti-Vaccination in Victorian England, 1853–1907." PhD diss., Johns Hopkins University, 2001.

26. ABSTRACT OF A DISSERTATION

To cite a dissertation abstract, list the work as you would a dissertation reference, but add the location of the abstract, including volume number and date, if applicable.

Engerman, David Charles. "America, Russia and the Romance of Economic Development." PhD diss., University of California, Berkeley, 1999. Abstract in *America since 1607* 678 (1999): 308t.

27. POEM

If a poem is included in a published anthology, cite it as a selection in an edited work.

Sadoleto, Jacopo. "The Poem of Jacobus Sadoletus on the Statue of Laocoon." In *The Gazer's Spirit: Poems Speaking to Silent Works of Art*, edited by John Hollander, translated by H. S. Wilkinson. Chicago: University of Chicago Press, 1995.

If the poem was published in a popular magazine, the citation should be modeled on the form for articles in a magazine.

Updike, John. "To a Well-Connected Mouse." *New Yorker,* January 6, 2003, 30.

28. COMPUTER SOFTWARE

To cite a software program, list the name of the software, then the version used, the publisher, and the location of the publisher. Do not separate the name of the software from the version used.

U.S. History: The American West CD-ROM Ver. Windows NT. Fogware Publishing, San Jose.

29. FILM OR VIDEOCASSETTE

A citation for a film or videocassette is similar to that for a book except that the title of the film goes first, followed by the media (videocassette, DVD, etc.), the name of the director (preceded with "Directed by"), and ending with the publication information.

In the Barracks. Videocassette. Directed by Hellmut Kirst. New York: The Scholar's Bookshelf, 1999.

30. MUSICAL SCORE

In order to cite a musical score, list the composer, the title, the editor or arranger, if applicable, and the publication information. If the score is part of a series, list the volume number and title of the series after the title of the score.

> Berio, Luciano. *Alternatim: per clarinetto, viola e orchestra*. Vienna: Universal Edition, 2001.

31. SOUND RECORDING

For the performance of a musical composition, list the name of the composer, the title of the piece, the performers, the recording company, and the number of the recording, followed by an indication of medium (compact disc, audiocassette, etc.).

> Rands, Bernard. *Le Tambourin, Suites 1 and 2*. Philadelphia Orchestra. New World Records 80392. Compact disc.

If the recording is of a speech or reading, list the speaker first, then the title of the recording, the publication information, and the medium.

> King, Martin Luther, Jr. *Martin Luther King at Zion Hill*. Los Angeles: Duotone Records, 1962. Audiocassette.

32. PHOTOGRAPH OR ILLUSTRATION

Cite a photograph or illustration from a printed work similarly to a selection of an edited work.

> Preller, Alexis. "Hieratic Women." In *A History of Art*, edited by Sir Lawrence Gowing. Rev. ed. Ann Arbor: Borders Press, 2002: 973.

If the artist is unknown, begin with the title or description of the work.

> "A Chavin hammered gold plaque." In *A History of Art*, edited by Sir Lawrence Gowing. Rev. ed. Ann Arbor: Borders Press, 2002: 479.

If you are not using a printed work as the source, then you must try to indicate where the work can be found, whether in a museum, archive, private collection, or building. Include the name of the artist or photographer (if known), the title of the work, the medium, the date of creation, and where the work can be found.

> Adams, Ansel. *The Golden Gate before the Bridge, San Francisco, California*. Gelatin silver print. 1980. National Gallery of Art, Washington, DC.

33. SLIDE

A citation for slides in a bibiography is much like a book citation. It should include the compiler of the collection, the title of the collection, the name of the editor (if any), the publication information, and the indication that the medium is "slides."

> Hammer, Elizabeth. *The Arts of Korea: A Resource for Educators*. Edited by Judith G. Smith. New York: Metropolitan Museum of Art, 2002. Slides.

34. LECTURE OR PUBLIC ADDRESS

If a lecture or public address has been published, then use the published source as your reference and follow the appropriate bibliographic citation. However, if the lecture or public address has not been published, then you should list the speaker, the title of the speech, the location, and the date.

Bremner, Eva. "From Heldenkaiser to Hausvater: Wilhelm I. as the King of Christmas." Paper presented at Young Scholars Forum: "Gender, Power, Religion: Forces in Cultural History" at the German Historical Institute, Washington, DC, March 31, 2001.

35. INTERVIEW OR ORAL HISTORY

When an interview has been published, you should cite it by listing the person interviewed, the title of the interview, the name of the interviewer, the publication, date, and page number.

Viola, Herman J. "Viola Records the View of the American Indian." Interview by Stephen Goode. *Insight on the News,* January 3, 2000.

When citing an unpublished oral history or interview, include the name of the speaker, the interviewer, the location of the interview or history, the date, and, if the interview is kept in an archive, the location of the transcript or recording, if any.

Coleman, William. Interviewed by the House Select Committee on Assassinations investigators. Washington, DC. August 2, 1978. http://historymatters.com/archive/jfk/hsca/unpub_testimony/contents.htm.

Internet Resources

36. WEB SITE

A Web site reference should begin with the author's name or, if none is listed, the name of the organization that is claiming responsibility for the material. Then put the title of the piece in quotes. Give the URL and then add, in parentheses, the date on which you accessed the Web site if the site is likely to have frequent substantive updates or if the material is particularly time sensitive (for example, legal material). Otherwise, do not include an access date.

Hooker, Richard. "The Idea of America." http://www.wsu.edu:8000/~dee/AMERICA/ (accessed January 14, 2003).

37. E-MAIL MESSAGE

In a bibliographic reference to an e-mail message, list the author and the subject header, mark that the source is a personal e-mail, and put the date on which the e-mail was sent.

Temple, Lynn. "Re: Question about the Bedford flag." Personal e-mail message, March 26, 2003.

38. LISTSERV MESSAGE

The format for citing a listserv message is like that for an e-mail message, except that you should substitute the e-mail address of the listserv for the "personal e-mail" notation after the date on which the message was sent.

Ten Dyke, Liz. "South Asians in 19th century USA." Listserv message, January 17, 2003. h-world@h-net.msu.edu.

39. NEWSGROUP MESSAGE

A newsgroup citation is similar to that of a listserv or e-mail message, except that you should include the location of the newsgroup.

Rosa, Domenico. "Vietnam's Women of War." Newsgroup message, January 19, 2003. soc.history.war.vietnam.

40. SYNCHRONOUS COMMUNICATION

Synchronous communications over the Internet should be cited by listing the author of the message — adding "(pseud.)" after the name if you know it to be a pseudonym — or the sponsor of the group, the title of the group (if any) or the indication that this was an instant message, the date on which the group was created (if applicable and known), the URL for accessing the group or messenger, and the date on which the communication occurred.

Absolute MUSH. absolute.spod.org:6250 (January 9, 2003).

Revising and Rewriting

Leave time in your writing schedule for revising your paper. Before writing your final draft, put the paper aside for a day or two (another reason to leave time) and then reread it. This way, you will gain a fresh perspective and may detect weaknesses that you hadn't noticed before.

A **rough draft** always needs smoothing out. As you reread your paper, ask these questions:

1. Is the paper clearly focused on its theme and thesis?
2. Do its parts clearly follow one another?
3. Is there adequate support for the major claims and interpretations?
4. Are the points made clearly and convincingly?

While you examine the overall structure of the paper for defects, you also need to look closely at the language itself. If you repeated yourself, eliminate the repetition. If you included material that is unrelated to your theme, discard it. Check the connections between paragraphs to see whether the reader will be able to follow your argument. Make sure that you have accomplished what you set out to do in your **introduction,** that you have sufficiently supported your thesis, and that your **conclusion** makes it clear that you have done so. Go over the footnotes or endnotes and the bibliography to check style and accuracy.

Finally, examine your writing for errors in spelling and grammar. **Proofread** carefully and slowly. At normal reading speed your eyes can go right by major errors. You are so familiar with your paper that you may not see what is on the page. Reading your paper aloud will help you catch unclear phrases. Showing it to a friend will let you know where your readers might have problems.

Sometimes **peer reviewing,** or reading a draft of another student's paper, is part of the work for the course. If your instructor gives specific guidelines for this assignment, follow them. (For more on peer reviewing, see the discussion that begins on p. 45.)

Word Processing: Advantages and Dangers

Changing what you have written either because it is wrong or because you think of a better way of saying it is the greatest advantage of composing with a computer. Read each sentence as it appears on the screen. Does it make sense? Does it say what you want it to say? Will your reader understand it? Does it take your thesis another step along the way? If not, revise it; don't wait until you have written more. If you wait, you will only entangle your weak sentence with others. When you go back to change the weak one, you will probably have to change surrounding sentences also so that they are connected to one another in a clear way.

The same advice for sentences holds true for paragraphs. Don't write too many paragraphs without rereading to see if they make sense together. Remember, you can only see one screen at a time. This can give you a tunnel-like vision of your paper. The paragraph on the screen may read well, but the one that just scrolled off the top of the screen may not be logically connected. Every few paragraphs, scroll back to earlier paragraphs (or even earlier pages) to ensure that whole sections of your paper hold together. If you lose a sense of the structure of any part of your paper, print it out and read it on the printed page. Don't let big pieces of your writing go by without rereading them — *and saving them.*

When you have finished a draft, print it out and read it as a whole. Mark any changes in red and save them on disk right away. If you don't do this, you may lose track of which changes you have and have not made. On the other hand, because rewriting is so easy on a computer, what is on your disk can quickly jump ahead of what you have printed. Be vigilant; otherwise, your "final" hard copy may not reflect all the changes that are on the disk.

Use Spell- and Grammar-Checkers with Caution.   It is a good idea to run these checking programs every time you finish a section of your paper. However, they are *not* replacements for your own *proofreading* of your work. They only catch spelling errors that are not other words — writing "no" when you mean "know" will satisfy the checker every time. Also, most grammar-checkers balk at some words and phrases that are just fine. Only you know what you mean to say, and only your eyes and brain can spot all of the spelling and grammar problems. Print out and carefully read each page of your work.

Formatting Your Paper.   Pay attention to the format of your paper — how it looks to the reader. Your instructor may require a special format. If not, here are several standards that are generally acceptable. You should create margins of about one inch on all four sides of each page. On your title page (which is *not* numbered) put (1) your name, (2) the course name and number, (3) the name of your instructor, (4) the date of your paper, and (5) the title of your paper. Text should be double-spaced — except for long (indented) quotes and footnotes, which are to be single-spaced. All pages following the title page should be consecutively numbered — including pages with illustrations, maps, graphs, and anything else. If you include visuals, mention them by number in your text — for example, "See Figure 6." Immediately below each visual, place the number and a brief description.

Example of a Research Paper

As a final aid in preparing your **research paper,** this chapter ends with a full-scale example. The examination of the research paper begins with a discussion of how the **topic, theme,** and **thesis** were chosen and then moves on to the **writing outline** that the student developed. Finally, there is the paper itself, including **endnotes** and a **bibliography,** all of which follow the rules and suggestions made earlier in this chapter.

Several aspects of the sample research paper are designed to aid students. Annotations in the margin help you to see what the text is trying to accomplish. Also in the margin are a series of subtitles to the paper. Note how each one represents a stage in the unfolding story and is related to part of the writing outline. Finally, a comment in the margin of each endnote tells you what point in the paper is being supported. As you read the paper, ask yourself about the point the author is making and how she is accomplishing the goal. Pay special attention to the way in which the parts are put together and how each section adds strength to the effort to describe and support the thesis. Read through the endnotes also to determine why a citation is full or shortened and to see the form used for writing citations. Note also the form of the bibliography. If anything is unclear, refer back to the earlier discussions of writing (Chapter 3) and research papers (Chapter 5).

This sample research paper can help you in two important ways. First, you can read the paper as a whole *before* you write your own. This will give you a clearer sense of what your paper should look like, how it should be developed, and the kind of **documentation** it should have. Second, you can refer to the paper *while* you are writing your own in order to answer specific questions about issues such as the introduction, continuity between paragraphs, the form of quotations and endnotes (or footnotes), the bibliography, and the conclusion.

How the Theme and Thesis Were Chosen

The theme chosen for this paper would fit a variety of courses: Pre–Civil War U.S. History, American Labor History, Women's History, and the History of Industrialization, among others. Within the framework of one such course, the student became curious about the lives of workers in the earliest factories. This curiosity led to a *topic* about industrialization in New England, where the student had grown up. Preliminary research indicated that textiles were the first goods to be made in factories, so the topic was narrowed to workers in that industry. When the student discovered that many of the earliest workers were young women who were the same age as she was, she decided to look at their lives in particular. At this point, her topic, "early industrialization in New England," has been narrowed to "women workers in early industrialization in New England." The largest number of these women worked in mills in Lowell, Massachusetts, so that town was chosen. (The student's research also made it clear that there were numerous sources that discussed Lowell mill workers.) The time period to be covered was the one during which women workers were the principal workforce in Lowell. Finally, the student discovered from preliminary research that in the early nineteenth century there was great concern about the impact of industrial work on American society and especially on women.

All of this narrowing led the student to her thesis: women workers in Lowell, though working under difficult conditions, used this work experience to increase their independence. Finally, the student chose a title that introduced the reader both to the general theme, "women workers in the Lowell, Massachusetts, textile mills, 1820–1850," and to her thesis, "wage slavery or true independence." Note that a thesis can take the form of a question. (See the sections on coming up with a theme and a thesis for your paper in Chapter 4, pp. 79–82.)

The Writing Outline for the Thesis

The writing outline was created from the student's **research outline** and subsequent research notes. (See the section on creating a research outline in Chapter 4, pp. 82–83.) The research phase had made clear that several important aspects of the thesis had to be examined in the paper. Several sources gave detailed accounts of the experiences of the women workers, showing both positive and negative aspects of their working lives. It became clear that this subject should have an important place in the paper. Sections 4, 5, and 6 of the outline focus on this subject. Section 4 talks about work life, section 5 social life, and section 6 the women's response to changes in the mills. Having decided on the importance of the work experience, it became necessary to give the reader an understanding of how these women came to be mill workers in the first place. Section 3 examines this subject. Showing how the women came to be mill workers required an explanation to the reader of where the mills themselves came from. This is necessary because the mills represent the first stage of industrialization in America. Sections 1 and 2 deal with industrialization. Section 7 covers the end of the period during which women workers predominated in textile work. The other two sections, of course, are the introduction and conclusion.

The subheadings within each section are divisions of the larger subject and determine the order in which a section will be developed. For example, section 4, "Life in a mill town," examines, in order, adjusting to life in a mill town, a typical workday, the work itself, the pay received, and the mill-owned boarding houses where the girls lived. Look at each part of the outline to see the function it serves and how the whole of the outline fully covers the important parts of the thesis. Try to be sure that your own outline sets the stage for writing the paper the way this one does.

SAMPLE WRITING OUTLINE

Wage Slavery or True Independence:
Women Workers in the Lowell, Massachusetts,
Textile Mills, 1820–1850

Introduction (thesis statement)
1. Attitudes toward industrialization in the United States
   a. Prejudice against industry by Americans
   b. Early industrialization in England
2. The origins of the textile industry in eastern Massachusetts
   a. The preindustrial economy in America
   b. Slater-type mills
   c. Plans for a textile mill in Lowell, Massachusetts
3. Recruiting women workers
   a. The choice of a female workforce
   b. Overcoming the prejudice against women working outside the home

    c. Building a "moral" community
    d. Why young women chose to work in the mills
  4. Life in a mill town
    a. Adjusting to life in the mills
    b. Typical workday
    c. Nature of work
    d. Rate of pay
    e. The boarding house
  5. Social life
    a. Leisure hours
    b. Female companionship
    c. The *Lowell Offering*
  6. Women workers' resistance to factory discipline
    a. "Turnouts"
    b. Slavery or independence?
  7. Declining conditions of work in the Lowell mills
    a. End of paternalism
    b. The coming of the Irish workers
Conclusion
    a. Young women's experience of early industrialization

Turning Research into Writing:
A Sample Research Paper

The full-scale example of a student research paper that concludes this chapter follows the rules and suggestions put forth earlier in the chapter. The **topic** ("women workers in early industrialization in New England") and **theme** ("women workers in Lowell, Massachusetts, textile mills, 1820–1850") were narrowed to form the **thesis.** This thesis—that women in Lowell used their difficult working conditions to gain independence—is reflected in the paper's title and writing outline and is supported throughout the paper.

Pay attention to the marginal comments that run down the sides of the pages of this sample paper. Compare them to the writing outline that you have just read. Note that each major section of the outline has a corresponding place in the paper itself. When you finish reading the paper, look at the marginal comments down the sides of the pages that contain the endnotes. Here you will see that each of the main points made in the paper is documented: each point has one or more accompanying notes that tell the reader where the information came from. (See the section on documenting sources earlier in this chapter.)

Unless your instructor has a special format, your title page should look something like this one. Whatever layout you choose, be sure to include: paper title, course name and number (and section, if necessary), instructor name, your name, and the date.

Wage Slavery or True Independence:

Women Workers in the Lowell, Massachusetts,

Textile Mills, 1820–1850

American History 200,

Section 4

Professor Jones

Jane Q. Student

May 29, 2003

1

This paper will examine the development of the textile industry in Lowell, Massachusetts, and the young women who served as its principal workforce between 1820 and 1850. It will describe how these women came to accept what was for them an unusual and difficult form of labor, but it will argue that they shaped this experience to serve their own purposes. Such a story helps to explain much about early industrialization in America and particularly about the role of women in the early factory system. The paper argues that these women workers were not mere laborers exploited by the mill owners but were actively engaged in expanding the constricted opportunities for women.

Until the early nineteenth century, the vast majority of Americans grew up in farm families. As the industrial revolution spread across England, rural Americans felt certain that the dark and dreary factory towns that were beginning to dot the English countryside would not arise in America. News coming from England contained reports that a permanent class of exploited workers was being created there. America, with its commitment to opportunity, would not, people were sure, experience such a fate. New England had been in the forefront of the struggle against British rule. Rural people in that region were especially proud of their independence and suspicious of anything that seemed to copy the ways of the English.[1]

New Englanders watched the rise of industrialization in England with concern. Changes in production there were most noticeable in the making of cloth. As late as the 1760s, English textile merchants were still making cloth by the age-old "putting out" system. They bought raw wool and hired women to spin it at home. When the wool had been spun into yarn, the merchant then sent it to weavers who also worked in their homes. In that decade, however, new machinery (the carding cylinder, spinning jenny, and most important, the water frame)

Introduction.

Statement of theme.

Statement of thesis.

Attitudes toward industrialization in the United States.

Superscript numbers refer to endnotes.

Background information.

2

was developed that made possible the shift of spinning and weaving from homes to what were called "factories." By 1800, many such factories had been established in England, usually employing children to do most of the work. Many of these children were orphans or "paupers" from families so poor that they could not even afford to feed them. Conditions in these factories were very bad, and stories of these dark and dangerous mills (some accurate, some exaggerated) filtered back to America reinforcing the prejudice against England and industry.[2]

The economy of New England early in the nineteenth century was tied to commerce and agriculture, not industry. The wealth of New England merchants had been made in foreign trade, and few of them saw the need to turn to other pursuits. Some worried that the development of American manufactures would cut down on the need to import foreign goods. Until the War of 1812, which cut the United States off from trade in English goods, most wealthy merchants in the Northeast were content to stay in the business that had made their riches.[3] Moreover, where would American factory workers come from? England had a large class of peasants who served as a pool of potential factory labor. In America, however, when land wore out or harvests were poor, Yankee farmers could move west to the vast territories being taken from Native Americans.

The origins of the textile industry in eastern Massachusetts.

While great changes in the production of textiles were taking place in England, most New Englanders still spun yarn at home and some also wove their own cloth. In most cases they were simply making clothes for their families. Much of this work was done by women. A spinning wheel was a possession of almost every household.[4] Despite their anti-industrial prejudice, however, New England farmers witnessed, in the first two decades of the nineteenth century, a slow shift in the way cloth was made in America. Home production gradually gave way to "putting out" and that system was eventually replaced by factory production. Why did this change occur?

3

Unlike most merchants in America, a few, like Samuel Slater and Francis Cabot Lowell, were impressed by the mechanization of English textile production and began to think about an American textile industry. Men like these noted the massive increase in productivity in the English textile industry. At first, Slater, and others who followed his lead, built small mills in rural villages and employed not children as in England but whole families. The building of Slater-type mills did not directly challenge the New England way of living. Most villages already contained small mills run by water power (streams pushing paddle wheels) that ground corn or wheat. Since the textile mills hired whole families who already lived in the villages, family and village life was not greatly altered.[5]

One new development in textile production, however, did raise troublesome questions about the impact of industrialization on America's rural way of life. This change came from a new type of mill. The first of its type was built in Waltham, Massachusetts, in 1813 by Francis Lowell and a small group of wealthy Boston merchants.[6] Three years earlier, Lowell had returned from a long trip to England. The British government would not allow the plans for the new power looms to be taken out of the country, but Lowell had paid close attention to their construction on his many tours of English mills and returned to America with enough knowledge in his head to eventually reproduce a machine comparable to the English power loom.[7]

In Waltham, Francis Lowell built a large mill that carried out both the spinning and weaving processes. In fact, every step of the production process was done in a series of connected steps. Waltham was not a village with a textile mill in it; it was a "mill town" in which the factory dominated the economic life of a rapidly growing city. Most significantly, Lowell's system of production brought important changes in the lives of his workers. He hired them as individuals, not as families, and many came from great distances to live and work in the new

Transition sentence introduces discussion of new type of mill.

4

mill town. When Lowell died in 1817, the small group of Boston businessmen who had invested in his mill at Waltham spread the new factory system to other places. Their biggest investment was in the small village of East Chelmsford about twenty-seven miles from Boston and lying along the swift-flowing Concord and Merrimack Rivers. There they built what was soon the biggest mill town in the nation with more than a dozen large integrated mills based upon mechanical looms. In honor of their friend, they called the new town Lowell. (See Figure 1, a map of Lowell in 1845.)[8]

The growth of Lowell between 1821 and 1840 was unprecedented.[9] A rapidly developing textile industry like the one at Lowell needed larger and larger numbers of people to work the mechanical looms and other machines in the factories. Given the prejudice against factory work in New England, how could large numbers of natives be drawn to work in the mills? It was a question that had been carefully pondered by the wealthy men who built the big textile mills at Lowell, Massachusetts.

Recruiting women workers.

The mill owners, aware of the negative view of English mill towns, decided to confront the problem by creating a *planned* community where workers would live in solid, clean housing rather than slums. Their source of workers would also be different. The rapidly running rivers that ran their mills were not near the major coastal cities. No large pool of potential laborers lived near their new town. The mill owners had to find a large group of people whose labor was not absolutely necessary to the farm economy. The solution to their labor problem came in the form of hundreds (later thousands) of young women who lived on the farms of the region.[10]

Several developments in the social and economic history of New England tended to make this group of workers available. Population growth was making it more and more difficult for farmers

5

Visual documentation of location of mills and boarding houses.

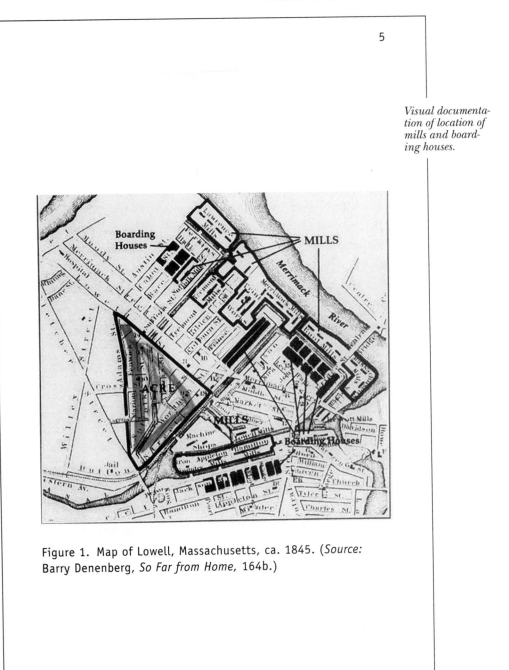

Figure 1. Map of Lowell, Massachusetts, ca. 1845. (*Source:* Barry Denenberg, *So Far from Home,* 164b.)

to find land close by for their sons (and their sons' families). Generations of the same family had hoped to live near one another. By the 1820s, however, many farms in New England, especially those on the less productive land of Maine and New Hampshire, had run out of good land and had to find sources of income outside of agriculture. While some farmers went west to find more fertile land and a less harsh climate, others sent their sons to work on neighboring farms, or as apprentices to craftsmen (shoemakers, blacksmiths, or leather workers). Extra cash was something that most farm families were in great need of.[11]

Problems of the farm community.

Another factor helped set the stage for the successful industrialization of textile production. This one was within the structure of the family itself and worked in favor of producing a new group of workers for the mills. The position of women (wives and, especially, daughters) in the family was an inferior one. Adult, property-holding males were citizens with full civil rights, but the same was not true for women *of any age.* The father of the family had the legal right to control most aspects of the lives of his wife and daughters. His wife could own no property. Her signature on a document meant nothing because only her husband could transact business. Daughters had even less independence. They were bound by social conventions to obey their fathers and rarely were able to earn money of their own. Even travel away from home was unusual. The idea that a woman's place was in the home was not merely a powerful concept, it was, with rare exceptions, a rule binding a woman's behavior. Although the work of daughters and wives was important to the family economy (it literally could not have functioned without their labor at field work, food preparation, cleaning, washing, etc.), they gained no independent income or freedom as a result. Indeed, so strong was the belief that daughters' lives would be bound by decisions made by their fathers, their older brothers, and, eventually, their husbands,

Subordinate status of women.

that many could not imagine for themselves a life of active, public involvement of the kind expected of men. For some women, however, their inferior position in family and society gave them an incentive to take hold of any opportunity to weaken their bonds of inferiority.[12]

Women's motives were economic as well as social. Very few opportunities for employment outside the home existed; teaching in a local school was one of the most common, but that was very poorly paid and lasted for only a few months a year. The new mill work was steady work, and it paid more than any alternative available to women.[13] Young girls could thus contribute to their family's welfare by sending home a portion of their pay. This economic motive added to their desire to move outside the traditional sphere of the family. For many of them, the chance to live away from home and with other young women like themselves offered an independence that was otherwise impossible.[14]

Hiring young women, of course, ran up against strong Yankee resistance. As noted above, fathers rarely allowed their daughters to leave home when they were young. According to the prejudices of the period, young women were unprepared for a life among adult, male strangers. Their "innocence" and "purity" had to be protected by their family. The goal held out for these girls (almost the only respectable one) was eventual marriage. To prepare for that, they had to learn wifely duties and practical household skills. God-fearing New England fathers were very reluctant to let their daughters leave the farm to live and work among strangers in a faraway town.[15]

Prejudice against women working outside the home.

To confront this prejudice, the mill owners created boarding houses around the mills where groups of girls would live and take their meals under the care of a boarding housekeeper who was usually an older woman, perhaps a widow. Strict boarding-house rules were laid down by the company; rules

8

that served the company's purposes but also reassured parents that their daughters' behavior would still be monitored even though they were away from home. For example, the young women could not have visitors in the late evening. (See Figure 2, a reproduction of boarding-house regulations.) Moreover, the girls would never grow into a permanent working class — something that no one wished to see — as it was expected that they would return to their homes for visits and after a year or two would go back to their villages. While they stayed in Lowell, their reputations (and thus their opportunity for marriage) would be protected by the town fathers.[16]

The mill owners did not advertise for help. They sent recruiters into the countryside to explain the special nature of Lowell and to soothe parents' fears. Because of the farmers' need for extra income, and the women's desire for independence, this effort was often successful.[17] Over the years, thousands of young women took the long trip by stagecoach or wagon from their rural homes to mill towns like Lowell.

Life in a mill town.

Upon first arriving in Lowell, the young girls were naturally nervous. They had not lived away from home or ever worked in a factory. They were not used to the atmosphere of a city. The boarding house was new also. Living with a strange woman (and probably her family), who might or might not be a caring mother-substitute, also required adjustment. The girls shared the home with a dozen or more other girls and usually roomed with three or four of them. Most were homesick for a time. While all this was happening, of course, the girls had to make the difficult adjustment to the rigorous rules and long hours at the mill.[18]

Mill work and the workday.

Mill work was not only an opportunity, like so much of early factory labor, it was hard work. The typical workday began at five a.m. and did not end until seven in the evening, or later. Thus the women worked an average of twelve hours a

9

*Visual documenta-
tion of boarding
house life.*

REGULATIONS

FOR THE

BOARDING HOUSES

OF THE

MIDDLESEX COMPANY.

THE tenants of the Boarding Houses are not to board, or permit any part of their houses to be occupied by any person except those in the employ of the Company.

They will be considered answerable for any improper conduct in their houses, and are not to permit their boarders to have company at unseasonable hours.

The doors must be closed at ten o'clock in the evening, and no one admitted after that time without some reasonable excuse.

The keepers of the Boarding Houses must give an account of the number, names, and employment of their boarders, when required; and report the names of such as are guilty of any improper conduct, or are not in the regular habit of attending public worship.

The buildings and yards about them must be kept clean and in good order, and if they are injured otherwise than from ordinary use, all necessary repairs will be made, and charged to the occupant.

It is indispensable that all persons in the employ of the Middlesex Company should be vaccinated who have not been, as also the families with whom they board; which will be done at the expense of the Company.

SAMUEL LAWRENCE, Agent.

JOEL TAYLOR, PRINTER, Daily Courier Office.

Figure 2. Rules for boarding houses where mill girls stayed. (*Source:* Merrimack Valley Textile Museum.)

day. They were given only thirty minutes for lunch and forty-five for dinner. Since they took their meals at the boarding house, the thirty minutes for lunch had to include a quick walk (perhaps a run) to and from the house, leaving only fifteen or twenty minutes for the meal.[19] The mills operated six days a week so that the only day off was Sunday, part of which was usually spent at church. Thus free time was confined to two or three hours in the evening (boarding-house rules required them to go to bed at ten) and to Sunday afternoon.[20] For many, however, this was still more leisure (and more freedom) than they would have had at home.

Despite a workday that, including meals, took up fourteen hours, most of the young women did not find the work very strenuous or particularly dangerous. As the mill owners had claimed, Lowell did not resemble the grimy, packed mill towns of England.[21] Still, the work was tedious and confining—doing the same operation over and over again and under the watchful eye of the overseer. In the ideal plan for Lowell, the overseer was to take the place of the absent father (just as the boarding-house widow was to be the substitute mother), someone responsible for seeing to the safety and welfare of the girls on the job. Of course, the overseer was also hired by the company to ensure that the mill ran smoothly and efficiently. He saw to it that the women worked steadily and recorded their hours of labor; any possibility of time off required his approval.[22]

The young women earned an average of three to four dollars a week from which their board of $1.25 a week was deducted.[23] At that time no other jobs open to women paid as well. As noted above, rural schoolteachers earned less than one dollar a week and taught for only three months of the year.[24] Three or four dollars a week was enough to pay their board, send badly needed money home, and still have enough left over for new clothes once in a while. Many women workers even established savings accounts, and some eventually left work with

11

several hundred dollars, something that they could never have done at home.[25]

   In Lowell the women became part of a growing city that had shops, social events, and camaraderie that were absent in their rural villages and farms. Most felt responsible to send part of their earnings home, but enough was left over to give them consumer choices unavailable to their rural sisters, cousins, and friends. Also, unlike farm and family chores, mill work offered free time on Sundays and in the evenings.[26]

Social life.

   Even though their free time was very limited, the women engaged in a wide variety of activities. In the evening they wrote letters home, entertained visitors (though there was little privacy), repaired their clothing, and talked among themselves. They talked of friends and relatives and also of conditions in the mill. They could go out to the shops, especially clothing shops. The mill girls at Lowell prided themselves on a wardrobe that, at least on Sunday, was not inferior to that of the wives of prosperous citizens.[27] One of the most surprising uses of their free time was the number of meetings attended by mill girls. There were evening courses that enabled the young women to extend their education beyond the few years of schooling they had received in the countryside. They could also attend lectures by prominent speakers. It was not unusual for the audience at serious presentations to be composed mostly of mill girls. In their spare time, they also read novels and essays. So strong was the girls' interest in reading that many mills put up signs warning "No reading in the mills."[28] Perhaps the most unusual pursuit of at least some mill girls was writing. Determined to challenge the idea that mill girls were mindless drones of the factory and lacked the refinement necessary to make them good wives, about seventy-five mill girls and women contributed in the 1840s to a series of publications that fea-

Leisure hours.

12

tured stories and essays by the workers themselves. Indeed, much of the editorial work was done by these women as well.[29]

The Lowell Offering.

The most well-known of these publications was the *Lowell Offering.* The *Offering* stayed away from sensitive issues concerning working conditions, and the mill owners certainly benefited from the reputation for seriousness that it earned their workers. Still, the women controlled the content of the publication and wrote on subjects (family, courtship, fashion, morality, nature, etc.) that interested them.[30] A few of the *Offering* writers even went on to literary careers, not the kind of future that most people expected of factory workers. Charles Dickens toured the mills in 1842 and later said of the girls' writing: "Of the merits of the *Lowell Offering,* as a literary production, I will

Example of a quotation with ellipsis. Short quotations are integrated into the text.

only observe . . . that it will compare advantageously with a great many English annuals."[31]

Though the *Offering* was a sign that something unusual was happening in this factory town, the women still worked in an industry that caused them hardship. In the early years, the owners had tried to keep up the image of the factory as a pleasant place. Buildings had many windows and much sunlight. The town had large green spaces and the atmosphere of a country village.[32] As time went on, however, the mill companies became more interested in profits and less concerned about their role as protectors of their young workers.

By the 1830s, tensions in the mills had begun to rise. Factory owners, observing a decline in the price of their cloth and the growth of unsold inventories, decided to lower their workers' wages.[33] When the reduction was announced in February 1834, the women workers circulated petitions among themselves pledging to stop work ("turn out") if wages were lowered.[34] When the leader of the petition drive at one mill was fired, many of the women protested. They left work and marched to the other mills to call out their workers. It is estimated that one-sixth of all women mill workers walked out as a

Women workers' resistance to factory discipline.

13

result. The strikers wrote another petition stating that "we will not go back into the mills to work until our wages are continued . . . as they have been."[35]

Although the "turn out" was brief and did not achieve its purpose, it did demonstrate the attitude of many of the women workers. They did not accept the owners' view that they were minors under their benevolent care. The petitions prepared by the strikers indicate that they thought of themselves as the equal of their employers. The sense of independence gained by factory work and cash wages led them to reject the idea that they were mere factory hands. Petitions referred to their "unquestionable rights," and to "the spirit of our patriotic ancestors, who preferred privation to bondage. . . ." One petition ended, "we are free, we would remain in possession of what kind providence has bestowed upon us, and remain *daughters of free men still*."[36] This language indicates that the women did not think of themselves as laborers complaining about low wages. They were free citizens of a republic and deserved respect as such. Because many of the women had relatives who had fought in the Revolutionary War, they felt that they were protecting not only their jobs but also their independence.

Example of a quotation with emphasis added.

Although the strike failed and these women did not really have the "independence" they were so proud of, this issue was so important to them that many left the mills and went home when it became clear that mill work required a lessening of their status. They had accepted mill work because life away from home and good wages gave them greater freedom. When mill work came to seem more like "slavery" (a comparison that also appeared in the petitions) than independence, many changed their minds. In 1836, another effort to lower wages led to an even larger "turn out."[37] The willingness of these young women to challenge the authority of the mill owners is a sign that their new lives had given them a feeling of mutual strength.[38]

14

Declining condi-
tions of work in
the Lowell mills.

Economic recession in the late 1830s and early 1840s led to the layoff of hundreds of the women workers. Many of the mills were forced to part-time schedules. In the 1840s and 1850s, the mill owners tried to maintain profits despite increased competition and lessened demand. They did so by intensifying the work process. The speed of the machinery was increased as was the number of machines tended by each worker. Paternalism was discarded. To save money, the companies stopped building boarding houses.[39] The look of Lowell changed as well. Mill buildings took up more of the green space that had been part of the original plan.

By 1850, Lowell did indeed look something like an English mill town. By then, however, the desire to pacify the fears of potential workers and their families was gone. Terrible famine in Ireland in 1845 and 1846 had caused a large number of Irish to immigrate to the United States.[40] As conditions in

The coming of
Irish workers.

the mills declined, more and more young Yankee women left the mills for home or other work. Their places were rapidly taken up by the very poor Irish for whom work of any kind in America was an opportunity, and who did not have the option of returning to their homes. Slowly, Lowell had become just another industrial city. It was dirty and overcrowded, and its mills were beginning to look run-down.

Conclusion.

By 1850, an era had passed. By then, most of the mill workers were recruited from newly arrived immigrants with backgrounds very different from those of the young New England women. During the period from the 1820s to the 1840s, however, young women from rural New England made up the majority of the textile workers in the area. At that time, an unusual era in the development of industrialization took place. Large textile mills with complex production systems were operated largely by young women who thought of themselves not as workers but as free citizens of a republic earning an indepen-

15

dent existence for a few years before returning to their homes. These women gave the mill owners the workforce that was needed to make the U.S. textile industry large and profitable. Many fortunes were made for investors living in Boston and other major cities.41 But the farmers' daughters profited as well. Not only did they earn more than earlier generations of women had been able to, but they did so outside the home.

Restatement of part of thesis.

 A great debate had raged during the 1830s and 1840s about the impact of industrialization on American life. Because of the general belief that women were weak, it was presumed that they would be taken advantage of as workers, especially as they were away from the protection of the male members of their families. Further, it was feared that mill work would "de-feminize" them and that young men would not marry them because they had not been brought up in an environment of modesty, deference to their fathers and brothers, and daily practice in domestic tasks such as cleaning, sewing, and cooking.[42] (Textile mill workers were known as "spinsters," a word that came to mean a woman who never married.) Seen from a longer perspective, however, the women showed these fears to be unfounded. Even more importantly, as effective workers they undermined the stereotype of women as frail and as thriving only in a domestic environment. While these young women helped make possible the industrialization of New England, at the same time they expanded their opportunities. Many women reformers and radicals in later years, as they raised the banner for equal rights for women in more and more areas of life, referred back to the example of the independent mill girls of the 1830s and 1840s who resisted pressures from their employers, gained both freedom and maturity by living and working on their own, and showed an intense desire for independence and learning.[43] Great fortunes were made from the textile mills of that era, but within those mills a generation of young women gained something even more precious: a sense of self-respect.

Summary.

Restatement of thesis.

16

Endnotes begin on a new page.

Endnotes

1. American attitudes toward industrialization in England and mill work in general.

  1. Caroline F. Ware, *The Early New England Cotton Manufacture* (Boston: Houghton Mifflin, 1931), 4–8; Barbara M. Tucker, *Samuel Slater and the Origins of the American Textile Industry: 1790–1860* (Ithaca: Cornell University Press, 1984), 38–41; Robert F. Dalzell, *Enterprising Elite: The Boston Associates and the World They Made* (Cambridge: Harvard University Press, 1987), 12–13; Jonathan Prude, *The Coming of Industrial Order: Town and Factory Life in Rural Massachusetts, 1810–1860* (Cambridge, UK: Cambridge University Press, 1983), 6–12; Allan Kulikoff, "The Transition to Capitalism in Rural America," *William and Mary Quarterly* 46 (1989): 129–30, 141–42.

2. The rise of industrialization in England.

  2. Tucker, *Slater,* 33–40.

3. The origins of industrialization in America.

  3. Dalzell, 41–42; Ware, 3–8, 62.

4. Home spinning in America.

  4. Thomas Dublin, *Women at Work: The Transformation of Work and Community in Lowell, Massachusetts, 1826–1860* (New York: Columbia University Press, 1979), 14; Adrienne D. Hood, "The Gender Division of Labor in the Production of Textiles in Eighteenth-Century Rural Pennsylvania," *Journal of Social History* 27 (Spring 1994), http://www.searchbank.com/infotrac/session/4/0/82904/37xrn_7.

Example of citation from the Web.

5. Slater-type mills and family production.

  5. Tucker, *Slater,* 79, 85, 99–100, 111; Barbara M. Tucker, "The Family and Industrial Discipline in Ante-Bellum New England," *Labor History* 21 (Winter 1979–80): 56–60.

6. The creation of Waltham mills.

  6. Dalzell, 26–30; Tucker, *Slater,* 111–16.

7. H. C. Lowell and power loom.

  7. Dalzell, 5–6.

8. The founding of Lowell.

  8. Tucker, *Slater,* 116–17.

9. The growth of Lowell.

  9. Dublin, 19–21, 133–35.

10. The owners' choice of a female workforce.

  10. Dublin, 26, 76; Benita Eisler, ed., *The "Lowell Offering": Writings by New England Mill Women (1840–1845)* (Philadelphia: Lippincott, 1977), 15–16.

17

11. Christopher Clark, "The Household Economy: Market Exchange and the Rise of Capitalism in the Connecticut Valley, 1800–1860," *Journal of Social History* 13 (Winter 1979): 175–76; Gail Fowler Mohanty, "Handloom Outwork and Outwork Weaving in Rural Rhode Island, 1810–1821," *American Studies* 30 (Fall 1989): 42–43, 48–49.

11. Problems of the farm economy.

12. Eisler, 16, 19, 62; Barbara Welter, "The Cult of True Womanhood," *American Quarterly* 18 (1966): 155, 162–65.

12. The inferior position of women.

13. Eisler, 16, 193; Clark, 178–79; Dalzell, 33.

13. Limited opportunities for women in New England.

14. Dublin, 40; Tucker, *Slater,* 255–56; Harriet H. Robinson, *Loom and Spindle* (1898; reprinted in *Women of Lowell,* New York: Arno Press, 1974), 194; Eisler, 61–63, 81–82.

14. Women's desire for independence.

15. On the influence of patriarchy see Tucker, *Slater,* 25–26; Robinson, 61; Welter, 152, 170–71. Also see *Sins of Our Mothers,* videocassette (Boston: WGBH/WNET/KLET/PBS, 1988).

15. Early nineteenth-century rural attitudes toward women.

Example of a film citation.

16. Dublin, 77–79; Eisler, 19–24.

16. Early Lowell paternalism.

17. Eisler, 18–19. On the decline of New England agriculture see Clark, 176; Ware, 14.

17. The method of recruiting women workers.

18. Dublin, 80; Eisler, 73–74.

18. Getting used to town life and the boarding house.

19. Dublin, 80; Robinson, 31; Lucy Larcom, "Among Lowell Mill Girls: A Reminiscence" (1881; reprinted in *Women of Lowell*), 602; Eisler, 75–77.

19. The nature of mill work and the workday.

20. See table of mill hours printed in Eisler, 30. Boarding-house curfew is listed in "Regulations for the Boarding Houses," contained in illustration on page 9. For a very negative view of work hours and conditions, see A Citizen of Lowell, *Corporations and Operatives: Being an Exposition of the Condition [of the] Factory Operatives* . . . (1843; reprinted in *Women of Lowell*), 15–19, 21.

20. Work hours and free time.

21. Larcom, 599–602; Eisler, 56–66.

21. Favorable comments on mill work by the Lowell mill girls.

22. "Factory Rules from the Handbook to Lowell, 1848," http://www.kentlaw.edu/ilhs/lowell.htm (accessed August 9, 1996).

22. The role of the overseer. (Example of a Web citation.)

23. Dublin, 66, 183, 185; Ware, 239.

23. The rate of women's pay.

## 18

24. Low alternative pay for women.

24. Ware, 240–42. For teachers' pay see Eisler, 193.

25. Savings accounts.

25. Elisha Bartlett, *A Vindication of the Character and Condition of the Females Employed in the Lowell Mills . . .* (Lowell, MA: Leonard Huntress, Printer, 1841), 21; Dublin, 188.

26. Free time.

26. Larcom, 599–600.

27. Leisure time and wardrobe.

27. Eisler, 49–50.

28. Reading and education.

28. Robinson, 91–93; Eisler, 113–32. For mill rules concerning reading, see Eisler, 31.

29. Women's writing.

29. Robinson, 97–102.

30. The Lowell Offering.

30. Eisler, 33–40; Dublin, 123–24, 129–30; Robinson, 114–20; Bertha Monica Stearns, "Early Factory Magazines in New England: The *Lowell Offering* and Its Contemporaries," *Journal of Economic and Business History* (August 1930): 690–91, 698.

31. Dickens commenting on the Lowell Offering.

31. Dickens is quoted in Robinson, 11. Also see Larcom, 609; Eisler, 41.

32. The early Lowell setting.

32. Larcom, 598, 609; Eisler, 63–65.

33. The tensions of the 1830s; lowered wages.

33. Dublin, 87–90.

34. The 1834 "turn out."

34. Robinson, 84; Dublin, 89–91.

35. Strikers' petitions.

35. Dublin, 91.

36. More quotes from petitions.

36. Dublin, 93. (Emphasis added to quotation.)

37. The 1836 "turn out."

37. Dublin, 98–99.

38. Mutual support.

38. Dublin, 44, 82–83, 103.

39. Declining working conditions.

39. Dublin, 108, 134; Robinson, 204, 208–9; Eisler, 215.

40. The workforce after 1845; Irish immigration.

40. Dublin, 140, 156, 197. On the decline of Lowell, see Dalzell, 69.

41. Profits for owners.

41. Dalzell, 60–61, 70–73.

42. The status of women.

42. Dublin 32; Welter, 151–74. For the contemporary debate about the impact of factory work on women, see these pamphlets: Bartlett, *A Vindication of the Character and Condition,* and A Citizen, *Corporations and Operatives.*

43. Lowell women activists and later movements.

43. Dublin, 127–29; Ware, 292.

19

Bibliography

Books

Bartlett, Elisha. *A Vindication of the Character and Condition of the Females Employed in the Lowell Mills*. . . . Lowell, MA: Leonard Huntress, Printer, 1841. Reprinted in *Women of Lowell*. New York: Arno Press, 1974.

Citizen of Lowell, A. *Corporations and Operatives: Being an Exposition of the Condition [of the] Factory Operatives*. . . . 1843. Reprinted in *Women of Lowell*. New York: Arno Press, 1974.

Dalzell, Robert F. *Enterprising Elite: The Boston Associates and the World They Made*. Cambridge: Harvard University Press, 1987.

Dublin, Thomas. *Women at Work: The Transformation of Work and Community in Lowell, Massachusetts, 1826–1860*. New York: Columbia University Press, 1979.

Eisler, Benita, ed. *The "Lowell Offering": Writings by New England Mill Women (1840–1845)*. Philadelphia: Lippincott, 1977.

Prude, Jonathan. *The Coming of Industrial Order: Town and Factory Life in Rural Massachusetts, 1810–1860*. Cambridge, UK: Cambridge University Press, 1983.

Robinson, Harriet H. *Loom and Spindle; Or, Life among the Early Mill Girls*. 1898. Reprinted in *Women of Lowell*. New York: Arno Press, 1974.

Tucker, Barbara M. *Samuel Slater and the Origins of the American Textile Industry: 1790–1860*. Ithaca: Cornell University Press, 1984.

Ware, Caroline F. *The Early New England Cotton Manufacture*. Boston: Houghton Mifflin, 1931.

Articles

Clark, Christopher. "The Household Economy: Market Exchange and the Rise of Capitalism in the Connecticut Valley, 1800–1860." *Journal of Social History* 13 (Winter 1979): 169–89.

Bibliography begins on a new page.

Citations are listed alphabetically under each heading.

Second and following lines of each citation are indented.

20

Hood, Adrienne D. "The Gender Division of Labor in the Pro-
    duction of Textiles in Eighteenth-Century Rural Pennsyl-
    vania." *Journal of Social History* 27 (Spring 1994).
    http://www.searchbank.com/infotrac/session/
    4/0/82904/3?xrn_7.
Kulikoff, Allan. "The Transition to Capitalism in Rural America."
    William and Mary Quarterly 46 (1989): 120–144.
Larcom, Lucy. "Among Lowell Mill Girls: A Reminiscence." 1881.
    Reprinted in *Women of Lowell.* New York: Arno Press, 1974.
Mohanty, Gail Fowler. "Handloom Outwork and Outwork Weaving
    in Rural Rhode Island, 1810–1821." *American Studies* 30
    (Fall 1989): 41–68.
Stearns, Bertha Monica. "Early Factory Magazines in New Eng-
    land: The *Lowell Offering* and Its Contemporaries." *Journal
    of Economic and Business History* (August 1930): 685–705.
Tucker, Barbara M. "The Family and Industrial Discipline in Ante-
    Bellum New England." *Labor History* 21 (Winter 1979–80):
    55–74.
Welter, Barbara. "The Cult of True Womanhood." *American Quar-
    terly* 18 (1966): 151–74.

Documents

"Factory Rules from the Handbook to Lowell, 1848." http://
    www.kentlaw.edu/ilhs/lowell.htm.

Nonwritten Sources

"Map of Lowell, showing the location of mills and boarding
    houses." In *So Far from Home,* by Barry Denenberg. New
    York: Scholastic, Inc., 1997: 164b.
*Middlesex Company Boarding-House Regulations of the Middlesex
    Company, ca. 1850.* The American Textile History Museum,
    Lowell, MA.
Sins of Our Mothers. Videocassette. Boston: WGBH/WNET/KCET/
    PBS, 1988.

Basic Reference Sources
for History Study
and Research

Chapter 4, "How to Research a History Topic," describes the ways of searching for information on a history topic in your library and on the Web. This appendix makes that job easier by grouping reference sources by type so that you know what *kind* of printed or online finding aid will get you where you want to go.

This list of reference sources is especially designed for undergraduate historical research. It contains several kinds of printed sources: (1) *reference works* (dictionaries, **encyclopedias, atlases, yearbooks**); (2) *guides* to biographies, articles in newspapers and **journals, book reviews,** and government documents; and (3) several hundred **subject bibliographies** arranged by topic. Reference works contain brief descriptions of aspects of your historical topic; guides and subject bibliographies lead you to specific studies of the theme itself. If, for example, your theme is nineteenth-century Asian immigration to the United States and you have narrowed it to "Chinese immigrant labor on the transcontinental railroad," the section of the subject bibliographies entitled "Asian Immigrant and Ethnic History" (p. 206) is a good place to begin.

Also included in this appendix is a section called "Digital Reference Sources" (see p. 212). Listed in this section are information sources on the **World Wide Web.** Most of your library's computer terminals will give you access to **CD-ROMs** owned by your library and to the Web. More and more historical research is likely to be done online, so it is important that you know your way around the universe of electronic information. For the present, however, more reliable background information on your theme is probably available in your library's *printed* reference works.

Many of the printed works cited in this appendix are likely to be available in the reference section of your college library. If your library is small, however, you may not find some of them. On the other hand if your school's library is large, you will have even more sources available to you.

Compilations and edited works are listed in the appendix by title to help you spot the works that seem most closely related to your topic. Following the title are the name of the editor or compiler (if available) and then publication information. When you have access to more than one edition of a work, it is usually best to use the most recent one. As always, the reference librarian is your best guide to your school's information resources.

Dictionaries, Encyclopedias, Atlases, and Yearbooks

These printed sources are general reference works that you can use to define and correctly spell important terms, gather general information on your theme, locate geographical areas, obtain statistical data, and much more. These sources are a good point at which to begin any historical investigation. You can also consult them for specific facts. However, these sources do not contain extensive examinations or interpretations of historical subjects, and therefore you should not depend on them for the substance of your work.

General Dictionaries

Webster's Third New International Dictionary. Springfield, Mass.: Merriam-Webster, 2002.

Oxford English Dictionary, 2d ed. Oxford: Clarendon Press, 1989. This is the most complete English-language dictionary. If you are tracing the historical development of the meaning of a word, it is an essential reference. If, however, you wish to determine the contemporary spelling or definition of a term, other general dictionaries are better sources. If the term is colloquial or is a recent derivation, be sure to use the most recent edition.

Historical Dictionaries

Historical dictionaries define only historical terms. Generally, they briefly describe the origin and general historical context of a term. Historical dictionaries that give extensive explanations of terms are similar to encyclopedias.

Concise Dictionary of American History. Ed. David W. Voorhees. New York: Scribner's 1983. This is an abridgment of the ten-volume *Dictionary of American History (see below).*

Oxford Dictionary of World Religions. Ed. John Bowker. Oxford: Oxford University Press, 1997.

Macmillan Concise Dictionary of World History. Comp. and ed. Bruce Wetterau. New York: Macmillan, 1986.

A Dictionary of Twentieth Century History, 1914–1990. Ed. Peter Teed. Oxford: Oxford University Press, 1992.

New Penguin Dictionary of Modern History, 1789–1945. Ed. Duncan Townson and Alan W. Palmer. Baltimore: Penguin Books, 1994.

Dictionary of American History. 3d ed. Ed. Stanley I. Kutler. 10 vols. New York: Thomson Learning, 2003.

The Harper Dictionary of Modern Thought. Ed. Alan Bullock and Stephen Trombley. New York: Harper & Row, 1988.

A Dictionary of Ancient History. Ed. Graham Speake. Oxford: Blackwell, 1994.

Oxford Dictionary of Byzantium. Ed. Alex P. Kazhdan. 3 vols. Oxford University Press, 1991.

A Dictionary of American History. Ed. Thomas L. Purvis. Oxford: Blackwell, 1995.

Dictionary of Contemporary History, 1945 to the Present. Ed. Duncan Townson. Oxford: Blackwell, 1999.

Specialized Dictionaries

A Dictionary of the Social Sciences. Ed. Craig J. Calhoun. New York: Oxford University Press, 2001.

The New Grove Dictionary of Music and Musicians. 2d ed. Ed. Stanley Sadie and John Tyrrell. 29 vols. New York: Macmillan, 2001.

Baker's Biographical Dictionary of Musicians. 9th ed. Ed. Nicolas Slonimsky and Laura Kuhn. 6 vols. New York: Schirmer, 2001.

The Oxford Dictionary of Philosophy. Comp. Simon Blackburn. Oxford: Oxford University Press, 1994.

Merriam-Webster's Geographical Dictionary. 3d ed. Springfield, Mass.: Merriam-Webster, 1997. This is a convenient source for determining the spelling, location, and description of geographical terms.

The Dictionary of Art. Ed. Jane Turner. New York: Grove Press, 1996.

General Encyclopedias

If your theme is a recent one, or if important new facts and interpretations have arisen in recent years, be sure to obtain the latest edition of whatever encyclopedia you use. If a recent edition is not available, check the annual supplements published by most good encyclopedias. Online versions of encyclopedias may be available to you.

Encyclopaedia Britannica. 15th ed. 32 vols. Chicago: Encyclopaedia Britannica Educational Corp., 2001. This is one of the best encyclopedias. It is also available on the Web at <www.britannica.com>.

Encyclopedia Americana. 30 vols. Danbury, Conn.: Grolier, 2002.

Collier's Encyclopedia. 24 vols. New York: Crowell Collier and Macmillan, 1996.

The Columbia Encyclopedia. 6th ed. Ed. Paul Lagassé. Detroit: Gale, 2000.

Historical Encyclopedias

The Encyclopedia of Ancient Civilizations of the Near East and Mediterranean. Ed. John Heywood. New York: M. E. Sharpe, 1997.

Harper Encyclopedia of the Modern World [1760 to present]. Ed. Richard B. Morris and Graham W. Irwin. New York: Harper & Row, 1970.

Encyclopedia of American History. 7th ed. Ed. Richard B. Morris and Jeffrey B. Morris. New York: Harper & Row, 1996.

The Encyclopedia of the Middle Ages. Ed. Norman F. Cantor. New York: Viking, 1999.

Women's Studies Encyclopedia: History, Philosophy, and Religion. Vol. 3. Ed. Helen Tierney. Westport, Conn.: Greenwood Press, 1999.

Encyclopedia of World History. 6th ed. Ed. Peter N. Stearns. Boston: Houghton Mifflin, 2001.

The Historical Encyclopedia of World Slavery. Ed. Junius P. Rodriguez. Santa Barbara, Calif.: ABC-Clio, 1997.

Specialized Encyclopedias

For encyclopedias of particular historical fields, see the subheadings under "Subject Bibliographies" (p. 192).

International Encyclopedia of the Social Sciences. Ed. David L. Sills. 19 vols. New York: Macmillan, 1968–1991. If your research takes you into fields such as political science, economics, anthropology, law, sociology, and psychology, this is an important sourcebook for you. A biographical supplement, published in 1979, includes biographies of famous social scientists.

Routledge Encyclopedia of Philosophy. Ed. Edward Craig. 10 vols. New York: Routledge, 1998.

Encyclopedia Judaica. Ed. Cecil Rovhand and Geoffrey Wigoder. 16 vols. Jerusalem: Keter Publishing, 1972. Reprint, New York: Coronet Books, 1994.

New Catholic Encyclopedia. 2d ed. Detroit: Gale, 2002.

Encyclopedia of Religion. Ed. Mircea Eliade. 16 vols. New York: Macmillan, 1993.

Encyclopedia of World Art. New York: McGraw-Hill, 1959–1983. Supplements, 1987.

Benet's Reader's Encyclopedia. 4th ed. Ed. Bruce Murphy. New York: HarperCollins, 1996.

New Encyclopedia of Islam. Ed. Cyril Glasse. Walnut Creek, Calif.: Alta Mira Press, 2001.

McGraw-Hill Encyclopedia of Science and Technology. 8th ed. Ed. Sybil P. Parker. New York: McGraw-Hill, 1998.

Encyclopedia of the United States in the Twentieth Century. Ed. Stanley Kutler. 4 vols. New York: Scribner's, 1996.

The New Grove Dictionary of Music and Musicians. 2d ed. Ed. Stanley Sadie and John Tyrrell. 29 vols. New York: Macmillan, 2001.

Encyclopedia of Bioethics. Rev. ed. Ed. Warren Thomas Reich. 5 vols. New York: Macmillan Library Reference, 1995.

General Atlases

The Times Atlas of the World: Comprehensive Edition. 10th ed. London: Times Publishing, 1999.

National Geographic Atlas of the World. 7th ed. Washington, D.C.: National Geographic Society, 1999.

See also *Merriam-Webster's Geographical Dictionary* under "Specialized Dictionaries" on page 181.

Historical Atlases

Muir's Historical Atlas: Ancient, Medieval, and Modern. London: George Philips, 1976.

Times Atlas of World History. 4th ed. New York: Hammond, 1993.

Atlas of American History. Ed. Kenneth T. Jackson. New York: Scribner's, 1984.

The Atlas of Medieval Man. Ed. Colin Platt. New York: Crescent Books, 1985.

The Complete Atlas of World History. 3 vols. New York: M. E. Sharpe, 1997.

Harper Atlas of World History. New York: HarperCollins, 1992.

Times Atlas of European History. Ed. Thomas Cussans. New York: Times/Harper-Collins, 1994.

Historical Atlas of the United States. Ed. Wilbur E. Garrett. Washington, D.C.: National Geographic Society, 1988.

Historical Atlas of Britain. Ed. Malcolm Falkus and John Gillingham. New York: Crescent Books, 1987.

Muir's Atlas of Ancient and Classical History. London: George Philips, 1982.

Atlas of World History. Rev. ed. Ed. Robert R. Palmer et al. Chicago: Rand McNally, 1995.

Atlas of the Greek World. Comp. Peter Levi. New York: Facts on File, 1980.

Atlas of the Roman World. Comp. Tim Cornell and John Matthews. New York: Facts on File, 1982.

Yearbooks

Statesman's Yearbook. New York: St. Martin's Press, 1864–. This and the following yearbooks provide up-to-date political information, especially of a governmental nature.

Political Handbook of the World. Ed. Arthur S. Banks and William Overstreet. New York: McGraw-Hill, 1927–.

United Nations Statistical Yearbook. New York: United Nations Statistical Office, 1949–. The *United Nations Demographic Yearbook* provides world and national population statistics.

Biography Collections

Printed biography collections consist of short biographies of well-known persons. They contain a general outline of the milestones and accomplishments of individuals who have made notable contributions to the times in which they lived or to posterity. Consulting these works is a useful first step in biographical research on persons central to your theme or in identifying characters peripheral to it. Each collection has different criteria for determining which individuals it includes. Take care to select the biography collection that is most likely to include the type of individual on whom you are seeking information. Some are also available on CD-ROM or online.

Guides to Biography Collections

Biography Index: A Cumulative Guide to Biographical Material in Books and Magazines. New York: H. W. Wilson, 1949–.

Biography and Genealogy Master Index. Ed. Miranda C. Herbert and Barbara McNeil. 8 vols. Detroit: Gale, 1980. Supplements issued annually. Also available on CD-ROM and online.

Biographical Dictionaries Master Index. Ed. Dennis LaBeau and Gary C. Tarbert. Detroit: Gale, 1975. Supplement, 1979.

American Biography Collections

American National Biography. Ed. John A. Garraty and Mark C. Carnes. 24 vols. New York: Oxford University Press and American Council of Learned Societies, 1999. Supplement, 2002. The newest and most extensive collection of U.S. biographies. To be updated online.

Dictionary of American Biography. New York: Scribner's, 1928–1996, including supplements. This collection includes both U.S. citizens and people who lived much of their lives in the United States even if they were not citizens. It lists only individuals who are no longer living. As in most biography collections, the date of original publication is the best key to determining who is included. Most of the original volumes were written between 1928 and 1936. If your subject died after 1930, check the numerous supplements. A one-volume work containing shortened versions of these biographies is published under the title *Concise Dictionary of American Biography,* 5th ed., 1997. An index was published in 1996.

Who Was Who in America: Historical Volume, 1607–1896. Chicago: Marquis, 1967. If you are uncertain about your subject's death date, check *Who Was Who in America: Index* (2002).

Who Was Who in America, with World Notables, 1897–2002. 14 vols. Chicago: Marquis, 2002. The years covered in each volume indicate the dates of death of those included in it. For example, if your subject died in 1945, he or she should be included in volume 2. For individuals who died before 1897, see the preceding citation.

Who's Who in America. Chicago: Marquis, 1897–. This volume covers living individuals. For purposes of historical research, you must obtain the older volumes or, preferably, use the *Who Was Who* collections.

Notable American Women 1607–1950: A Bibliographical Dictionary. Ed. Edward T. James. 3 vols. Cambridge, Mass.: Harvard University Press, 1971. Supplemented by *Notable American Women: The Modern Period.* 1980. This volume includes women who died between 1951 and 1975.

Research Guide to American Historical Biography. Ed. Suzanne Niemeyer. New York: Beacham, 1990.

Biographical Directory of the American Congress, 1774–1996. Washington, D.C.: Government Printing Office, 1996.

Biographical Directory of the United States Executive Branch, 1774–1989. Westport, Conn.: Greenwood Press, 1990.

Who's Who of American Women. Chicago: Marquis, 1958–.

Dictionary of American Negro Biography. Ed. Rayford W. Logan and Michael Winston. New York: Norton, 1982.

American Men and Women of Science. New York: Bowker, 1906–.

American Diaries: An Annotated Bibliography of Published American Diaries and Journals. Detroit: Gale, 1983–1987.

The Encyclopedia of American Biography. Ed. John Garraty and Jerome Sternstein. New York: HarperCollins, 1996.

British and Canadian Biography Collections

Dictionary of National Biography. Ed. Leslie Stephen and Sidney Lee. Oxford: Oxford University Press, 1908–. A summary of this large multivolume collection can be found in *A Concise Dictionary of National Biography, from Earliest Times to 1985.*

Who's Who. London: Allen & Unwin, 1849–. Annual. This volume covers *living* individuals. For historical research, you must choose a year during which your subject was most active, or preferably use the *Who Was Who* collection that follows.

Who Was Who. Vol. 1, 1897–1915; vol. 2, 1916–1928; vol. 3, 1929–1940; vol. 4, 1941–1950; vol. 5, 1951–1960; vol. 6, 1961–1970; vol. 7, 1971–1980; vol. 8, 1981–1990; vol. 9, 1991–1995; vol. 10, 1996–2000. A cumulative index for 1897–1990 was published in 1991. (See annotation to *Who Was Who in America, with World Notables,* for further information.)

Canadian Who's Who. 37 vols. Toronto: University of Toronto Press, 2002.

Dictionary of Canadian Biography. Toronto: University of Toronto Press, 1966–. An index to this multivolume work is listed below.

Dictionary of Canadian Biography: Index. Volumes I to XII, 1000 to 1900. Toronto: University of Toronto Press, 1991.

National Biography Collections

Most national biography collections deal with contemporary personages. However, such collections may be useful for research into recent history or for obtaining information on the early careers of contemporary figures. Here is a brief selection.

Dictionary of Canadian Biography. Toronto: University of Toronto Press, 1966–.

Dictionary of African Historical Biography. Ed. Mark R. Lipschultz and R. Kent Rasmusson. Berkeley: University of California Press, 1986.

Dictionary of African Biography. New York: Reference Publications, 1977–1995.

Japan Biographical Encyclopedia and Who's Who. Tokyo: Rengo Press, 1958–1965.

Australian Dictionary of Biography. Ed. Douglas Pike et al. 16 vols. Carlton, Victoria: Melbourne University Press, 1966–.

International Biography Collections

International biography collections list persons of all national origins.

Current Biography. New York: H. W. Wilson, 1940–. This work covers living persons. Older volumes may list individuals who are now of historical significance. Useful only for historical research for the period since the 1930s. To locate the volume you need, check *Current Biography: Cumulated Index, 1940–2000.*

International Who's Who. London: Europa, 1935–.

New York Times Obituary Index, 1858–1968, 1969–1980. New York: New York Times, 1970, 1980. Current volumes published by Meckler, 1990–.

Who's Who in the World. Chicago: Marquis, 1971–.

The Continuum Dictionary of Women's Biography. Expanded ed. Ed. Jennifer S. Uglow. New York: Continuum, 1989.

Dictionary of International Biography. Cambridge: England International Biographical Centre, 1985.

Dictionary of Scientific Biography. Ed. Charles C. Gillispie. 16 vols. New York: Scribner's, 1970–1980. Includes index.

Newspaper Directories and Indexes

If you determine that a particular newspaper is especially important to your research, the best way to locate back issues is to check a newspaper directory. These directories can tell you in which libraries that newspaper can be found and how complete the collection is. Remember, the newspaper directory is useful only if you know the name of the paper for which you are looking. You might be able to obtain the newspapers you need if they are on microfilm or microfiche. Some newspaper directories and indexes are available on CD-ROM and online.

Newspaper Directories

American Newspapers, 1821–1936: A Union List of Files Available in the United States and Canada. Ed. Winifred Gerould. New York: H. W. Wilson, 1937. Also available on microfilm. Ann Arbor: University Microfilms, 1966.

Newspapers on Microfilm: A Union Check List. Ed. George Schwegman Jr. Washington, D.C.: Library of Congress, 1963. This volume is supplemented by *Newspapers in Microform: United States, 1948–1984.*

African Newspapers in Selected American Libraries: A Union List. Washington, D.C.: Library of Congress, 1965.

Latin American Newspapers in United States Libraries. Ed. Steven M. Charno. Austin: University of Texas Press, 1969.

Newspaper Indexes

Once you have access to a particular newspaper, you must determine which issues contain articles on your theme. If your theme is a specific event, then merely check the issues of the newspaper published at the time of or shortly after the event. However, if you are seeking articles about an event that was not confined to a particular day or week (for example, the stock market crash of 1929), then you will have to check newspaper issues covering many weeks or even months. An indispensable aid in such a task is the newspaper index.

If you know the year in which the event occurred, then a newspaper index can tell you the days in that year when a particular paper contained related articles or editorials. The only problem with newspaper indexes is that so few of them exist. If there is no index to the paper you wish to read, check the index of another newspaper. This will tell you the dates on which that newspaper carried articles on your subject. You can then go back to the newspaper in which you were initially interested and read it for those dates. In most cases, you will find what you need. Some newspaper indexes are now available on the Web at the newspapers' home pages or through your library's Web sites.

New York Times Index. New York: New York Times, 1913–. This is usually the best source for beginning students. Most libraries have files of the *New York Times,* and the index has been extended back to 1851. Some libraries have Internet access to all of the articles themselves. In this case you can search by keyword.

New York Daily Tribune Index. New York: Tribune Association, 1841–1907.

Palmer's Index to The Times [of London] *Newspaper,* 1790–1941. London: 1868–1943. For more recent coverage, there is a CD-ROM and electronic access.

Official Index to The Times [of London]. London: 1907–.

Christian Science Monitor Index. Corvallis, Ore.: 1960–. Because this index goes back only to 1960, it is of limited use for historical research.

Periodical Guides and Indexes

Periodical guides describe the location and general content of **periodicals.** Like newspaper guides, they are most useful if you already know which periodical you need and you want to find out where collections of it are located. Many periodical indexes are available on the World Wide Web (see "Digital Reference Sources," pp. 212–31).

Periodical Guides

Historical Periodicals: An Annotated World List of Historical and Related Serial Publications. Ed. Eric H. Boehm and Lalit Adolphur. Santa Barbara, Calif.: ABC-Clio, 1961. This volume is succeeded by the directory that follows.

Historical Periodicals Directory. Ed. Eric H. Boehm, Barbara H. Pope, and Marie Ensign. Vol. 1 *United States and Canada.* Vol. 2, *Europe (West).* Vol. 3, *Europe*

(East). Vol. 4, *Latin America.* Vol. 5, *Australia and New Zealand.* Santa Barbara, Calif.: ABC-Clio, 1981–1986.

Ulrich's International Periodicals Directory. 41st ed. New York: Bowker, 2003.

Magazines for Libraries. 11th ed. New York: Bowker, 2002. This guide describes each publication and helps to determine which are best for historical research.

General Periodical Indexes

General periodical indexes list articles that have appeared in periodical publications. Usually organized by subject, they contain all of the articles on a given topic that appeared in the periodicals that are indexed. When you choose an index, be sure that it covers the kind of periodical likely to contain articles on your theme and that the articles are written for a serious or scholarly audience. There are also many electronic databases that index periodicals. Be sure to check your library's databases and also the World Wide Web.

Historical Abstracts. Ed. Eric H. Boehm. Part A, *Modern History (1450–1914).* Part B, *The Twentieth Century (1914–Present).* Santa Barbara, Calif.: ABC-Clio, 1955–. This is the best source for articles in history journals. It covers a wide range of subjects. A brief description of each article is included. After 1964, it does not include articles on United States or Canadian history. Also available on CD-ROM.

America: History and Life: A Guide to Periodical Literature. Santa Barbara, Calif.: ABC-Clio, 1965–. Supplement, 1980. A brief description of each article is included. It covers the United States and Canada. Also available on CD-ROM and online.

Readers' Guide to Periodical Literature. New York: H. W. Wilson, 1900–. Supplements in 1915 and 1923. These volumes cover the twentieth century. Be selective when using them because many of the periodicals included are written for a popular rather than a scholarly audience. However, the magazines listed are valuable as records of popular opinions and interests.

Nineteenth Century Readers' Guide to Periodical Literature. New York: H. W. Wilson, 1944. With supplementary indexing from 1900 to 1922.

Public Affairs Information Service Bulletin or *PAIS International in Print.* New York: P.A.I.S., 1915–. This work emphasizes periodicals and other publications in the social sciences and includes many government publications.

The Combined Retrospective Index to Journals in History, 1838–1974. Ed. Annadel N. Wile. Washington, D.C.: Carrollton, 1977.

Social Science and Humanities Index. New York: H.W. Wilson, 1907–1973.

Poole's Index to Periodical Literature, 1802–1881. Boston: Houghton Mifflin, 1891. There is a supplement covering 1882–1906.

Social Sciences Index. New York: H. W. Wilson, 1974–. For the period prior to 1974, see *Social Science and Humanities Index.*

Humanities Index. New York: H. W. Wilson, 1974–. For the period prior to 1974, see *Social Science and Humanities Index.*

Historical Periodicals

Some of the best-known historical periodicals are published in the United States, Britain, and Canada and written for professional and student researchers. Some of these journals, such as the *American Historical Review,* have their own cumulative indexes and thus can be useful places to begin a search. There are also many highly specialized periodicals. For example, most state historical societies publish journals. Be sure to examine periodical indexes that include the journals most closely related to your theme. Many periodicals are becoming available on the World Wide Web (see "Digital Reference Sources," pp. 212–31).

U.S., British, and Canadian Historical Journals

Agricultural History
American Historical Review
American Jewish History
The American Journal of Legal History
American Quarterly
The Americas
Bulletin of the Institute of Historical Research
Business History Review
Cambridge Historical Journal
Canadian Historical Review
Canadian Journal of History
Central European History
China Quarterly
Common Place
Comparative Studies in Society and History
Current History
Daedalus
Diplomatic History
Early Medieval History
Economic History Review
Economic Journal
Eighteenth Century Studies
English Historical Review
Ethnohistory
Feminist Studies
Film and History
French Historical Studies
Gender and History

Hispanic American Historical Review
The Historian
Historical Journal
Historical Methods
Historical Research
History
History and Theory
History of Education Quarterly
History of Political Economy
History of Religions
The History Teacher
International Journal of African Historical Studies
International Review of Social History
Irish Historical Studies
Isis
Journal of African History
Journal of American History
Journal of American Studies
Journal of Asian Studies
Journal of Black Studies
Journal of British Studies
Journal of Canadian Studies
Journal of Contemporary History
Journal of the Early Republic
Journal of Ecclesiastical History
Journal of Economic History
Journal of Environmental History
Journal of the History of Biology
Journal of the History of Ideas

Journal of Imperial and
  Commonwealth History
Journal of Interdisciplinary History
Journal of Japanese Studies
Journal of Latin American History
Journal of Modern History
Journal of Near Eastern Studies
Journal of Negro History
Journal of Political Thought
Journal of Popular Culture
The Journal of Psychohistory
Journal of Religious History
Journal of Social History
Journal of Southern History
Journal of Sports History
Journal of Urban History
Journal of Women's History
Journal of World History
Labor History
Latin American Research Review

Mid-America
Middle East Review
Oral History Review
Pacific Affairs
Pacific Historical Review
Past and Present
Political Studies
The Public Historian
Renaissance Quarterly
Russian History
Scottish History Review
Slavic Review
Slavic Studies
Social History
Social Science History
Speculum
Transactions of the Royal
  Historical Society
Western Historical Quarterly
William and Mary Quarterly

Book Review Indexes

Historical periodicals usually contain reviews of recently published books on historical subjects. If you wish to know the content of a particular book or to find out what historians thought of a book, you can look up the reviews. The indexes in the following list organize book reviews by author, title, and sometimes by subject. They indicate which periodicals reviewed the book and in what issue. If the index is annual, you will need to know the year of publication of the book in which you are interested. Most books are reviewed within one to two years after publication. Book reviews are also available on CD-ROM (see "Digital Reference Sources," pp. 212–31).

Index to Book Reviews in Historical Periodicals. Metuchen, N.J.: Scarecrow Press, 1974–1977.

Combined Retrospective Index to Book Reviews in Scholarly Journals, 1886–1974. 15 vols. Arlington, Va.: Carrollton Press, 1982.

Book Review Digest. New York: H. W. Wilson, 1905–. Monthly.

Index to Book Reviews in the Humanities. Detroit: Gale, 1960–1990. Annual.

Book Review Digest: Author/Title Index, 1905–1974. Ed. Leslie Dunmore-Lieber. 4 vols. New York: H. W. Wilson, 1976.

New York Times Book Review Index, 1896–1970. 5 vols. New York: New York Times, 1973.

National Library Service Cumulative Book Review Index, 1905–1974. 6 vols. Princeton: National Library Service Co., 1975.

Book Review Index. Detroit: Gale, 1965–. Bimonthly.

Book Review Index: Master Cumulation, 1965–1984. Ed. Gary C. Tarbert and Barbara Beach. 10 vols. Detroit: Gale, 1985.

Government Publications
and Public Documents

Listed here are English-language guides to books, pamphlets, speeches, treaties, hearings, reports, and so on, published by public agencies. If your research topic is related to governmental affairs at any level, these works can lead you to documents and publications by or about the agencies you are studying. The major publications of the U.S. government are available at many libraries. Many U.S. government documents are also available on the World Wide Web.

International Agencies

Guide to League of Nations Publications: A Bibliographical Survey of the Work of the League, 1920–1947. Comp. Hans Aufricht. New York: Columbia University Press, 1951.

United Nations Documents Index. New York: United Nations Library, 1950–1977, 1998–. These volumes are supplemented by *UNDOC: Current Index.*

Foreign Government Publications

Great Britain, Parliament: Parliamentary Debates. London: 1803–.

Canada, Parliament: Parliamentary Debates. Ottawa: 1867–.

U.S. Government Publications

A great many U.S. government documents are also available at a variety of sites on the World Wide Web.

Introduction to United States Government Information Sources. 6th ed. Ed. Joe Morehead and Mary Fetzer. Englewood, Colo.: Libraries Unlimited, 1999.

Subject Guide to Major United States Government Publications. Comp. William J. Wiley. Chicago: American Library Association, 1987.

Guide to United States Government Publications. Ed. Donna Andriot. Farmington Hills, Mich.: Documents Index, 1985. Cumulative bimonthly supplements.

Monthly Catalogue of United States Government Publications. Washington, D.C.: Government Printing Office, 1895–.

United States Congressional Committee Hearings Index, 1833–1969. Washington, D.C.: Congressional Information Service, 1981–.

United States Congressional Committee Prints Index from Earliest Publications through 1969. 5 vols. Washington, D.C.: Congressional Information Service, 1980.

United States Serial Set Indexes: American State Papers . . . 1789–1969. Washington, D.C.: Congressional Information Service, 1975.

(For sources on local U.S. history, see "Sources for Family History Research" in Appendix B, pp. 234–35.)

Subject Bibliographies

A subject bibliography lists printed works on a particular topic. The subject bibliographies listed here are those that (1) are written especially for students, (2) are of recent publication or republication and therefore likely to be in newer library collections, (3) contain predominantly or solely works in the English language, and (4) are general rather than specialized. If the title of a bibliography indicates that it is annotated, this means that it not only *lists* books on a particular topic but also provides a brief description of their contents. (In some instances, helpful sources that are not bibliographies have been included.)

Disciplines Other than History

The following bibliographies list works in fields other than history. If an important aspect of your research topic falls under other major branches of knowledge, you might find valuable materials in nonhistorical publications.

Sources of Information in the Social Sciences. Ed. William H. Webb. Chicago: American Library Association, 1986.

Sources of Information in the Humanities. 4 vols. Chicago: American Library Association, 1985.

The Humanities: A Selective Guide to Information Sources. 5th ed. Ed. Ron Blazek and Elizabeth Aversa. Englewood, Colo.: Libraries Unlimited, 2000.

The Social Sciences: A Cross-Disciplinary Guide to Selected Sources. 3d ed. Ed. Nancy L. Herron. Englewood, Colo.: Libraries Unlimited, 2002.

Specialized Branches of History

Encyclopedia of Medical History. Ed. Roderick E. McGrew. New York: McGraw-Hill, 1985.

Dictionary of the History of Ideas. Ed. Philip P. Wiener. 5 vols. New York: Scribner's, 1973–1974.

History of Psychology: A Guide to Information Sources. Ed. Wayne Viney, Michael Wertheimer, and Marilyn Lou Wertheimer. Detroit: Gale, 1979.

Isis Cumulative Bibliography: A Bibliography of the History of Science from Isis Critical Bibliographies. 1913–1965 (1971); 1966–1975 (1980); 1976–1985 (1989); 1986–1995 (1997). London: History of Science Society.

Bibliography of the History of Medicine. Bethesda, Md.: National Library of Medicine, 1965–. Also available on the World Wide Web. <igm.nih.gov>.

New Oxford History of Music. 2d ed. 10 vols. Oxford: Oxford University Press, 1999–2001.

The Harper Encyclopedia of Military History: From 3500 B.C. to the Present. Ed. Ernest R. Dupuy and Trevor N. Dupuy. New York: Harper & Row, 1993.

The Holocaust: An Annotated Bibliography. Ed. Harry James Cargas. Haverford, Pa.: Catholic Libraries Association, 1985.

The New Standard Jewish Encyclopedia. Ed. Geoffrey Wigoder. Garden City, N.Y.: Facts on File, 1992.

Psychohistorical Inquiry: A Comprehensive Research Bibliography. Ed. William J. Gilmore. New York: Garland, 1984.

Encyclopedia of the Industrial Revolution. Ed. Thomas Heinrich. 3 vols. New York: M. E. Sharpe, 2002.

Companion Encyclopedia of the History of Medicine. New York: Routledge, 1997.

Encyclopedia of the Holocaust. Ed. Israel Gutman. 4 vols. New York: Macmillan, 1995.

The Cold War, 1945–1991. Ed. Benjamin Frankel. 3 vols. Detroit: Gale, 1992.

Dictionary of Concepts in History. By Harry Ritter. Westport, Conn.: Greenwood Press, 1986.

Church History: An Introduction to Research, Reference Works, and Methods. Ed. James E. Bradley and Richard A. Muller. Grand Rapids, Mich.: Erdmans, 1996.

General World History

This large section of the appendix contains the basic source material for historical research—history bibliographies. Once you have chosen your research topic and theme, consulting these bibliographies and the reference collection of your library should be your initial step in finding sources. For convenience, the list of subject bibliographies is separated according to the chronological period or geographical area that the works cover. The bibliographies themselves break down the topics even further.

Don't expect to find an entire bibliography dedicated to your particular theme. Choose bibliographies that cover the period or area into which your theme falls. Remember, your library will probably not have all of these books. If the most promising bibliography is not there, try a different work. Like other reference sources, some of these works are available in digital form.

American Historical Association: A Guide to Historical Literature. Ed. Mary Beth Norton. Oxford: Oxford University Press, 1995. This work has chapters on all periods and areas and on many specialized topics.

Historical Abstracts. Ed. Eric H. Boehm. Part A, *Modern History (1450–1914).* Part B, *The Twentieth Century (1914–Present).* Santa Barbara, Calif.: ABC-Clio, 1955–. This is the best source for articles in history journals. Also available on CD-ROM and on the World Wide Web.

World Historical Fiction Guide. Ed. Daniel McGarry and Sarah White. Metuchen, N.J.: Scarecrow Press, 1973. If you are studying historical novels, this is an important source.

Serial Bibliographies and Abstracts in History: An Annotated Guide. Ed. David Henige. Westport, Conn.: Greenwood Press, 1986.

Bibliographies in History. Santa Barbara, Calif.: ABC-Clio, 1988.

Reference Sources in History: An Introductory Guide. 2d ed. Ed. Ronald H. Fritze. Santa Barbara, Calif.: ABC-Clio, 2003.

World History from Earliest Times to 1800. Ed. H. Judge. Oxford: Oxford University Press, 1988.

Encyclopedia of Nationalism. Ed. Alexander Motyl. New York: Academic Press, 2000.

Slavery and Slaving in World History, A Bibliography, 1900–1991. Ed. Joseph C. Miller. New York: M. E. Sharpe, 1997–1998.

Ancient History

The Cambridge Ancient History. Cambridge: Cambridge University Press, 1923–1939, 1951–1954, 1970–2000. This is a multivolume work with extensive bibliographies.

The Oxford History of the Classical World. Ed. John Boardman et al. Oxford: Oxford University Press, 1988–. An excellent bibliography is included.

The Encyclopedia of Ancient Egypt. Ed. Margaret Bunson. New York: Gramercy, 1999.

Civilizations of the Ancient Near East. Ed. Jack S. Sasson. New York: Scribner's, 1995.

Civilizations of the Ancient Mediterranean: Greece and Rome. Ed. Michael Grant and Paul A. Cimbala. New York: Scribner's, 1988.

Encyclopedia of Early Christianity. Ed. Everett Ferguson et al. New York: Garland, 1998.

The Oxford Encyclopedia of Ancient Egypt. Ed. Donald B. Redford. Oxford: Oxford University Press, 2001.

Medieval History

A Guide to the Study of Medieval History. Ed. Louis J. Paetow. New York: F. S. Crofts & Sons, 1931. This guide is updated in a supplement by Gray C. Boyce (published by the Medieval Academy of America, 1980) and by the next item.

Literature of Medieval History, 1930–1975. Ed. Gray C. Boyce. 5 vols. Millwood, N.Y.: Kraus International, 1981.

Cambridge Medieval History. Cambridge: Cambridge University Press, 1911–1936.

The New Cambridge Medieval History. Ed. Rosamond McKitterick. 7 vols. New York: Cambridge, 1995–2000.

Dictionary of the Middle Ages. Ed. Joseph R. Strayer. 13 vols. New York: Scribner's, 1998.

The Middle Ages: A Concise Encyclopedia. Ed. H. R. Loyn. New York: Thames and Hudson/Norton, 1991.

Atlas of Medieval Europe. Ed. Angus Konstern and Roger Kean. New York: Facts on File, 2000.

Dictionary of Medieval Civilization. Ed. Joseph Dahmus. New York: Macmillan, 1984.

The Encyclopedia of the Middle Ages. Ed. Norman F. Cantor. New York: Viking, 1999.

Medieval France: An Encyclopedia. Ed. William W. Kibler et al. New York: Garland, 1995.

Early Modern and Modern European History

The Longman Handbook of Modern European History, 1763–1997. Ed. Chris Cook and John Stevenson. New York: Longman, 1998.

Modern European History: 1789 to the Present. New York: M. Weiner, 1986.

The European Powers in the First World War: An Encyclopedia. Ed. Spencer C. Tucker. New York: Garland, 1999.

Cambridge Modern History. Cambridge: Cambridge University Press, 1902–1911; reissued, 1970. These history volumes have large bibliographies. *The New Cambridge Modern History,* however, has no bibliography.

A Bibliography of Modern History. Ed. John Roach. Cambridge: Cambridge University Press, 1968. This bibliography was created to accompany *The New Cambridge Modern History.*

Renaissance and Reformation: Reference Library Cumulative Index. Detroit: U.X.L., 2002.

Reformation Europe: A Guide to Research. Ed. Steven Ozment. St. Louis: Center for Reformation Research, 1982.

Renaissance Humanism, 1300–1550: A Bibliography of Materials in English. Ed. Benjamin Kohl. New York: Garland, 1985.

Modern European Imperialism: A Bibliography of Books and Articles, 1815–1972. Comp. John P. Halstead. Boston: G. K. Hall, 1974.

Women in Western European History: A Select Chronological, Geographical and Topical Bibliography from Antiquity to the French Revolution. Ed. Linda Frey, Marsha Frey, and Joanne Schneider. Westport, Conn.: Greenwood Press, 1982. Supplement, 1986.

Women in Western European History: A Select Chronological, Geographical, and Topical Bibliography: The Nineteenth and Twentieth Centuries. Ed. Linda Frey and Marsha Frey. Westport, Conn.: Greenwood Press, 1984.

The Columbia Dictionary of European Political History since 1914. Ed. John Stevenson. Berkeley: University of California Press, 1992.

The Oxford Encyclopedia of the Reformation. Ed. Hans J. Hillerbrand. New York: Oxford University Press, 1996.

Encyclopedia of European Social History [1350–2000]. Ed. Peter N. Stearns. New York: Scribner's, 2000.

Modern Europe: France, Italy, Spain, Germany, Scandinavia

Historical Dictionary of the French Fourth and Fifth Republics, 1946–1991. Ed. Wayne Northcutt. Westport, Conn.: Greenwood Press, 1992.

Dictionary of Modern Italian History. Ed. Frank J. Coppa. Westport, Conn.: Greenwood Press, 1985.

Modern Italian History: An Annotated Bibliography. Comp. Frank J. Coppa and William Roberts. Westport, Conn.: Greenwood Press, 1990. A companion to *Dictionary of Modern Italian History.*

Historical Dictionary of Modern Spain, 1700–1988. Ed. Robert W. Kern. Westport, Conn.: Greenwood Press, 1990.

Nazism, Resistance, and the Holocaust in World War II: A Bibliography. Ed. Vera Laska. Metuchen, N.J.: Scarecrow Press, 1985.

Modern Germany: An Encyclopedia of History, People and Culture, 1871–1900. Ed. Dieter K. Buse. New York: Garland, 1998.

Historical Dictionary of Germany. Ed. Wayne C. Thompson, Susan L. Thompson, and Juliet S. Thompson. Metuchen, N.J.: Scarecrow Press, 1994.

France. Ed. Frances Chambers. Santa Barbara, Calif.: ABC-Clio, 1990.

Dictionary of Scandinavian History. Ed. Byron J. Nordstrom. Westport, Conn.: Greenwood Press, 1986.

Scandinavian History: 1520–1970. Comp. Stewart P. Oakley. London: Historical Association of London, 1984.

British History

British History to 1789

A Bibliography of English History to 1485. Ed. Edgar B. Graves. Oxford: Clarendon Press, 1975.

The Blackwell Encyclopedia of Anglo-Saxon England. Ed. Michael Lapidge. New York: Blackwell, 2000.

Medieval England: An Encyclopedia. Ed. Paul E. Szarmch et al. New York: Garland, 1998.

Tudor England: An Encyclopedia. Ed. Arthur F. Kinney et al. New York: Garland, 2000.

Women in Early Modern England, 1500–1700. Ed. Jacqueline Eales. New York: Garland, 1998.

A Bibliography of British History, Stuart Period, 1603–1714. Ed. Mary Keeler. Oxford: Clarendon Press, 1970.

Early Modern British History, 1485–1760. Comp. Helen Miller and Aubrey Newman. London: Historical Association of London, 1970.

The Kings of Medieval England, c. 560–1485: A Survey and Research Guide. Ed. Larry W. Usilton. Lanham, Md.: Scarecrow Press, 1996.

British History since 1789

The Cambridge History of the British Empire. Cambridge: Cambridge University Press, 1929–1988.

The Oxford History of England: Consolidated Index. Comp. Roger Raper. Oxford: Clarendon/Oxford University Press, 1995.

British History since 1760: A Select Bibliography. Comp. Ian R. Christie. London: Historical Association of London, 1970.

A Bibliography of British History, 1789–1851. Ed. Lucy Brown and Ian R. Christie. Oxford: Clarendon Press, 1977.

A Bibliography of British History, 1914–1989. Ed. Keith Robbins. Oxford: Clarendon Press, 1996.

Modern England, 1901–1984: A Bibliographical Handbook. Comp. Alfred F. Havighurst. Cambridge: Cambridge University Press, 2002.

British Economic and Social History: A Bibliographical Guide. 3d ed. Ed. W. H. Chaloner and R. C. Richardson. Manchester, Eng.: Manchester University Press, 1995.

Victorian Britain: An Encyclopedia. Ed. Sally Mitchell. New York: Garland, 1988.

The Cambridge Historical Encyclopedia of Great Britain and Ireland. Ed. Christopher Haigh. Cambridge: Cambridge University Press, 1990.

A Bibliography of British History, 1851–1914. Ed. Henry J. Hanham. Oxford: Oxford University Press, 1989.

Irish, Scottish, and British Empire History

A Dictionary of Irish History since 1800. Ed. D. J. Hickey and J. E. Doherty. Totowa, N.J.: Barnes & Noble, 1980.

A Bibliography of Works Relating to Scotland, 1916–1950. Ed. P. D. Hancock. Edinburgh: Edinburgh University Press, 1959–1960.

Cambridge History of the British Empire. Comp. John Rose, Arthur Newton, and Ernest Benians. Cambridge: Cambridge University Press, 1929–1988.

A Chronicle of Irish History since 1500. Ed. J. E. Doherty and D. J. Hickey. Savage, Md.: Rowman and Littlefield, 1990.

East European History

The American Bibliography of Slavic and East European Studies. Stanford, Calif.: American Association for the Advancement of Slavic Studies, 1956–.

Poland's Past and Present: A Select Bibliography of Works in English. Ed. Norman Davies. Newtonville, Mass.: Oriental Research Partners, 1977.

Yugoslavia: A Comprehensive English-Language Bibliography. Ed. Francine Friedman. Wilmington, Del.: Scholarly Resources, 1993.

Encyclopedia of Eastern Europe. Ed. Richard Frucht. New York: Garland, 2000.

Russian (and Soviet) History

A Bibliography of Works in English on Early Russian History to 1800. Comp. Peter A. Crowther. New York: Barnes & Noble, 1969.

Books in English on the Soviet Union, 1917–1973: A Bibliography. Comp. David L. Jones. New York: Garland, 1975.

The Rise and Fall of the Soviet Union: A Selected Bibliography of Sources in English. Ed. Abraham J. Edelheit and Hershel Edelheit. Westport, Conn.: Greenwood Press, 1992.

The American Bibliography of Slavic and East European Studies. Stanford, Calif.: American Association for the Advancement of Slavic Studies, 1956–. Also available online.

Russia and the Former Soviet Union: A Bibliographic Guide to English Publications, 1986–1991. Ed. Helen F. Sullivan and Robert H. Burger. Englewood, Colo.: Libraries Unlimited, 1994.

An Atlas of Russian History: Eleven Centuries of Changing Borders. Ed. Allen F. Chew. New Haven: Yale University Press, 1970.

The Modern Encyclopedia of Russian and Soviet History. Gulf Breeze, Fla.: Academic International Press, 1976–. Plus supplements.

The Soviet Union: A Biographical Dictionary. Ed. Archie Brown. New York: Macmillan, 1991.

Soviet Foreign Policy, 1918–1945: A Guide to Research and Research Materials. Ed. Robert H. Johnston. Wilmington, Del.: Scholarly Resources, 1997.

Dictionary of the Russian Revolution. Ed. George Jackson. Westport, Conn.: Greenwood Press, 1989.

The Russian Revolution, 1905–1921: A Bibliographic Guide to the Works in English. Ed. Murray Frame. Westport, Conn.: Greenwood Press, 1995.

Ukraine: A Bibliographic Guide to English Language Publications. Ed. Bohdan Wynar. Englewood, Colo.: Ukrainian Academic Press, 1990.

African History[1]

The Encyclopedia of Precolonial Africa. Ed. Joseph O. Vogel. Walnut Creek, Calif.: Alta Mira Press, 1997.

An Atlas of African History. Ed. J. D. Fage. New York: Africana, 1978.

Cambridge History of Africa. 8 vols. Cambridge: Cambridge University Press, 1975–1986.

Encyclopedia of Africa South of the Sahara. Ed. John Middleton. 4 vols. New York: Scribner's, 1997.

Africa and the World: An Introduction to the History of Sub-Saharan Africa from Antiquity to 1840. By Lewis H. Gann and Peter Duignan. 1972. Reprint, Lanham, Md.: University Press of America, 1999.

South African History: A Bibliographic Guide with Special Reference to Territorial Expansion and Colonization. Ed. Naomi Musiker. New York: Garland, 1984.

Dictionary of African Historical Biography. Ed. Mark R. Lipschultz and R. Kent Rasmusson. Berkeley: University of California Press, 1986.

Near and Middle Eastern History

The Islamic Near East and North Africa: An Annotated Guide to Books in English for Non-Specialists. Ed. David W. Littlefield. Littleton, Colo.: Libraries Unlimited, 1977.

Books on Asia from the Near East to the Far East: A Guide for General Readers. Ed. Eleazir Birnbaum. Toronto: University of Toronto Press, 1981.

Middle East and Islam: A Bibliographical Introduction. Geneva: Inter Documentation, 1979. Supplement, 1986.

Encyclopedia of Islam. Ed. C. E. Botsworth et al. Leiden, Neth.: E. J. Brill, 1960–. Available on CD-ROM (1999).

The Cambridge Encyclopedia of the Middle East and North Africa. Ed. Trevor Mostyn. Cambridge: Cambridge University Press, 1988.

---

[1]For the northern African states that border on the Mediterranean, see "Near and Middle Eastern History."

The Oxford Dictionary of Byzantium. Ed. Alexander P. Kazhdan. 3 vols. Oxford: Oxford University Press, 1991.

Oxford Encyclopedia of the Modern Islamic World. New York: Oxford University Press, 1995. Covers the eighteenth century to the present.

General Asian History

Encyclopedia of Asian History. Ed. Ainslis T. Embree. 4 vols. New York: Scribner's, 1988.

Cumulative Bibliography of Asian Studies, 1941–1965, 1966–1970. Boston: G. K. Hall, 1972.

Bibliography of Asian Studies. Ann Arbor: Association for Asian Studies, 1956–. Check online for recent materials.

Encyclopedia of China: The Essential Reference to China, Its History and Culture. Ed. Dorothy Perkinson. New York: Facts on File, 2000. No bibliographies.

Indian, Pakistani, and Sri Lankan History

India: A Critical Bibliography. Ed. J. Michael Mahar. Tucson: University of Arizona Press, 1980.

Cambridge History of India. New York: Macmillan, 1922–1953. Supplement, 1968. See bibliography at end of volumes.

A Historical Atlas of South Asia. Ed. Joseph E. Schwartzberg. New York: Oxford University Press, 1992.

A Dictionary of Indian History. Ed. Sachchidananda Bhattacharya. New York: Braziller, 1977.

South Asian Civilizations: A Bibliographical Synthesis. Ed. Maureen Patterson. Chicago: University of Chicago Press, 1981.

Cambridge Encyclopedia of India, Pakistan, Sri Lanka, Nepal, Bhutan and the Maldives. Ed. Francis Robinson. Cambridge: Cambridge University Press, 1989.

Southeast Asian History

Southeast Asia: A Critical Bibliography. Ed. Kennedy G. Tregonning. Tucson: University of Arizona Press, 1969.

Vietnam: A Guide to Reference Sources. Ed. Michael Cotter. Boston: G. K. Hall, 1977.

The Wars in Vietnam, Cambodia, and Laos, 1945–1982: A Bibliographic Guide. Ed. Richard Dean Burns and Milton Leitenberg. Santa Barbara, Calif.: ABC-Clio, 1992.

Vietnam Studies: An Annotated Bibliography. Ed. Carl Singleton. Lanham, Md.: Scarecrow Press, 1997.

Chinese History

Modern China: An Encyclopedia of History, Culture, and Nationalism. Ed. Wang Ke-wen. New York: Garland, 1998.

Dictionary of Chinese History. Ed. Michael Dillon. London: Frank Cass, 1979.

Chinese History: A Bibliography. Ed. Leona Rasmussen Phillips. New York: Gordon Press, 1978.

China Bibliography: A Research Guide to Reference Works about China Past and Present. Ed. Harriet T. Zurndorfer. Honolulu: University of Hawaii Press, 1999.

Japanese and Korean History

Japan and Korea: A Critical Bibliography. Ed. Bernard Silberman. Westport, Conn.: Greenwood Press, 1982.

The Cambridge Dictionary of Japan. Vol. 4, *Early Modern Japan.* Ed. John Whitney Hall. Cambridge: Cambridge University Press, 1991.

Japanese History and Culture from Ancient to Modern Times: Seven Basic Bibliographies. Ed. John Dower and Timothy George. New York: Markus Wiener, 1997.

Japanese Studies from Pre-History to 1990: A Bibliographical Guide. Ed. Richard Perren. Manchester, Eng.: Manchester University Press, 1992.

Studies on Korea: A Scholar's Guide. Ed. Han-kyo Kim. Honolulu: University of Hawaii Press, 1980.

Modern Japan: An Encyclopedia of History, Culture and Nationalism. Ed. James Huffman. New York: Garland, 1998.

Latin American and Caribbean History

Encyclopedia of Latin American History and Culture. Ed. Barbara Tenenbaum. New York: Scribner's, 1995.

A Guide to the History of Brazil, 1500–1822: The Literature in English. Ed. Francis A. Dutra. Santa Barbara, Calif.: ABC-Clio, 1980.

Handbook of Latin American Studies. Cambridge, Mass.: Harvard University Press, 1936–1947; and Gainesville: University of Florida Press, 1948–. Annual volume.

The Complete Caribbeana, 1900–1975: A Bibliographical Guide to the Scholarly Literature. Ed. Comitas Lambros. Millwood, N.Y.: KTO Press, 1978.

The Cambridge Encyclopedia of Latin America and the Caribbean. Ed. Simon Collier et al. Cambridge: Cambridge University Press, 1992.

Latin America and the Caribbean: A Critical Guide to Research Sources. Ed. Paula H. Covington et al. Westport, Conn.: Greenwood Press, 1992.

Index to Latin American Periodical Literature, 1929–1960, 1961–1965, 1966–1970. Boston: G. K. Hall, 1962, 1975, 1980.

Latin America: A Guide to Economic History, 1830–1930. Ed. Stanley Stein and R. Cortés Conde. Berkeley: University of California Press, 1977.

Latin American Politics: A Historical Bibliography. Santa Barbara, Calif.: ABC-Clio, 1986.

A Reference Guide to Latin American History. Ed. James D. Henderson et al. New York: M. E. Sharpe, 2000.

The Oxford Encyclopedia of Mesoamerican Cultures: The Civilizations of Mexico and Central America. Ed. David Carrasco. Oxford: Oxford University Press, 2001.

Canadian History

Encyclopedia Canadiana. Toronto: Grolier, 1977.

Bibliographia Canadiana. Comp. Claude Thibault. Don Mills, Ont.: Longman Canada, 1973.

The Oxford Companion to Canadian History and Literature. Comp. Norah Story. Toronto: Oxford University Press, 1967. Supplement, 1973.

Canadian Reference Sources: A Selective Guide. 2d ed. Ed. Dorothy E. Ryder. Ottawa: Canadian Library Association, 1973. Supplement, 1981.

Canada since 1867: A Bibliographical Guide. Ed. J. L. Granatstein and Paul Stevens. Toronto: Samuel Stevens, 1977.

Western Canada since 1870: A Select Bibliography and Guide. Ed. Alan F. J. Artibise. Vancouver: University of British Columbia Press, 1978.

Bibliography of Ontario History, 1867–1976: Cultural, Economic, Political and Social. By Olga B. Bishop. 2 vols. Toronto: University of Toronto Press, 1980. Supplement, 1976–1986. Toronto: Dunburn Press, 1989.

Economic History of Canada: A Guide to Information Sources. Ed. Trevor J. O. Dick. Detroit: Gale, 1978.

Historical Atlas of Canada. Ed. R. Cole Harris and Donald Kerr. Toronto: University of Toronto Press, 1987.

The Canadian Encyclopedia, 2000. Ed. James H. March. Toronto: McClelland and Stewart, 2000.

U.S. History

The bibliographies of U.S. history are arranged by topics of special interest to students.

Many items in this first group have separate chapters on specialized topics.

Harvard Guide to American History. Rev. ed. Ed. Oscar Handlin et al. Cambridge, Mass.: Harvard University Press, 1979. Chapters six through thirty contain detailed reading lists for many periods and topics in U.S. history.

The Reader's Companion to American History. Ed. Eric Foner and John A. Garraty. Boston: Houghton Mifflin, 1991.

The American Historical Association's Guide to Historical Literature. 3d ed. Ed. Mary Beth Norton. 2 vols. Ithaca: Cornell University Press, 1995. This guide contains a large section on U.S. history.

Writings on American History. Washington, D.C.: American Historical Association, 1956; and Millwood, N.Y.: KTO Press, 1974–1990. The original series of volumes covers (with two brief lapses) books and articles written between 1902 and 1961. The new series is now annual and covers only articles written since 1962. Coverage of books is continued in the next item.

Writings on American History, 1962–1973: A Subject Bibliography of Books and Monographs. Comp. James R. Masterson. 10 vols. White Plains, N.Y.: Kraus International, 1985.

Writings on American History, 1962–1973: A Subject Bibliography of Articles. Ed. James J. Dougherty. 4 vols. Millwood, N.Y.: KTO Press, 1976.

America: History and Life. Santa Barbara, Calif.: ABC-Clio, 1954–. After 1965, titled *America: History and Life: A Guide to Periodical Literature.* Each volume now has four parts: (1) abstracts of journal articles, (2) an index to book reviews, (3) a bibliography of articles and dissertations, and (4) an annual index. The best source for articles on U.S. history. Also on CD-ROM.

United States History: A Bibliography of the New Writings on American History. Ed. Louise Merriam and J. W. Oberly. Manchester, Eng.: Manchester University Press, 1995.

Encyclopedia of American History. 2d ed. Ed. Richard B. Morris. New York: HarperCollins, 1996.

Dictionary of American History. Ed. James T. Adams and Roy V. Coleman. New York: Scribner's, 1942–1961. Revised, 1976. Supplement, 1996.

Concise Dictionary of American History. Ed. David W. Voorhees. New York: Scribner's, 1983. This is an abridgment of the *Dictionary of American History.*

Handbook for Research in American History: A Guide to Bibliographies and Other Reference Works. 2d ed. Ed. Francis Paul Prucha. Lincoln: University of Nebraska Press, 1994.

Encyclopedia of American Political History: Studies of the Principal Movements and Ideas. Ed. Jack P. Greene. 3 vols. New York: Scribner's, 1984.

Recently Published Articles. Washington, D.C.: American Historical Association, 1976–1990.

(For sources on the U.S. government, see "U.S. Government Publications," p. 191.)

Regional, State, County, and Local U.S. History

The sources listed here can be supplemented by the appropriate sections of the *Harvard Guide to American History, Writings on American History,* and *America: History and Life.* For local histories, also see Appendix B, "Sources for Family History Research" (pp. 234–35).

Directory of Historical Organizations in the United States and Canada, 2002. 15th ed. Comp. Mary Bray Wheeler. Nashville: American Association for State and Local History, 2002. This volume includes the addresses of state and local historical societies. A continuing publication.

Directory of State and Local History Periodicals. Comp. Milton Crouch and Hans Raum. Chicago: American Library Association, 1977.

A Bibliography of American County Histories. Comp. P. William Filby. Baltimore: Genealogical Publishing, 1985.

State Censuses: An Annotated Bibliography to Censuses of Population Taken after 1790 by States and Territories of the United States. Ed. Henry J. Dubester. New York: Burt Franklin, 1969.

Encyclopedia of Urban America. Ed. Neil L. Shumsky. Santa Barbara, Calif.: ABC-Clio, 1998.

Encyclopedia of Southern Culture. Ed. Charles Reagan Wilson and William Ferris. Chapel Hill: University of North Carolina Press, 1989.

United States Local Histories in the Library of Congress: A Bibliography. Ed. Marion J. Kaminkow. 5 vols. Baltimore: Magna Carta, 1975.

Genealogical and Local History Books in Print. 5th ed. 4 vols. Washington, D.C.: Genealogical Books in Print, 1996–1997.

Encyclopedia of the American West. 4 vols. New York: Simon and Schuster/ Macmillan, 1996.

Encyclopedia of the Confederacy. Ed. Richard N. Current. 4 vols. New York: Scribner's, 1998.

Encyclopedia of Local History. Ed. Carol Kammen. Walnut Creek, Calif.: Alta Mira Press, 2000.

Specific Periods

Colonial Wars of North America, 1512–1763: An Encyclopedia. Ed. Alan Gallay. New York: Garland, 1995.

Encyclopedia of the United States in the Nineteenth Century. Ed. Paul Finkelman. 3 vols. New York: Scribner's, 2001.

The Blackwell Encyclopedia of the American Revolution. Ed. Jack P. Greene. Cambridge, Mass.: Basil Blackwell, 1994.

Encyclopedia of the North American Colonies. Ed. Jacob E. Cooke. New York: Scribner's, 1993.

The Encyclopedia of Colonial and Revolutionary America. Ed. John Faragher. New York: Facts on File, 1989.

The American Revolution, 1775–1783: An Encyclopedia. New York: Garland, 1993.

James Madison and the American Nation, 1751–1836: An Encyclopedia. Ed. Robert A. Rutland. New York: Scribner's, 1994.

The United States in the First World War: An Encyclopedia. Ed. Anne C. Venzon. New York: Garland, 1999.

Historical Dictionary of the Progressive Era, 1890–1920. Ed. John D. Buenker. Westport, Conn.: Greenwood Press, 1988.

Encyclopedia of the United States in the Twentieth Century. Ed. Stanley Kutler. 4 vols. New York: Scribner's, 1996.

The Penguin Dictionary of Contemporary American History, 1945 to the Present. Ed. Stanley Hochman and Eleanor Hochman. New York: Penguin, 1997.

Diplomatic History

A large number of U.S. foreign policy documents are available on the World Wide Web.

Foreign Affairs Bibliography: A Selected and Annotated List of Books on International Relations [1919–1972]. New York: Harper & Row, 1933, 1943, 1953; and Bowker, 1964. Vol. 1 covers 1919–1932; vol. 2, 1932–1942; vol. 3, 1942–1952; vol. 4, 1952–1962; vol. 5, 1962–1972.

Foreign Relations of the United States. U.S. Department of State. Washington, D.C.: Government Printing Office, 1861–. These volumes are issued regularly and contain actual diplomatic correspondence. These are *primary* sources rather than bibliographies.

Guide to American Foreign Relations since 1700. 2d ed. Ed. Robert Beisner. Santa Barbara, Calif.: ABC-Clio, 2001.

Writing about Vietnam: A Bibliography of the Literature of the Vietnam Conflict. Ed. Sandra M. Wittman. Boston: G. K. Hall, 1989.

Encyclopedia of United States Foreign Relations. Ed. Bruce Jentleson and Thomas Patterson. Oxford: Oxford University Press, 1997.

Cambridge History of American Foreign Relations. Ed. Bradford Perkins et al. 4 vols. New York: Cambridge University Press, 1995. Also available on CD-ROM.

A Bibliography of United States–Latin American Relations since 1810. Ed. David F. Trask et al. Lincoln: University of Nebraska Press, 1968. Supplement, 1979.

Dictionary of American Diplomatic History. Ed. John E. Findling. Westport, Conn.: Greenwood Press, 1989.

Origins, Evolution and Nature of the Cold War: An Annotated Bibliography. Ed. J. L. Black. Santa Barbara, Calif.: ABC-Clio, 1985.

Labor, Business, and Economic History

Labor in America: A Historical Bibliography. Santa Barbara, Calif.: ABC-Clio, 1985.

American Working Class History: A Representative Bibliography. By Maurice F. Neufeld, Daniel J. Leab, and Dorothy Swanson. New York: Bowker, 1983.

Biographical Dictionary of American Labor. Rev. ed. Ed. Gary Fink. Westport, Conn.: Greenwood Press, 1984.

Labor Unions. Ed. Gary Fink. Westport, Conn.: Greenwood Press, 1977. Contains a brief history and bibliography for each major union.

A Financial History of the United States [to 1900]. Ed. Jerry W. Markham. New York: M. E. Sharpe, 2002.

Gale Encyclopedia of United States Economic History. Ed. Thomas Carson. Detroit: Gale, 1999.

Biographical Dictionary of American Business Leaders. Ed. John Ingham. 4 vols. Westport, Conn.: Greenwood Press, 1983.

American Economic History: An Annotated Bibliography. Ed. John Braeman. Englewood Cliffs, N.J.: Salem Press, 1994.

Encyclopedia of American Economic History. Ed. Glen Porter. 3 vols. New York: Scribner's, 1980.

Dictionary of United States Economic History. Ed. James S. Olson. Westport, Conn.: Greenwood Press, 1992.

African American History

Africana: The Encyclopedia of the African and Afro-American Experience. Ed. Kwame Anthony Appiah. New York: Perseus Group, 1999.

Encyclopedia of African-American Religions. Ed. Larry G. Murphy et al. New York: Garland, 1993.

Black/White Relations in American History: An Annotated Bibliography. Ed. Leslie V. Tischauser. Lanham, Md.: Scarecrow Press, 1998.

Encyclopedia of Black America. Ed. W. Augustus Low and Virgil A. Clift. New York: DaCapo Press, 1988.

Afro-American History: A Bibliography. Ed. by Dwight L. Smith. Santa Barbara, Calif.: ABC-Clio, 1981.

Dictionary of American Negro Biography. Ed. Rayford W. Logan and Michael Winston. New York: Norton, 1982.

Dictionary of Afro-American Slavery. Ed. Randall M. Miller and John David Smith. Westport, Conn.: Greenwood Press, 1997.

Black Women in America: An Historical Encyclopedia. Bloomington: Indiana University Press, 1994.

Encyclopedia of African-American Culture and History. Ed. Jack Salzman, David L. Smith and Cornel West. New York: Simon and Schuster/Macmillan, 1996. Supplement, 2000.

Mexican American and Puerto Rican History

A Bibliography for Chicano History. Comp. Matt S. Meier and Feliciano Rivera. Westport, Conn.: Greenwood Press, 1984.

Bibliography of Mexican-American History. Comp. Matt S. Meier. Westport, Conn.: Greenwood Press, 1984.

Dictionary of Mexican American History. Ed. Matt S. Meier and Feliciano Rivera. Westport, Conn.: Greenwood Press, 1981.

Puerto Ricans on the United States Mainland. Ed. Francesco Cordasco. Totowa, N.J.: Rowman and Littlefield, 1972.

The Puerto Ricans: An Annotated Bibliography. Ed. Paquita Vivó. New York: Bowker, 1973.

An Annotated, Selected Puerto Rican Bibliography. Comp. Enrique R. Bravo. New York: Columbia University Press, 1972.

Historical Dictionary of Puerto Rico and the United States Virgin Islands. Comp. Kenneth Farr. Metuchen, N.J.: Scarecrow Press, 1973.

Women's History

Encyclopedia of Women in American History. Ed. Joyce Appleby et al. 3 vols. New York: M. E. Sharpe, 2002.

Notable American Women, 1607–1950: A Biographical Dictionary. Ed. Edward T. James. 3 vols. Cambridge, Mass.: Harvard University Press, 1974. Supplemented by *Notable American Women: The Modern Period.* Cambridge, Mass.: Harvard University Press, 1980. This volume includes women who died between 1951 and 1975.

The American Woman in Colonial and Revolutionary Times, 1565–1800: A Syllabus with Bibliography. By Eugenie Leonard et al. Westport, Conn.: Greenwood Press, 1975.

Women's Magazines, 1693–1968. Comp. Cynthia White. London: Michael Joseph, 1970.

The Female Experience in Eighteenth- and Nineteenth-Century America: A Guide to the History of American Women. Ed. Jill K. Conway. New York: Garland, 1982.

The Female Experience in Twentieth-Century America: A Guide to the History of American Women. Ed. Jill K. Conway. New York: Garland, 1991.

Women's Studies Encyclopedia: History, Philosophy, and Religion. Vol. 3. Ed. Helen Tierney. Westport, Conn.: Greenwood Press, 1999.

Handbook of American Women's History. 2d ed. Ed. Angela M. Howard and Frances M. Kavenik. Thousand Oaks, Calif.: Sage, 2000.

General Immigrant and Ethnic History

Use general immigrant and ethnic history bibliographies if you are researching the history of a minority group not listed separately in this appendix or if you are unsure which group you wish to study.

Harvard Encyclopedia of American Ethnic Groups. Ed. Stephen Thernstrom et al. Cambridge, Mass.: Harvard University Press, 1980.

A Comprehensive Bibliography for the Study of American Minorities. By Wayne C. Miller. 2 vols. New York: New York University Press, 1976.

American Immigrant Cultures. Ed. David Levinson and Melvin Ember. 2 vols. New York: Macmillan, 1997.

Encyclopedia of American Immigration. Ed. James Ciment. 4 vols. New York: M. E. Sharpe, 2001.

European Immigrant and Ethnic History

European Immigration and Ethnicity in the United States and Canada: A Historical Bibliography. Ed. David L. Brye. Santa Barbara, Calif.: ABC-Clio, 1983.

German American History and Life: A Guide to Information Sources. Ed. Michael Kereztesi and Gary Cocozzoli. Detroit: Gale, 1980.

Hungarians in the United States and Canada: A Bibliography. Ed. Joseph Szeplaki. Minneapolis: Immigration History Research Center, 1977.

The British in America 1578–1970: A Chronology and Fact Book. Ed. Howard B. Furer. Dobbs Ferry, N.Y.: Oceana, 1972. Covers the English, Scotch, Welsh, and Scotch-Irish.

The Italian-American Experience: An Encyclopedia. Ed. Salvatore J. LaGumina et al. New York: Garland, 1999.

Asian Immigrant and Ethnic History

Asian American Studies: An Annotated Bibliography and Research Guide. Ed. Hyung-Chan Kim. Westport, Conn.: Greenwood Press, 1989.

Asians in America: A Selected, Annotated Bibliography. Ed. Isao Fujimoto. Davis: University of California Press, 1983.

Dictionary of Asian American History. Ed. Hyung-Chan Kim. Westport, Conn.: Greenwood Press, 1986.

Native American History

Native Americans: An Encyclopedia of History, Culture and Peoples. 2 vols. Santa Barbara, Calif.: ABC-Clio, 1998.

A Bibliographical Guide to the History of Indian-White Relations in the United States. Ed. Francis Paul Prucha. Chicago: University of Chicago Press, 1977. Continued in the next item.

Indian-White Relations in the United States: A Bibliography of Works Published 1975–1980. Ed. Francis Paul Prucha. Lincoln: University of Nebraska Press, 1982.

Handbook of American Indians North of Mexico. Ed. Frederick W. Hodge et al. 1910. Reprint, New York: Rowman and Littlefield, 1979.

Encyclopedia of Native American Tribes. Ed. Carl Waldman. New York: Checkmark Books, 1999.

The Gale Encyclopedia of Native American Tribes. Ed. Sharon Malinowski. 4 vols. Detroit: Gale, 1998.

Native American Periodicals and Newspapers, 1828–1982: Bibliography, Publishing Record, and Holdings. Comp. Maureen Hardy. Westport, Conn.: Greenwood Press, 1984.

Ethnographic Bibliography of North America. Ed. George P. Murdock and Timothy J. O'Leary. 5 vols. New Haven: HRAF Press, 1990. Updated on CD-ROM.

Handbook of North American Indians. Ed. William C. Sturtevant. 17 vols. Washington, D.C.: Smithsonian Institution, 1978–2001.

Cambridge History of the Native Peoples of the Americas. Vol. 1. Ed. Bruce Triggas and Wilcomb Washburn. New York: Cambridge University Press, 1997.

Social, Cultural, Intellectual, and Religious History

Social Reform and Reaction in America: An Annotated Bibliography. Santa Barbara, Calif.: ABC-Clio, 1984.

Encyclopedia of American Social History. Ed. Mary K. Cayton, Elliott J. Gorn, Peter W. Williams. 3 vols. New York: Scribner's, 1993.

A Dictionary of American Social Change. By Louis Filler. Malabar, Fla.: Kreiger, 1982.

Urban America: A Historical Bibliography. Ed. Neil L. Shumsky and Timothy Crimmins. Santa Barbara, Calif.: ABC-Clio, 1983.

Urban History. Ed. John D. Buenker. Detroit: Gale, 1981.

United States Cultural History: A Guide to Information Sources. By Philip I. Mitterling. Detroit: Gale, 1980.

Encyclopedia of Lesbian and Gay Histories and Cultures. New York: Garland, 1999.

Encyclopedia of the American Religious Experience. Ed. Charles H. Lippy. New York: Scribner's, 1988.

A Companion to American Thought. Ed. Richard W. Fox and James T. Kloppenberg. Oxford: Blackwell, 1998.

The Cambridge History of American Theater. Ed. Don B. Wilmeth. 3 vols. Cambridge: Cambridge University Press, 1998–2000.

Constitutional, Legal, and Military History

Encyclopedia of the American Military. Ed. John E. Jessup. 3 vols. New York: Scribner's, 1994.

The Literature of American Legal History. Ed. William E. Nelson and John P. Reid. New York: Oceana, 1985.

Encyclopedia of the American Judicial System. Ed. Robert J. Janosik. New York: Scribner's, 1987.

Encyclopedia of the American Constitution. 2d ed. Ed. Leonard Levy. 6 vols. New York: Macmillan, 2000.

Reference Guide to United States Military History, 1607–1815. Ed. Charles R. Shrader. New York: Replica Books, 1999.

Dictionary of the Vietnam War. Ed. James S. Olson. Westport, Conn.: Greenwood Press, 1988.

The United States in the First World War: An Encyclopedia. New York: Garland 1999.

Guide to the Sources of United States Military History. By Robin Higham. Hamden, Conn.: Archon Books, 1975. Supplements, 1981, 1986, 1993, 1998.

America and the IndoChina Wars, 1945–1990: A Bibliographic Guide. Ed. Lester Brune. Claremont, Calif.: Regina Books, 1991.

American Naval History: A Guide. Ed. Paolo E. Coletta. Lanham, Md.: Scarecrow Press, 1998.

Political History

Political Parties and Elections in the United States: An Encyclopedia. Ed. L. Sandy Maisel. 2 vols. New York: Garland, 1991.

Guide to the Presidency. 3d ed. Ed. Michael Nelson. Washington, D.C.: Congressional Quarterly, 2002.

Guide to United States Elections. 3d ed. Ed. John L. Moore. Washington, D.C.: Congressional Quarterly, 1994.

The American Presidency: A Historical Bibliography. Santa Barbara, Calif.: ABC-Clio, 1984.

Herbert Hoover: A Bibliography of His Times and Presidency. Comp. Richard D. Burns. Wilmington, Del.: Scholarly Resources, 1991.

Dwight D. Eisenhower: A Bibliography of His Times and Presidency. Comp. R. Alton Lee. Wilmington, Del.: Scholarly Resources, 1991.

Encyclopedia of the American Left. Ed. Mari J. Buhle. Oxford: Oxford University Press, 1998.

Historical Dictionary of the Progressive Era, 1890–1920. Ed. John D. Buenker. Westport, Conn.: Greenwood Press, 1988.

American Reform and Reformers: A Biographical Dictionary. Ed. Randall M. Miller and Paul A. Cimbala. Westport, Conn.: Greenwood Press, 1996.

Encyclopedia of the American Presidency. New York: Simon and Schuster, 1994.

Protest, Power and Change: An Encyclopedia of Non-Violent Action. . . . New York: Garland, 1997.

Encyclopedia of American Political History: Studies of the Principal Movements and Ideals. Ed. Jack P. Green. 3 vols. New York: Scribner's, 1984.

Miscellaneous Topics in United States History

Dickinson's American Historical Fiction. 5th ed. Ed. Virginia B. Gerhardstein. Metuchen, N.J.: Scarecrow Press, 1986.

American Family History: A Historical Bibliography. Santa Barbara, Calif.: ABC-Clio, 1984.

Biographical Dictionary of American Sports. Ed. David L. Porter. Westport, Conn.: Greenwood Press, 1995.

Encyclopedia of American Agricultural History. By Edwin I. Schapsmeier and Frederick H. Schapsmeier. Westport, Conn.: Greenwood Press, 1975.

A Subject Bibliography of the History of American Higher Education. Comp. Mark Beach. Westport, Conn.: Greenwood Press, 1984.

The History of Science and Technology in the United States: A Critical and Selective Bibliography. Ed. Mare Rothenberg. New York: Garland, 1993.

The Craft of Public History: An Annotated Select Bibliography. By David F. Trask and Robert W. Pomeroy III. Westport, Conn.: Greenwood Press, 1983.

Encyclopedia of Environmental Issues. Ed. Craig Allin. Pasadena, Calif.: Salem Press, 2000.

History of the Mass Media in the United States: An Encyclopedia. Ed. Margaret A. Blanchard. Chicago: Fitzroy Dearborn, 1998.

Sources for Historical Statistics

World Statistical Data

Historical Tables, 58 B.C.–A.D. 1990. By Sigfrid H. Steinberg. New York: Tuttle, 1991.

Statistics Sources. 26th ed. Detroit: Gale, 2002.

The International Almanac of Electoral History. 3d ed. By Thomas Mackie and Richard Rose. Washington, D.C.: Congressional Quarterly, 1991.

Demographic Yearbook. New York: United Nations Statistical Office, 1949–. Annual. Also available on CD-ROM.

Population Index. Princeton: Office of Population Research, 1935–. Also available on the Web.

Statistical Yearbook. New York: United Nations Statistical Office, 1949–.

European Statistical Data

European Political Facts, 1900–1996. 4th ed. By Christopher Cook and John Paxton. New York: St. Martin's Press, 1998.

The Gallup International Public Opinion Polls. By George H. Gallup. New York: Random House, 1976. France: 1939, 1944–1975.

International Historical Statistics: Europe, 1750–2000. Ed. B. R. Mitchell. New York: Palgrave Macmillan, 2003.

African, Asian, Latin American, and Middle Eastern Statistical Data

Statistical Abstract of Latin America. Ed. James W. Wilkie. Los Angeles: U.C.L.A. Center of Latin American Studies, 1955–.

The Arab World, Turkey and the Balkans, 1878–1914: A Handbook of Historical Statistics. Ed. Justin McCarthy. Boston: G. K. Hall, 1982.

International Historical Statistics: The Americas: 1750–1988. Ed. B. R. Mitchell. New York: Stockton Press, 1998.

International Historical Statistics: Africa, Asia and Oceania: 1750–1993. Ed. B. R. Mitchell. New York: Stockton Press, 1998.

British Statistical Data

Abstract of British Historical Statistics. By B. R. Mitchell. Cambridge: Cambridge University Press, 1976.

Annual Abstract of Statistics. London: Central Statistical Office of Great Britain, 1915/1928–.

British Labour Statistics: Historical Abstract, 1886–1968. London: Great Britain Department of Employment and Productivity, 1971.

The British Voter: An Atlas and Survey since 1885. By Michael Kinnear. London: Batsford, 1981.

Twentieth-Century British Political Facts, 1900–2000. By David Butler and Gareth Butler. New York: Palgrave MacMillan, 2000.

The Gallup International Public Opinion Polls: Great Britain, 1937–1975. By George H. Gallup. Westport, Conn.: Greenwood Press, 1977.

British Historical Statistics. Ed. B. R. Mitchell. Cambridge: Cambridge University Press, 1988.

U.S. and Canadian Statistical Data

Historical Statistics of the United States, Colonial Times to 1970. Washington, D.C.: Bureau of the Census, 1976, and Government Printing Office, 1989. Also available on CD-ROM and the Web.

Statistical Abstract of the United States. Washington, D.C.: Government Printing Office, 1878–. Annual. Also available on the Web.

Historical Statistics of Canada. By M. C. Urquhart. Ottawa: Statistics Canada, 1983. Also available on the Web.

Bureau of the Census Catalog of Publications, 1790–1972. Washington, D.C.: Bureau of the Census, 1974.

American Statistics Index . . . : A Complete Guide and Index to the Statistical Publications of the United States Government. Washington, D.C.: Congressional Information Service, 1973–.

Federal Population Censuses 1790–1890: A Catalogue of Microfilm Copies of the Schedules. Washington, D.C.: National Archives Trust Fund Board, 1979. Catalogs of the 1900 and 1910 censuses were published in 1978 and 1982.

The Gallup Poll. By George H. Gallup. New York: Random House and Scholarly Resources, 1935–.

The Gallup Poll Cumulative Index: Public Opinion, 1935–1997. Wilmington, Del.: Scholarly Resources, 1999.

Guides to Photographs, Microfilms, Microforms, Movies, Recordings, and Oral History

A large number of the audio and video recordings mentioned in these works are becoming available on the World Wide Web.

Guide to Microforms in Print: Author, Title. Westport, Conn.: Microform Review. Annual since 1961.

Guide to Microforms in Print: Subject. Westport, Conn.: Microform Review. Annual since 1961. Now published by K. G. Saur Verlag, Munich.

Catalog of National Archives Microfilm Publications. Washington, D.C.: N.A.R.S., 1974–.

List of National Archives Microfilm Publications, 1947–1974. Washington, D.C.: N.A.R.S., 1974. Supplemented by:

Supplementary List of National Archives Publications, 1974–1982. Washington, D.C.: N.A.R.S., 1982.

Subject Guide to Microforms in Print. Ed. Albert J. Diaz. Washington, D.C.: Microcard Editions, 1962–.

Library of Congress Catalog: Music and Phonorecords. Washington, D.C.: Library of Congress, 1953–1989.

The Oral History Collection of Columbia University. Ed. Elizabeth Mason and Louis M. Starr. New York: Columbia University Oral History Research Office, 1979.

Oral History in the United States: A Directory. Comp. Gary L. Shumway. New York: Oral History Association, 1971. Locates and describes oral history collections.

Oral History Index: An International Directory of Oral History Interviews. Westport, Conn.: Meckler, 1990.

Picture Sources. Ed. Ernest H. Robl. New York: Special Libraries Association, 1983.

Microform Research Collections. 2d ed. Ed. Suzanne Cates Dodson. Westport, Conn.: Meckler, 1984.

Pamphlets in American History: A Bibliographical Guide to the Microfilm Collections. 4 vols. Sanford, N.C.: Microfilming Corp. of America, 1979–1983.

Newspapers on Microfilm: United States, 1948–1983. Washington, D.C.: Library of Congress, 1984.

Directory of Oral History Collections. Ed. Allen Smith. Phoenix: Oryx, 1988.

American Periodical Series, 1741–1900. Ann Arbor: University Microfilms, 1946–1978.

American Culture Series, 1493–1875. Ann Arbor: University Microfilms, 1979.

Guides to Dissertations, Archives, and Manuscripts

Dissertation Abstracts International. Ann Arbor: University Microfilms, 1938–. Annual. Also available online.

A Guide to Archives and Manuscripts in the United States. Ed. Philip C. Hamer. New Haven: Yale University Press, 1965.

Directory of Archives and Manuscript Repositories in the United States. Phoenix: Oryx, 1988. This volume updates the preceding one. Also available online.

Guides to Archives and Manuscript Collections in the United States: An Annotated Bibliography. Comp. Donald L. DeWitt. Westport, Conn.: Greenwood Press, 1994.

The National Union Catalog of Manuscript Collections. Washington, D.C.: Library of Congress, 1959–. Also available online: <lcweb.loc.gov/coll/nucmc>.

Digital Reference Sources

A universe of sources is available in digital form for use in historical research. This digital information can be sorted by **search engines,** allowing you to sift through a tremendous amount of historical material from your home or school library. The **home page** or original search page of your library's **online catalog** will indicate how much of this digital material you can access. Some of this material will be in your library, but much will be outside of it on the **World Wide Web.** (For an explanation of how to search your library's online catalog, see Chapter 4, pp. 84–90.)

As you already know, the Web is huge. The best researcher is able to explore only a small fraction of the billions of Web pages. Your goal is to use the best search tools and the best search terms in order to find the best material on your theme in a reasonable amount of time. Mentioned in this section are tools for general searching (engines and **directories**), major research sites (gateways), and specialized sites where historical materials are located. Searching can be a frustrating experience; there is no substitute for good search skills. It is wise to try several different ways of searching because no one search path will bring you to all of the available material. (For more on search techniques, see Chapter 4, pp. 93–103.) A poor choice of search terms can bring you reams of irrelevant information or none at all. Whenever you *do* get to a promising site, evaluate its usefulness with the "Guidelines for Evaluating Web Sites" on page 107. Always remember to **bookmark** a useful site.

Each search engine and each site on the Web has a specific **URL** (Uniform Resource Locator), and you must type it *exactly* in the search line of your **Web browser.** *The URLs listed here were current as of January 2003.* URLs can change. If they do, you should receive a message with a forwarding address, though, unfortunately this is not always the case.

A Student's Online Guide to History Reference Sources at bedfordstmartins.com/ benjamin offers access to an easy-to-navigate hypertext version of the digital reference sources listed here, as well as complete contact information for state, local, and professional history organizations.

Databases on CD-ROM and on the World Wide Web

Until recently, many libraries purchased databases on **CD-ROMs.** Many major databases are now also available on the World Wide Web. Because it is almost always easier to find what you are looking for if it is in your own library, check with the librarian before you seek databases on the Web.

The databases listed here are still most commonly found on CD-ROMs. Some contain statistical information; most refer to journal articles providing either the **full text** of an article or a **citation** indicating where the article can be found. Be sure to check the **date range** of the database (for more on date range, see p. 88). In time, most of these databases will probably be on the Web. If a database is listed here with a URL, it is already available on the Web.

Statistics

Historical Statistics of the United States: Colonial Times to 1970.

Statistics Masterfile. This is a digital version of the printed reference work.

Statistical Abstract of the United States. U.S. Census Bureau. U.S. Government. <www.census.gov/prod/www/statistical-abstract-us.html>. This database offers census information by year.

Statistical Resources on the Web. <www.lib.umich.edu/govdocs/stats.html>. This database provides statistics from the United States and from around the world, linking to many of the most important compilers of statistical information.

Journal Indexes

Journal indexes are among the best databases for finding articles in history journals. Some offer abstracts; others provide full text. No one index covers everything, so you should experiment with many and see what results you find.

America: History and Life: United States and Canada. When researching American and Canadian history, start with this database, which references articles drawn from international journals.

Arts and Humanities Citation Search. This database covers a broad range of art and humanities journals and allows you to search by subject, title, author, and the materials cited in each piece.

Expanded Academic ASAP. This database covers many academic disciplines but includes many abstracts and the full text of some articles of particular interest to historians.

Historical Abstracts: World History since 1450, not U.S. or Canada. When researching post-1450 historical topics that do not focus on American or Canadian history, start with this database, which complements *America: History and Life: U. S. and Canada.*

History Cooperative. This database makes available online many recent issues of major historical journals in *JSTOR*, as well as smaller journals, with multimedia enhancements.

Index to Early American Periodicals. This database features articles written in American periodicals during the eighteenth, nineteenth, and early twentieth centuries.

Ingenta. This database surveys both academic and professional journals, many of which are available online with full-text articles.

JSTOR. This database includes the full text of over 200 academic journals, including many of the most prominent historical journals. However, the most current issues are not available.

LexisNexis Academic. This database covers journals, magazines, news providers, and legal materials, and it is particularly useful for researching current events.

Project Muse. This database includes the full text of recent articles in over 200 journals across many academic disciplines, including history.

ProQuest. This database features abstracts for a wide range of media and subjects, including history.

Reader's Guide Retrospective. This is an index of popular American and Canadian magazines printed between 1890 and 1982.

Social Sciences Citation Index. Like the *Arts and Humanities Citation Search,* this database covers a broad range of social science journals and allows you to search by subject, title, author, and the materials cited in each piece.

Search Engines

Search engines provide a line for entering your search terms, and skill with keyword searching is crucial (for more on keyword searching, see Chapter 4, pp. 99–102). Many of these search engines allow you to search for images, including maps and photographs of artifacts, as well as text. Be aware, however, that some search engines, including Kanoodle and Overture, allow sponsors to pay for placement.

About:
  <www.about.com>
Alta Vista:
  <www.altavista.com>
Ask Jeeves:
  <www.ask.com>
Dogpile:
  <www.dogpile.com>
Excite:
  <www.excite.com>
Google:
  <www.google.com>
HotBot:
  <www.hotbot.com>
Infoseek:
  <infoseek.go.com>
Kanoodle:
  <www.kanoodle.com>
Lycos:
  <www.lycos.com>
Metacrawler:
  <www.metacrawler.com>
Northern Light:
  <www.northernlight.com>
Overture:
  <www.overture.com>
Profusion:
  <www.profusion.com>
Search:
  <www.search.com>
Teoma:
  <www.teoma.com>

Webcrawler:
  <www.webcrawler.com>
Yahoo!:
  <www.yahoo.com>

Indexes and Directories

These are enormous lists of Web sites organized by subject. Find the category closest to "History" and follow the links, moving from the more general to the more specific. Bookmark relevant sites or write down their URLs so that you can find them again.

First Search. <www.oclc.org>. This site allows you to search library holdings of over 48 million bibliographic records and 70 databases from around the world.

Librarians' Index to the Internet. <lii.org>. Organized by the Librarians of California, this site offers directories to reference works and many topics of interest to historians.

My Virtual Reference Desk. <www.refdesk.com>. RefDesk links to over 20,000 sites, organized by category, for use by both students and scholars.

WWW Virtual Library. <www.vlib.org>. This site sorts links by academic discipline, with several regional history categories.

Gateway Sites to History Materials

These sites focus on history and have a large number of links to specialized history sites. As with the indexes and directories, start with the most general category and follow the links that lead to subsections of that category until you find a site that by time period, geographical area, or subject is close to your theme. Bookmark relevant sites or write down their URLs so that you can find them again.

Academic Info: World History Gateway. <www.academicinfo.net/hist.html>. This site categorizes and annotates links to history Web sites but also allows you to search by keyword.

American Studies Crossroads Project (American Studies Association). <www.georgetown.edu/crossroads/>. This site features material for both teachers and students of history, including multimedia learning tools, a community area for discussion, and links to other sites.

Best of History Web Sites. <www.besthistorysites.net>. This annotated site uses a ranking system to guide users through Internet resources in history.

Directory of Historical Resources (History Database, Los Angeles). <www.history.la.ca.us/hddirect.htm>. This site features an extensive database of Web sites relating to history and historical research.

History Guide. <www.historyguide.de/>. This site offers links, bibliographies, journals, and materials relating primarily to American and European history.

History Matters (George Mason University). <historymatters.gmu.edu>. This site features articles, reference materials, and primary sources relating to American history.

The History Net. <www.TheHistoryNet.com/>. This site is a portal with particular strength in military history.

History Resource Center: Modern World (The Gale Group). <www.galegroup.com/ modernworld/>. This site is a virtual library requiring a subscription for access.

Internet History Sourcebooks Project (Paul Halsall, Fordham University). <www .fordham.edu/halsall/>. This site features primary texts from all periods of history, including special sourcebooks for Islamic, Indian, African, and East Asian history.

National Archives and Records Administration. <www.archives.gov/index.html>. This site, which houses U.S. government records, allows for catalog searches and for some online access to the materials.

Organization of American Historians. <www.oah.org/>. The OAH features links to many historical organizations and research sources.

Tennessee Tech History Web Site. <www2.tntech.edu/history/>. This site is useful for many matters relating to the study of history; its links include primary source documents, news, and grant applications.

Voice of the Shuttle History Page. <www.qub.ac.uk/english/shuttle/history.html>. This site organizes sources in an easily searchable format.

World History Archives. <www.hartford-hwp.com/archives/>. This site organizes links geographically and topically, presenting a balance to Western-centered history.

World History Association. <www.thewha.org/>. This site is a central location for announcements, links, publications, and competitions relating to the field of world history.

World History Center (Northeastern University). <www.whc.neu.edu/>. This site is developing an extensive World History Network to serve as a portal to global history research.

World History Compass. <www.worldhistorycompass.com/>. This site, which organizes annotated links geographically and by subject, includes countries often underrepresented on such sites.

WWW-Virtual Library, History. <www.ukans.edu/history/VL/>. This site organizes an extensive list of sites by topic, epoch, and geography, with useful subdivisions to help users pinpoint information and resources.

Archives of Texts and Documents

At these sites, specific historical texts (books, articles, primary documents) and, in a few cases, images and sound, are available. Online access to these archives is free—though this is not always the case for downloading or printing selections. Some of these sites also offer links to other history archives.

American Memory: Historical Collections for the National Digital Library. <memory .loc.gov/ammem/amhome.html>. This site is run by the Library of Congress and features more than 7 million documents relating to American history.

American Studies at the University of Virginia. <xroads.virginia.edu>. This site offers a variety of multimedia and hypertext sources, exhibits, time lines, and other resources of use for studying American history, with a special section on the 1930s.

American Studies Crossroads Project (American Studies Association). <www .georgetown.edu/crossroads/>. This site features material for both teachers and students of history, including multimedia learning tools, a community area for discussion, and links to other sites.

ARC (Archival Research Catalog). <www.archives.gov/research_room/arc>. This site allows users to search for archival materials around America.

The Avalon Project. <www.yale.edu/lawweb/avalon/avalon.htm>. This site covers documents in law, history, and diplomacy from many periods in American history and is organized by century.

Berkeley Digital Library SunSITE. <sunsite.berkeley.edu/>. This site features texts and images, including classical and medieval works, the Emma Goldman papers, and a strong collection relating to California.

The British Library. <www.bl.uk>. This site offers online access to historical newspapers, special exhibits, Magna Carta, and the Gutenberg Bible, available at the British Library in London.

California Digital Library: A Co-Library of the Campuses of the University of California. <www.cdlib.org>. This site features digital resources, including e-journals, databases, and materials, relating to the history of California.

Colorado Digitalization Project. <www.cdpheritage.org>. This site features a variety of media, including maps, letters, and government documents, relating to the history of Colorado.

Columbus and the Age of Discovery. <muweb.millersv.edu/~columbus/>. This site features over 1,100 articles about Columbus and cross-cultural encounters.

Demography and Population Studies. <demography.anu.edu.au/VirtualLibrary/>. This site links to census figures, journals, and demography conferences.

Don Mabry's Historical Text Archive. <historicaltextarchive.com/>. This site features articles and links to a variety of topics but is especially extensive in military and diplomatic history.

Duke University Rare Book, Manuscript, and Special Collections Library. <scriptorium.lib.duke.edu>. This site presents highly specialized and in-depth collections of digital materials on a variety of subjects but especially in the areas of advertising, the history of women, African American history, and Native American history.

Early Canadiana Online. <www.canadiana.org>. This site is a centralized, rapidly growing collection of documents relating to Canadian history through the early twentieth century.

Electronic Text Center. <etext.lib.virginia.edu/>. This site offers searchable e-books and collections, including the writings of George Washington, information relating to the Plymouth Colony, and the Salem witchcraft trials, as well as materials in a variety of languages.

The EServer: History and Historiography. <eserver.org/history/>. This site features diverse and interesting articles.

Eurodocs: Primary Historical Documents from Western Europe. <library.byu.edu/~rdh/eurodocs/>. This site provides an extensive collection of documents from European history, beginning with the Middle Ages and continuing to the present day.

Everglades Digital Library. <everglades.fiu.edu/library/index.html>. This site is dedicated to the study of the environment of southern Florida and offers historical and scientific information relating to the Everglades.

Hanover Historical Texts Archive. <history.hanover.edu/project.htm>. This site offers primary documents relating to world history but is particularly strong in European history.

Internet History Sourcebooks Project. <www.fordham.edu/halsall/>. This site features primary texts from all periods of history, including special sourcebooks for Islamic, Indian, African, and East Asian history.

Internet Public Library. <www.ipl.org>. This site offers free access to magazines, newspapers, and over 20,000 books through the Web.

National Library of Canada. <www.nlc-bnc.ca/initiatives/>. This site features an inventory of Canadian digital initiatives with links to Internet resources about Canadian scholarship.

National Library of Medicine: History of Medicine Division. <www.nlm.nih.gov/hmd/hmd.html>. This site features images, texts, and exhibits relating to all aspects of the history of medicine.

Perseus Project. <www.perseus.tufts.edu>. This site features primary source materials, including literary documents from ancient Greece, ancient Rome, and the English Renaissance, both in translation and the original.

SAGE (Selected Archives at Georgia Tech and Emory Digital Archive Project). <sage.library.emory.edu>. This site displays online multimedia exhibitions.

University of Michigan Documents Center. <www.lib.umich.edu/govdocs/index.html>. This site includes information, statistics, legislation, and news relating to each level of government.

University of Pennsylvania Digital Library. <digital.library.upenn.edu/books/>. This site's Online Books page features over 18,000 books but highlights banned books, female writers, and foreign language texts.

The World War One Document Archive. <www.lib.byu.edu/~rdh/wwi>. This site includes government documents, maps, photographs, biographies, and other relevant materials.

Specialized History Topics

These sites are usually dedicated to particular historical topics. Here you will find historical documents (primary and secondary, print and nonprint) and links to similar kinds of sites. Only a small number of the several thousand such sites are listed here. Unless one is close to your theme, begin your search in the directories and gateway sites.

Asia

Academic Info: Chinese History. <www.academicinfo.net/chinahist.html>. This site offers selected, annotated links to chronologies, databases, bibliographies, journals, and dictionaries.

The Asia Society. <www.asiasociety.org/>. This site focuses on the cultures of contemporary Asia, providing information on current politics, news, business, and cultural exhibits.

Asian Division, Area Studies (Library of Congress). <lcweb.loc.gov/rr/asian/>. This site includes information on the Library of Congress's Asian studies collections, as well as a Korean bibliography and a Japanese Documentation Center with a searchable database.

Chinese History Research Site (University of California, San Diego). <orpheus .ucsd.edu/chinesehistory/>. This site includes a primary source guide, archives, links, book reviews, and a bibliography (after the Qing period), as well as information on contemporary research by scholars worldwide.

Digital Asia Library. <digitalasia.library.wisc.edu/>. This site features a searchable catalog for online documents about Asian history and culture.

Digital South Asia Library. <dsal.uchicago.edu/>. This site categorizes resources useful in South Asian research, including documents, books, newspapers, references, journals, bibliographies, and maps.

East Asian Library (University of Pittsburgh). <www.library.pitt.edu/libraries/ eastasian/eastasian.html>. This site is a prominent specialist library.

Harvard Korean Studies Bibliography. <www.fas.harvard.edu/~korbib/>. This site, which covers the late sixteenth century to the present in a searchable online database, features over 80,000 references.

Indonesia: Society and Culture, World Wide Web Virtual Library (Australian National University). <coombs.anu.edu.au/WWWVLPages/IndonPages/WWWVL -Indonesia.html>. This site organizes annotated links to resources in Indonesian studies, including information on Islam in Indonesia.

J Guide: Stanford Guide to Japan Information Resources. <jguide.stanford.edu/>. This site covers all aspects of Japanese culture and history, with extensive links.

Japanese Studies Resources (East Asian Collection, Duke University Libraries). <www.lib.duke.edu/ias/eac/japanesestudies.html>. This site offers an extensive compilation of bibliographies, journals, dictionaries, reference works, materials, and listservs useful to the study of Japan.

John Fairbank Memorial Chinese History Virtual Library. <www.cnd.org/ fairbank/>. This site offers information about the Qing period, the Republican era, and the People's Republic of China.

The Korea Institute (Harvard University). <www.fas.harvard.edu/~korea/index _home.html>. This sites features links to and news about contemporary Korean studies.

Korean History (Korean Studies at the University of California, Berkeley). <ist -socrates.berkeley.edu/~korea/history.html>. This site offers a brief yet comprehensive look at the history of Korea, with time lines, illustrations, and explanations of terms.

South Asia Resource Access on the Internet [SARAI] (Columbia University). <www.columbia.edu/cu/libraries/indiv/area/sarai/>. This site offers links to journals, organizations, and topical guides on South Asian history.

Southeast Asian Archive (University of California, Irvine). <www.lib.uci.edu/ libraries/collections/sea/sasian.html>. This site offers virtual exhibits and annotated links to Southeast Asian resources.

Vietnam War Bibliography (Clemson University). <hubcap.clemson.edu/ ~eemoise/bibliography.html>. This site offers an extensive list of books and articles relevant to various topics in the study of the Vietnam War.

The Wars for Vietnam: 1945 to 1975 (Vassar College). <vietnam.vassar.edu/>. This site, created for an undergraduate course, includes an overview of the Vietnam War, documents for study, and links to other useful sites.

Africa

Africa South of the Sahara: Selected Internet Resources (Stanford University). <www
-sul.stanford.edu/depts/ssrg/africa/guide.html>. This site organizes links
relevant to African cultures and history by country and topic.

African Studies Association. <www.africanstudies.org/>. This site includes the association's publications, activities, and conferences and includes links to
relevant resources.

Association of Concerned Africa Scholars. <www.prairienet.org/acas/>. This site includes the association's publications, action alerts on policy problems, and
a list of scholars on contemporary issues in Africa.

Internet African History Sourcebook (Paul Halsall, Fordham University). <www
.fordham.edu/halsall/africa/africasbook.html>. This site includes primary
texts and articles relating to all periods of African history.

Middle East and Islam

ABZU: Guide to Resources for the Study of the Ancient Near East. <www.etana.org/
abzu/>. This site offers a searchable catalog with links to Internet resources
relating to the ancient Near East.

Internet Islamic History Sourcebook (Paul Halsall, Fordham University). <www
.fordham.edu/halsall/islam/islamsbook.html>. This site organizes primary
source materials and articles relating to all periods of the history of Islam.

Middle East Studies Internet Resources (Columbia University Libraries). <www
.columbia.edu/cu/lweb/indiv/mideast/cuvlm/index.html>. This site categorizes a variety of research links and materials about the Middle East by geography and subject.

Oxford Centre for Islamic Studies (Oxford University). <www.oxcis.ac.uk/>. This
site includes information on the center's publications and activities, as well
as a notice board.

Question of Palestine: History (United Nations). <www.un.org/Depts/dpa/ngo/
history.html>. This UN multimedia document discusses the history of Palestine since 1917.

Resources in Middle East Studies. <www-lib.haifa.ac.il/www/subj/mideast/
mideast.html>. This site categorizes material by subject and geography but
excludes information on Israel.

YIVO Institute for Jewish Research (New York). <www.yivoinstitute.org/>. This site
features material relevant to the study of Jewish history, as well as the institute's publications and upcoming events.

Ancient Europe

Academic Info: Ancient History. <www.academicinfo.net/histanc.html>. This site
offers annotated links to materials on ancient Greece, Rome, India,
Mesopotamia, China, and Egypt, as well as information on archaeology.

Academic Info: Classical Studies. <www.academicinfo.net/classics.html>. This site
offers annotated links to materials on the languages, literatures, art, cultures, and histories of ancient Greece and Rome.

The Ancient Greek World (University of Pennsylvania Museum of Archaeology and Anthropology). <www.museum.upenn.edu/Greek_World/Index.html>. This site offers text and images that explore the history and culture of ancient Greece.

Centre for the Study of Ancient Documents (Oxford University). <www.csad.ox.ac .uk/index.html>. This site presents information on and links to the materials and scripts of ancient writing.

Egyptology Resources (University of Cambridge). <www.newton.cam.ac.uk/ egypt/>. This site features texts, images, and links to organizations, publications, archaeological digs, and museums about Egypt.

Exploring Ancient World Cultures (University of Evansville). <eawc.evansville .edu/index.htm>. This site offers primary sources about and links to the ancient Near East, India, Egypt, China, Greece, Rome, Islam, and Europe.

Illustrated History of the Roman Empire. <www.roman-empire.net/>. This site is an extensive text with chronologies, forums, and maps.

Internet Ancient History Sourcebook. <www.fordham.edu/halsall/ancient/asbook .html>. This site offers articles and primary texts relating to the study of ancient history.

Medieval Europe

The Labyrinth: Resources for Medieval Studies (Georgetown University). <labyrinth.georgetown.edu/>. This site allows you to search bibliographies, discussion groups, images, and primary and secondary works by category.

NetSERF: The Internet Connection for Medieval Resources (Catholic University of America). <www.netserf.org/>. This site features almost 2,000 annotated links relating to medieval history.

Early Modern Europe

Britannia History Index: Reformation and Restoration [England, 1486–1689]. <britannia.com/history/h70.html>. Britannia offers documents, chronologies, articles, biographies, and links relating to England during the Reformation, Civil War, and Restoration.

Center for Reformation and Renaissance Studies. (University of Toronto). <www .library.utoronto.ca/crrs/index.htm>. This site links to early modern history resources and organizations.

Columbus and the Age of Discovery (Millersville University). <muweb.millersville .edu/~columbus>. This site offers over 1,100 articles about Columbus and cross-cultural encounters.

Exploring the French Revolution (Center for New Media, George Mason University History Project, CUNY). <chnm.gmu.edu/revolution/>. This site features essays, a time line, and a variety of primary source materials, including texts, songs, and images, on the French Revolution.

ITER: Gateway to the Middle Ages and Renaissance (University of Toronto). <iter.utoronto.ca/>. This site features a searchable database of medieval and Renaissance materials.

Renascence Editions [Renaissance]. <www.uoregon.edu/~rbear/ren.htm>. This site gives online access to texts printed in English between the late fifteenth century and the end of the eighteenth century.

Society for Renaissance Studies. <www.sas.ac.uk/srs/>. This site lists information on the society's activities and publications.

Web Gallery of Art. <gallery.euroweb.hu/>. This site offers images and information about the history of European art from 1150 to 1800.

Modern Europe

Britannia History Index: The Age of Empire. <www.britannia.com/history/h80.html>. This site offers documents, chronologies, articles, biographies, and links relating to Great Britain during the Age of Empire (1689–1901).

Cold War International History Project (Woodrow Wilson International Center for Scholars). <cwihp.si.edu/>. This site lists publications and information relating to the study of international relations during the Cold War.

Eighteenth-Century Resources — History (Rutgers-Newark). <newark.rutgers.edu/~jlynch/18th/history.html>. This site features annotated links and is particularly strong in American and British history.

Institute of Contemporary British History (University of London). <ihr.sas.ac.uk/icbh/>. This site features seminar papers and organizational information.

Italian Life under Fascism (University of Wisconsin, Madison). <www.library.wisc.edu/libraries/dpf/Fascism/Home.html>. This online exhibit features materials from the Fry Collection, organized thematically.

Links of Interest to Historians of Germany (H-German, H-Net network). <www.h-net.org/~german/research/links.html>. This site offers links to organizations, funding opportunities, libraries and archives, document centers, and areas of research.

Russian and East European History (Tennessee Tech History Web Site). <www2.tntech.edu/history/russee.html>. This site offers a variety of links relating to contemporary and historical eastern Europe.

Southwark Spanish Civil War Collection (University of California, San Diego). <orpheus.ucsd.edu/speccoll/collects/southw.html>. This site includes propaganda posters, children's drawings, newspapers, poems, and other primary resources.

United States Holocaust Memorial Museum. <www.ushmm.org/>. This site offers multimedia exhibits and historical information relating to the Holocaust, World War II, and genocide.

The Victorian Web. <65.107.211.206/victov.html>. This site organizes links relating to Victorian culture, history, and politics in Great Britain.

World War II Links on the Internet (University of California, San Diego). <history.acusd.edu/gen/ww2_links.html>. This site offers annotated links relating to the Second World War.

WWI: The World War I Document Archive (Brigham Young University). <www.lib.byu.edu/~rdh/wwi/>. This site includes government documents, maps, photographs, and biographies.

Canada

Association for Canadian Studies. <www.acs-aec.ca/>. This site offers information on, publications about, links to, and programs on contemporary and historical Canada.

Canadian Archival Resources on the Internet (University of Saskatchewan). <www.usask.ca/archives/menu.html>. This site allows you to search archives and historical Internet resources relating to Canada.

The Canadian Encyclopedia. <www.thecanadianencyclopedia.com/>. This site allows you to search information relating to Canadian history.

Canadian Historical Association. <www.cha-shc.ca/>. This site details activities, publications, and resources for Canadian scholars of history.

Canadian History and Studies (Tennessee Tech History Web Site). <www2.tntech.edu/history/canada.html>. This site offers links relating to Canadian history, divided into such categories as libraries, reference sources, journals, maps, and government documents.

National Library of Canada. <www.nlc-bnc.ca/2/index-e.html>. This site offers wide-ranging collections of primary source materials and research guides.

WWW-VL History: Canadian History. <www.ukans.edu/history/VL/CANADA/canada.html>. This site features links relating to Canadian history, divided by category.

Latin America

Ancient Mesoamerican Civilizations (University of Minnesota). <www.angelfire.com/ca/humanorigins/index.html>. This site covers ancient Mesoamerican politics, culture, writing, government, and astronomy, with links to other sites of interest.

Columbus and the Age of Discovery (Millersville University). <muweb.millersville.edu/~columbus>. This site offers over 1,100 articles about Columbus and cross-cultural encounters.

Handbook of Latin American Studies (HLAS) Online (U.S. Library of Congress). <lcweb2.loc.gov/hlas/>. This site is an updated, annotated, online bibliography.

Latin American Network Information Center (University of Texas). <info.lanic.utexas.edu/>. This site organizes contemporary cultural and political information relating to Latin America.

Latin American Studies Association. <lasa.international.pitt.edu/>. The site includes links and includes information about the organization.

Mystery of the Maya (Canadian Museum of Civilization). <www.civilization.ca/civil/maya/mminteng.html>. This site is a multimedia exhibit on the culture and civilization of the Maya.

The Perry-Castañeda Library Map Collection. <www.lib.utexas.edu/maps/index.html>. This site includes an extensive collection of maps covering the world.

Templo Mayor Museum. <archaeology.la.asu.edu/tm/index2.php>. This site guides you through the halls of the museum, dedicated to ancient Mexican history and artifacts.

The United States, General Information

Academic Info: United States History Resources. <www.academicinfo.net/histus
.html>. This site includes gateways, reference materials, and topical sites
with annotated links.

The African-American Mosaic Exhibition (Library of Congress). <www.loc.gov/
exhibits/african/afam001.html>. This online multimedia exhibit guides
the reader through African American history.

Africans in America [African American history since 1450]. <www.pbs.org/
wgbh/aia/>. This site covers the history of slavery in America from 1450 to
1865 with articles and primary source materials in a multimedia format.

American Memory: Historical Collections for the National Digital Library (Library of
Congress). <memory.loc.gov/>. This site features more than 7 million documents relating to American history.

American Studies Crossroads Project (American Studies Association).. This site includes materials for both teachers and students of history, including multimedia learning tools, a commu-
nity area for discussion, and links to other sites.

Avalon Project: Documents in Law, History and Diplomacy (Yale Law School).
<www.yale.edu/lawweb/avalon/avalon.htm>. This site covers documents in
law, history, and diplomacy from many periods in American history, organized by century.

Bibliographies in Women's History and Studies (University of Maryland).. This
site includes bibliographies for many topics relating to women's studies.

Congressional Archives (University of Oklahoma). <www.ou.edu/special/
albertctr/archives/>. This site includes photographs, oral histories, and extensive documents.

Documenting the American South (University of North Carolina, Chapel Hill).
. This site features electronic primary sources relating
to the American South before 1920.

Environmental History. <www2.tntech.edu/history/envir.html>. This site includes links relating to environmental history.

The Evolution of the Conservation Movement [United States, 1850–1920].
<memory.loc.gov/ammem/amrvhtml/conshome.html>. This site traces the
history of environmental conservation ideas and political action in the
United States between 1850 and 1920, with primary texts, government
statutes, and images.

History Resource Center: U.S. (The Gale Group). <www.galegroup.com/
HistoryRC/index.htm>. This site requires a subscription to use its integrated text and commentary.

U.S. Senate Historical Office. <www.senate.gov/artandhistory/history/common/
generic/Senate_Historical_Office.htm>. This site features essays, photographs, and statistics relating to the U.S. Senate.

U.S. Supreme Court Opinions. <www.findlaw.com/10fedgov/judicial/supreme
_court/opinions.html>. This site allows you to search Supreme Court opin-
ions.

United States Historical Census Data Browser (University of Virginia).. This site allows you to search census data from

1790 to 1960, with links to more recent population statistics and census information.

WWW-VL History: United States. <www.ukans.edu/history/VL/USA/index.html>. This site categorizes links and materials by media, topic, and era.

The United States, Seventeenth and Eighteenth Centuries

George Washington Papers at the Library of Congress, 1741–1799 (Library of Congress). <memory.loc.gov/ammem/gwhtml/gwhome.html>. This site allows you to search and browse digitized versions of George Washington's manuscript papers.

Museum of African Slavery (Johns Hopkins University). <jhunix.hcf.jhu.edu/~plarson/smuseum/welcome.htm>. This site offers a scholarly investigation into and resources about the atrocities of African slavery.

NativeWeb. <www.nativeweb.org/>. This site, which is updated and expanded regularly, features information about Native American studies.

Omohundro Institute for Early American History and Culture. <www.wm.edu/oieahc/>. This site includes access to the papers of John Marshall and links to other resources relating to early American history.

Plimoth-on-Web: Plimoth Plantation's Web Page [Colonial America, 1620–1692]. <www.plimoth.org>. This site features multimedia educational materials about colonial America and the Plymouth Colony.

Salem Witch Trials (University of Virginia). <etext.virginia.edu/salem/witchcraft/home.html>. This site includes documents and maps relating to the Salem witch trials, as well as a historical overview and links to relevant organizations and archives.

The United States, Nineteenth Century

The Abolition Movement (Library of Congress). <www.loc.gov/exhibits/african/afam005.html>. This site is a multimedia exhibit, guiding users through African American history, particularly the abolition movement.

African-American Perspectives. <memory.loc.gov/ammem/aap/aaphome.html>. This site is a database of the Daniel A. P. Murray Pamphlet Collection, which focuses on the late nineteenth and early twentieth centuries in America.

African-American Religion: A Documentary History Project (Amherst College). <www.amherst.edu/~aardoc/menu.html>. This site, which spans 1441 to the present, includes limited information and sample documents; the project will ultimately be published in printed form.

African American Women Writers of the 19th Century (Digital Schomburg). <digital.nypl.org/schomburg/writers_aa19/>. This site offers the full text of poetry, essays, novels, and other writings by African American women during the nineteenth century.

The Age of Imperialism. <www.smplanet.com/imperialism/toc.html>. This site offers a brief but detailed narrative and links about American imperialism in the late nineteenth and early twentieth centuries.

The American Civil War Homepage (University of Tennessee). <sunsite.utk.edu/civil-war/warweb.html>. This site links to images, documents, secondary works, local studies, bibliographies, and other materials relating to the Civil War.

American Civil War Resources. <spec.lib.vt.edu/civwar/>. This site links to manuscript collections, dissertation information, print collections, and a guide to manuscript resources.

Antebellum American History, 1812–1864 (University of Colorado). <web.uccs.edu/~history/index/antebellum.html>. This site organizes the antebellum years by time and topic, with links and illustrations.

Anti-Imperialism in the United States, 1898–1935 (Jim Zwick). <www.boondocksnet.com/ai/index.html>. This site offers essays, bibliographies, and links to materials on anti-expansionary influences in the early twentieth century.

Center for the Study of Southern Culture (University of Mississippi). <www.olemiss.edu/depts/south>. This site offers publications and a media archive.

Civil War Resources on the Internet: Abolitionism to Reconstruction, 1830's–1890's (Rutgers University). <www.libraries.rutgers.edu/rul/rr_gateway/research_guides/history/civwar.shtml>. This site offers selected and partially annotated links to documents, listservs, bibliographies, studies, and images relating to the Civil War.

Core Historical Literature of Agriculture (Cornell University). <chla.library.cornell.edu/>. This site, which serves as a collection of agricultural texts from the nineteenth and twentieth centuries, includes over 800 monographs.

Crucible of Empire: The Spanish-American War (PBS). <www.pbs.org/crucible/>. This site is a multimedia teaching tool for exploring the Spanish-American War.

Documenting the American South (University of North Carolina). <docsouth.unc.edu/>. This site includes primary sources relating to the American South before 1920.

The Dred Scott Case (Washington University Libraries). <www.library.wustl.edu/vlib/dredscott/>. This site features the papers of the Dred Scott case, as well as a chronology and information about the papers.

Explore Your Family History at Ellis Island (American Family Immigration History Center). <www.ellisisland.org/>. This site presents information about immigration through Ellis Island and allows you to search for arrivals.

The Gilded Page. <www.wm.edu/~srnels/gilded.html>. This site offers documents, genre descriptions, and other links to materials relating to the American Gilded Age (1870–1898).

The Great Chicago Fire. <www.chicagohs.org/fire/intro/gcf-index.html>. This site includes essays, images, and primary documents about the fire of 1871.

Immigration: The Changing Face of America (Library of Congress). <memory.loc.gov/ammem/ndlpedu/features/immig/oldflash.html>. This site is a multimedia exhibit of immigration to America from many different parts of the world.

Making of America (University of Michigan). <moa.umdl.umich.edu>. This site offers scanned images of primary text documents—over 8,500 books and 50,000 journal articles—from nineteenth-century America, particularly focused on social history.

Marriage, Women, and the Law. <www.rlg.org/scarlet>. This site, a primary source archive of nineteenth-century family law, focuses on the legal treatment of women in America from 1815 to 1914.

Nineteenth Century Documents Project (Furman University). <alpha.furman.edu/ ~benson/docs/>. This site focuses on regional issues, especially inter-American tensions in South Carolina.

Southern Historical Collection (University of North Carolina). <www.lib.unc.edu/ mss/shcgl.html>. This site offers documents, databases, and journals.

Tangled Roots: A Project Exploring the Histories of Americans of Irish Heritage and Americans of African Heritage (Yale University). <www.yale.edu/glc/ tangledroots/>. This site examines the interwoven history of Irish Americans and African Americans from the seventeenth century to the present.

United States Historical Census Data Browser (University of Virginia). <fisher.lib .virginia.edu/census/>. This site allows you to search census data from 1790 to 1960, with links to more recent population statistics and census information.

Valley of the Shadow: Two Communities in the American Civil War (Edward Ayers et al., University of Virginia). <www.iath.virginia.edu/vshadow2/>. This site presents a northern county and a southern county and their fates throughout the Civil War, offering primary sources and secondary narrative and analysis.

Vaudeville and Popular Entertainment [1870–1920]. <lcweb2.loc.gov/ammem/ vshtml/vshome.html>. This site collects and organizes Library of Congress digital multimedia holdings about vaudeville in America.

Western History Association. <www.unm.edu/~wha/>. This site includes links of interest to scholars of the American West and information about the organization's events and publications.

WestWeb: Western History (CUNY). <www.library.csi.cuny.edu/westweb/>. This site includes primary sources, links, time lines, and bibliographies relating to the history of the American West.

Whole Cloth: Discovering Science and Technology through American History (Smithsonian Institution). <www.si.edu/lemelson/centerpieces/whole_cloth/>. This site offers information relating to the history of American textiles in a multimedia format.

Women and Social Movements in the United States, 1775–2000 (Binghamton University, SUNY). <womhist.binghamton.edu>. This site contains bibliographies, links, and over 900 primary source documents relating to women and social movements in America.

The United States, Twentieth Century

Ad*Access (Duke University) [Historical Advertisements, United States, 1911–1955]. <scriptorium.lib.duke.edu/adaccess/>. This site features 7,000 advertisements from the early twentieth century.

America in the 1930's (American Studies Program, University of Virginia). <xroads.virginia.edu/~1930s/DISPLAY/displayframe.html>. This site offers audio, visual, and textual sources to survey the culture and politics of the time.

American Cultural History: 1920–1929 (Kingwood College Library). <www .nhmccd.edu/contracts/lrc/kc/decade20.html>. This site offers a hypertext narrative explaining the primary cultural and political events of the 1920s.

American Life Histories: Manuscripts from the Federal Writers' Project, 1936–1940. <memory.loc.gov/ammem/wpaintro/wpahome.html>. This site includes 2,900 life histories, searchable by keyword or state.

Civil Rights Documentation Project (University of Southern Mississippi). <www-dept.usm.edu/~mcrohb/>. This site features an oral history bibliography, oral history transcripts, and a civil rights timetable.

Clash of Cultures in the 1910s and 1920s (Ohio State University). <www.history.ohio-state.edu/projects/clash>. This site explains the cultural turmoil of the early twentieth century by focusing on the Scopes trial, Prohibition, immigration restriction, the Ku Klux Klan, and the "New Woman."

Cold War International History Project (Woodrow Wilson International Center for Scholars). <cwihp.si.edu/>. This site lists publications and information relating to the study of international relations during the Cold War.

Cold War Policies, 1945–1991 (University of San Diego). <history.acusd.edu/gen/20th/coldwar0.html>. This site includes outlines and links relating to Cold War policies, organized chronologically.

The Counterculture of the Sixties. <www.geocities.com/SoHo/Studios/2914/>. This site includes primary sources, time lines, quotes, biographies, and analysis of the upheaval of the 1960s.

Documents from the Women's Liberation Movement (Duke University). <scriptorium.lib.duke.edu/wlm/>. This site offers a searchable database of primary text from the 1960s and 1970s.

Documents Relating to American Foreign Policy in Vietnam (Mount Holyoke College). <www.mtholyoke.edu/acad/intrel/vietnam.htm>. This Web site compiles primary and secondary sources relating primarily to Vietnam, with some focus on World War II.

The Fifties Web. <www.fiftiesweb.com/fifties.htm>. This site focuses on American popular culture in the 1950s, particularly music, film, and television, with a bibliography of other sources.

The Gallup Organization. <www.gallup.com>. This site offers access to the results of Gallup opinion polls.

The Korean War (Project Whistlestop). <www.trumanlibrary.org/whistlestop/study_collections/korea/large/>. This site includes a history of the war, official documents, links, and teaching materials.

Martin Luther King Jr. Papers Project (Stanford University). <www.stanford.edu/group/King/>. This site, which features materials relating to the life and works of Dr. King, includes reference materials, his writings, audio files, chronologies, and analysis.

The Media History Project. <www.mediahistory.umn.edu/>. This site includes chronologies, articles, songs, quizzes, definitions, and links.

The New Deal Network (Franklin and Eleanor Roosevelt Institute/Columbia University). <newdeal.feri.org/>. This site includes over 900 documents and 5,000 images, as well as bibliographies and information about the era.

The Oyez Project: United States Supreme Court Multimedia Database. <oyez.nwu.edu/>. This site, which covers the Supreme Court from 1955 to the present, includes information about the justices and key events and allows you to search cases.

The President John F. Kennedy Assassination Records Collection (National Archives). <www.archives.gov/research_room/jfk/index.html>. This site offers documentation of the assassination and its investigation.

Red Scare, 1918–1921 (Baruch College, CUNY). <newman.baruch.cuny.edu/digital/redscare/default.htm>. This site includes a searchable image database.

Roper Center for Public Opinion Research (University of Connecticut). <www.ropercenter.uconn.edu/>. This site offers access to the data gathered from Roper opinion polls, archived collections, and the Roper magazine.

Rutgers Oral History Archive of World War Two. <history.rutgers.edu/oralhistory/orlinf.htm>. This site features interviews with survivors of World War II and links to other resources.

Schomburg Center for Research in Black Culture (New York Public Library). <www.nypl.org/research/sc/sc.html>. This site includes oral histories and online exhibits.

The Sixties Project (University of Virginia). <lists.village.virginia.edu/sixties/>. This site includes back issues of the *Viet Nam Generation Journal.*

Vietnam War Bibliography (Clemson University). <hubcap.clemson.edu/~eemoise/bibliography.html>. This site offers a list of books and articles relevant to the study of the Vietnam War.

Vietnam War Internet Project. <www.vwip.org/vwiphome.html>. This site offers documents about, images of, newsgroups on, and links to the events of and debates surrounding the Vietnam War.

The Wars for Vietnam: 1945 to 1975 (Vassar College). <vietnam.vassar.edu/>. This site, created for an undergraduate course, offers an overview of the Vietnam War, documents for study, and links.

W. E. B. Du Bois Institute for Afro-American Research (Harvard University). <www.fas.harvard.edu/~dubois/>. This site offers links to recent projects and research, including databases, bibliographies, and other materials.

Woman Suffrage and the 19th Amendment (National Archives). <www.archives.gov/digital_classroom/lessons/woman_suffrage/woman_suffrage.html>. This site offers primary documents relating to the women's suffrage movement.

World War II Links on the Internet (University of San Diego). <history.acusd.edu/gen/ww2_links.html>. This site offers annotated links relating to World War II.

World War II Resources on the Internet (Miami University). <www.lib.muohio.edu/inet/subj/history/wwii/>. This site offers annotated links to primary and secondary materials that focus on pivotal themes and moments in World War II.

Digital History Journals

In addition to hundreds of print history journals on the Web (that is, journals that were originally in printed form), there are e-journals—journals found *only* on the Web. If they are searchable, you can quickly discover if these journals have articles related to your theme. Some e-journals offer a discussion list where readers send in their comments on the articles or on other readers' comments. Most e-journals are new, and not many articles have been written for them yet. Some print journals that have moved to the Web make back issues available online. In either case, the title of the journal can help you decide if it is likely to cover your theme.

Directory of Scholarly Electronic Journals and Academic Discussion Lists. <dsej.arl .org/index.html>. This directory allows you to search journals relevant to your chosen theme.

The Early America Review [Eighteenth century]. <www.earlyamerica.com/ review/index.html>. This directory, under the auspices of Archiving Early America, offers articles and book reviews about eighteenth-century America and is devoted to placing primary source material relating to colonial America online.

Electronic Antiquity: Communicating the Classics. <scholar.lib.vt.edu/ejournals/ ElAnt>. This directory offers articles and book reviews relating to ancient Greece and Rome.

Essays in History (edited by graduate students at the University of Virginia). <etext.lib.virginia.edu/journals/EH>. This directory offers essays relating to many historical topics and time periods.

The North Star: A Journal of African American Religious History. <northstar .vassar.edu>. This directory offers documents, articles, bibliographies, book reviews, and announcements relevant to the study of African American religious history.

Renaissance Forum: An Electronic Journal of Early-Modern Literary and Historical Studies. <www.hull.ac.uk/Hull/EL_Web/renforum>. This directory features historical and literary articles and book reviews relating to early modern Europe.

Electronic Discussion Lists in History

If you want to talk online about history to other students or faculty—or to anybody who is interested—you should join a discussion list—that is, a **listserv.** To join, visit <www.h-net.org>, select a specific discussion network of interest, and then click on "Subscribe!" After entering your name, your e-mail address, and the name of your school, you will receive an e-mail confirmation with further information. The home site for history discussion lists is <www .h-net.org/lists>. Here are the names and topics of some of the larger discussion groups.

H-Africa [African history and culture]

H-Afro-Am [African American studies]

H-AHC [Association of History and Computing]

H-Albion [British and Irish history]

H-AmIndian [American Indian history and culture]

H-AmRel [American religious history]

H-Amstdy [American studies]

H-Asia [Asian studies and history]

H-Business [History of business and commerce]

H-Canada [Canadian history and studies]

H-Childhood [History of childhood and youth]

H-CivWar [U.S. Civil War history]

H-Demog [Demographic history]

H-Diplo [Diplomatic history and international affairs]

H-Education [History of education]

H-Environment [Environmental history]

H-Ethnic [Ethnic and immigration history]

H-Film [Cinema history and the uses of media]

H-History-and-Theory [Philosophy of history]

H-Holocaust [Holocaust studies]

H-Ideas [Intellectual history]

H-Labor [Labor history]

H-LatAm [Latin American history]

H-Law [Legal and constitutional history]

H-Local [State and local history]

H-Mediterranean [Modern and contemporary Mediterranean history]

H-Minerva [Women and the military]

H-OIEAHC [Colonial and early American history]

H-Pol [U.S. political history]

H-Rural [Rural and agricultural history]

H-Sci-Med-Tech [History of science, medicine, and technology]

H-South [History of the U.S. South]

H-USA [International study of the United States]

H-War [Military history]

H-Women [Women's history]

H-World [World history]

A P P E N D I X   B

Useful Information
for the Historian

Historical Sources
in Your Own Backyard

Some of the most rewarding kinds of historical research concern people, events, and places that you can almost reach out and touch. The history of your family, of the town you grew up in, or of events that shaped your parents' lives can be uncovered not only in a library but in a nearby museum or in a local history archive filled with old photographs, land deeds, birth registers, and personal correspondence. Every state in the United States and every province in Canada has its own historical society with a library of books, photographs, and documents on the state's or province's history. Every city and most towns, even small ones, have a historical society or a museum where they keep the documents and artifacts that tell the story of the town's past.

Wherever your school is located, you are probably not more than a short drive from a local history archive. If your research concerns the town or area where your school is located, look up the address of the local historical society and visit it. One of the most enjoyable aspects of history research is to hold in your hand an actual document or artifact that makes the past come alive—a 150-year-old land deed, a photograph of the center of town in 1890, a record player from 1918, a letter from a mother to her daughter written in 1838.

If you live or go to school in a large city or if you want to research the history of a county or an area of a state or province, many records are available to you. Each state and province and each county within that state or province will have its own archive of historical materials. Each city will have at least one such archive. Cities and towns also have private historical societies. There are thousands of state and province, county, and local museums and archives. The best way to locate the major archives is to look them up in *Directory of Historical Organizations in the United States and Canada,* published by the American Association for State and Local History. This directory lists many hundreds of organizations. It has an index that arranges organizations alphabetically by the name of the place whose history they record. The archives are also listed alphabetically by subject if their collection of documents or artifacts is specialized in some way—say a town that was an important battlefield in the Civil War. The name, address, and telephone number of each organization is listed along with a brief description of the kind of materials it contains. Many archives have also created Web sites and can be located online.

How to Research Your Family History

One of the most pleasurable kinds of historical research is investigating your own family's history. Moreover, to research it is to re-create a portion of the historical experience of our nation. Because most of our ancestors came from other nations, a family history also will connect us with the historical experience of other lands. By studying the history of your family, you become aware of your own place within these broader historical experiences. Perhaps most important, knowledge of your family's history and its meaning can give you a strong sense of your cultural roots that will strengthen you throughout your lifetime.

The best sources—in many cases the only sources—of information on the history of your family are the recollections, understandings, and long-term possessions of your relatives. Researching a family history involves investigating these sources as thoroughly and creatively as possible. This kind of research involves (1) familiarizing yourself with the general history of the nations and regions, and of the specific times and places, in which your ancestors lived; (2) studying all available family records, such as diaries, photographs, and heirlooms; and most important, (3) interviewing all available family members.

The interview is the core of a family history because, in most instances, it is the only way of uncovering the nature of your family's life. Without the recollections of your relations, you would not be able to discover more than a handful of names, dates, and places—only the barest outline of your family's history.

In preparing for this crucial aspect of family research, you must familiarize yourself with the basic history of your family so that you can place in proper context the information you obtain from the people you interview. You will need to prepare your questions beforehand, focusing on important aspects of family life and of the larger social and political life surrounding the family. Be sure that your questions establish the basics: the names, relationships, and principal home and workplace activities of each member of the family in each generation, going as far down the trunk and out on the limbs of the family tree as possible given the scope of your project and the memories of your relatives. Look for information that will enable you to make comparisons between generations of your family and between it and other families. Investigate such topics as the type of dwelling and neighborhood, parent-child and husband-wife relationships, authority and status patterns, income and social mobility. When you come across major family events—immigration, military service, job and residence changes, involvement in political movements—probe the reasons for them, because they will illuminate the ties between your family and the nation's history.

When actually conducting the interview, use your prepared questions, taking care to make them as broad as possible—for example, "What was the neighborhood like when you lived there?" not simply "What was your address in 1936?" When you get an answer that seems to lead in the direction of important material, ignore your prepared questions temporarily and probe further. However, never interrupt an answer, even when the response seems unimportant. Your informants are the experts on their lives, and their self-perceptions—even if illogical or factually incorrect—are essential ingredients of family history. Finally, because the intricate web of your relatives' feelings is as important as the milestones of their lives, it is best to tape-record the interview if possible rather than rely on written notes. Record it all and then collect from your tapes the information that, on the one hand, best reflects your informants' testimony about their lives and, on the other, enables you to say something of importance about those lives and the times in which they were lived.

If important pieces are missing from the story—your great-grandfather's birthplace, for instance, or the age at which your grandmother married—you can try to supplement your own family's records with official ones. Listed below are the best sources for family history research. Many of them are also available on the World Wide Web.

Sources for Family History Research

Printed Reference Sources

How to Climb Your Family Tree: Genealogy for Beginners. Baltimore, Md.: Genealogical Publishing, 1997.

The Researcher's Guide to American Genealogy. Ed. Val D. Greenwood. Baltimore, Md.: Genealogical Publishing, 1990.

American Families: A Research Guide and Historical Handbook. Westport, Conn.: Greenwood Press, 1991.

State Censuses: An Annotated Bibliography of Censuses of Population Taken after 1790 by States and Territories of the United States. New York: Burt Franklin, 1969.

A Bibliography of American County Histories. Baltimore, Md.: American Genealogical Publishing, 1985.

Federal Population Censuses: A Catalogue of Microfilm Copies of Schedules [1790–1920]. Washington, D.C.: Library of Congress.

Biography and Genealogy Master Index. Detroit: Gale, 1980. Supplements annually. Now on CD-ROM and the World Wide Web.

Genealogical and Local History Books in Print. Comp. and ed. Marian Hoffman. 4 vols. Baltimore, Md.: Genealogical Publishing, 1996–1997.

In Search of Your European Roots: A Complete Guide to Tracing Your Ancestors in Every European Country. Ed. Angus Baxter. Baltimore, Md.: Genealogical Publishing, 1994.

Encyclopedia of [U.S.] Local History. Walnut Creek, Calif.: Alta Mira, Press, 2000.

Finding Your Hispanic Roots. Ed. George Riskamp. Baltimore, Md.: Genealogical Publishing, 1997.

State Census Records. Ed. Ann S. Lainhart. Baltimore, Md.: Genealogical Publishing, 1992.

American Passenger Arrival Records: A Guide to the Records of Immigrants Arriving at American Ports by Sail and Steam. Ed. Michael Tepper. Baltimore, Md.: Genealogical Publishing, 1993. (Also see the National Archives and Records Administration Web site listed below.)

Guide to Naturalization Records of the United States. Ed. Christina K. Shaefer. Baltimore, Md.: Genealogical Publishing, 1997.

Digital Reference Sources

U.S. GOVERNMENT RESOURCES

National Archives and Records Administration's Genealogy Page. <www.nara.gov/genealogy/genindex.html>. This very large Web site tells you where different kinds of U.S. government records are kept and how you can find information in them. It also contains a large list of genealogical resources on the World Wide Web.

American Family Immigration History Center. <www.ellisisland.records.org>.

GENERAL GENEALOGICAL RESOURCES

Cyndi's List of Genealogy Sites on the Internet. <CyndisList.com>. The largest list of sites and links on the Web.

The Church of Jesus Christ of Latter-Day Saints Family Search Genealogy Service. <www.familysearch.org>.

The Genealogy Home Page. <www.genhomepage.com>.

Gendex: WWW Genealogical Index. <www.gendex.com/gendex>.

Ancestry Plus. <www.gale.ancestry.com/ggmain.htm>.

State and Local History. <www2.tntech.edu/history/state.html>.

Grammar and Style Manuals

If you know that your background in grammar and composition is weak, or if you need more specific information concerning report writing, here are a few manuals that should help.

Hacker, Diana. *A Pocket Style Manual.* 4th ed. Boston: Bedford/St. Martin's, 2004.

Hacker, Diana. *Rules for Writers.* 5th ed. Boston: Bedford/St. Martin's, 2003.

Lunsford, Andrea. *The St. Martin's Handbook.* 5th ed. Boston: Bedford/St. Martin's, 2003.

Rampolla, Mary Lynn. *A Pocket Guide to Writing in History.* 4th ed. Boston: Bedford/St. Martin's, 2004.

University of Chicago Press. *The Chicago Manual of Style.* 15th ed. Chicago: University of Chicago Press, 2003.

Glossary

Abstract: A brief description of the contents of a scholarly article.

Appendix: Information placed after the end or conclusion of a research paper or book. This information (for example, charts, tables, visuals, etc.) is separated because it is too long to place within the paper or book itself.

Archive: A place in which public records or historical documents are preserved. On the Web: a site where historical documents are available in digital form.

Artifact: A physical object created in the past.

Atlas: A bound collection of maps, often including illustrations, informative tables, or textual matter.

Bias: An attitude or prejudice that influences the way in which a subject is interpreted.

Bibliography: An alphabetical list, often with descriptive or critical notes, of works relating to a particular subject, period, or author; in student papers, a list of the works referred to or consulted.

Biography: A written history of a person's life.

Bookmark: A place on a Web browser (usually near the top) where you can click on any Web site that is on your screen and record the URL for future use.

Book review: An essay that comments on a particular work or a series of works on a single subject.

Browser: *See* Web browser.

Call number: A combination of characters assigned to a library book to indicate its place on a shelf.

Catalog: A complete listing of items, such as books, arranged systematically with descriptive details. *See also* Library catalog.

CD-ROM: A compact disc capable of containing a large amount of data that is read by a computer. May contain text, statistics, pictures, and audio and video files.

Chart: A visual display of quantitative information. Common examples are bar charts and pie charts.

Chat room: An open forum on the Web, a place where individuals can comment on current messages. Older messages are not preserved. To take part in a more organized and recorded discussion, subscribe to a listserv. *See also* Listserv.

Cheating: *See* Plagiarism.

Chronological organization: A research paper that is organized by date.

Citation: A reference to a source of information used in preparing a written assignment; usually takes the form of a footnote or endnote. *See also* Documentation.

Conclusion: The final section of a written document in which the writer summarizes findings and interpretations.

Context: The text that surrounds a particular statement and affects the statement's meaning.

Continuity: As a component of writing, continuity is the coherent flow of an author's arguments as the author moves from one point to another.

Counterevidence: Evidence that contradicts your thesis.

Cyclical school: School of historical thought that believes history repeats itself. According to this school, essential forces of nature and human nature are changeless, so past patterns of events repeat themselves endlessly.

Database: A large collection of data organized for rapid search and retrieval, as by a computer.

Date range: The time period covered by a large collection of books, articles, newspapers, and other documents.

Demography: The study of changes in population and the reasons for those changes.

Directory: On a computer, an organized list of files and folders. On the Web, a kind of search engine. *See also* Search engine; Subject index.

Dissertation: An extended, usually written, treatment of a subject; specifically one submitted for a doctorate.

Documentation: The use of historical or other evidence to support a statement or argument; usually takes the form of footnotes or endnotes or material such as pictures, graphs, tables, or copies of documents.

Draft: A preliminary sketch, outline, or version of an essay or paper.

Ellipsis: The omission of words from a quotation; also, the punctuation (. . .) that indicates the omission.

Encyclopedia: A work that contains information on all branches of knowledge or that comprehensively treats a particular branch of knowledge; usually comprises articles arranged alphabetically by subject. Online encyclopedias can be searched electronically.

Endnote: A note of reference, explanation, or comment placed at the end of an essay or paper. *See also* Documentation.

Essay exam: A test that requires a complete, well-organized written answer on a particular topic.

Ethnohistory: The study of ethnic groups and how they evolve.

Evidence: *See* Primary document; Secondary source.

Footnote: A note of reference, explanation, or comment placed below the text on a printed page. *See also* Documentation.

Full-text database: An electronic database that contains all of the text of a written source rather than merely information for finding the source.

Graph: A precise drawing, usually taking the form of a series of points and lines that make visual the numerical changes in the relationship between two or more things.

Historian: A student or writer of history, especially someone who produces a scholarly examination of a historical topic.

Historical novel: A work of fiction based on actual events and people.

Historiography: The study of changes in the methods, interpretations, and conclusions of historians over time.

Home page: The first page of a Web site, with links to other parts of the site or to other sites.

Hyperlink: A one-step connection between two different pages on the World Wide Web. Hyperlinks appear on your screen as click-on boxes or icons or as highlighted or underlined text.

Identification exam: A test that requires the brief identification of a person, place, object, or event and an explanation of its importance.

Index: An alphabetical list of persons and subjects and the page numbers where they are discussed in a book. For electronic indexes, *see* Subject index.

Interlibrary loan: The lending of a book by one library to another.

Internet: A worldwide network of computers that can transfer information back and forth. *See also* World Wide Web.

Introduction: The beginning section of a book or multipage paper. It sets out the writer's theme or thesis.

Journal: A periodical containing articles on scholarly topics. For students: a written record, created by a student, of some aspect of a course.

Keyword: A word that represents a core aspect of a subject to be researched. Keywords are used to search online catalogs and electronic databases found in libraries and on the World Wide Web.

Library catalog: A catalog that organizes all the holdings of a library; most library catalogs are electronic and can be searched by title, author, or keyword.

Library stacks: Shelves on which a library's books and journals are stored.

Link: *See* Hyperlink.

Linking paragraph: A paragraph that indicates how and why an essay is moving from one important point to another.

Linking sentence: A sentence that ties together the points made in two paragraphs. It almost always comes at the end of one paragraph or at the beginning of the very next one.

Listserv: An e-mail discussion list to which individuals who have a special interest in the topic of the list subscribe. Many listservs are moderated: someone organizes the messages by date and topic. Messages are preserved so that you can read previous exchanges between subscribers.

Microfiche: A sheet of microfilm containing pages of printed matter in reduced form.

Microfilm: A film bearing a photographic record on a reduced scale of printed or other graphic matter.

Monograph: A scholarly study of a specific topic.

Multiple-choice exam: A test consisting of questions with several possible answers, one of which is the correct or best answer.

Note cards: Small cards (3-by-5 or 4-by-6) that are convenient for note taking and the indexing of notes when researching.

Objective exam: A test consisting of factual questions for which there is only one correct answer for each question.

Online catalog: An electronic catalog that enables the user to search the holdings of a library, and possibly other libraries and databases, from a computer.

Paraphrase: A restatement of a passage, idea, or work in different words. Like direct quotations, paraphrases of original work require proper documentation. *See also* Plagiarism.

Peer editing: *See* Peer reviewing.

Peer reviewing: Examining the work (usually written work) of a classmate or colleague. The purpose is to offer constructive comments so that the work can be improved.

Periodical: A publication with a fixed interval between issues.

Periodical database: A large collection of articles from journals, magazines, or newspapers in electronic, searchable form.

Plagiarism: Stealing and presenting the ideas or words of another as one's own; using material without crediting its source; presenting as new and original an idea or product derived from an existing source. Plagiarism is a serious act of academic dishonesty. *See also* Paraphrase; Quotation.

Plug-ins: Computer software that enhances the capability of a Web browser or other program.

Postmodernism: A philosophy or school of history that questions whether we can truly uncover the past.

Primary document, primary source: Firsthand evidence that records the words of someone who participated in or witnessed the events described or of someone who received his or her information from direct participants.

Progressive school: School of historical thought that believes human history illustrates neither endless cycles nor divine intervention but continual progress. According to this school, the situation of humanity is constantly improving.

Proofreading: A careful rereading of written work to correct errors of style or grammer.

Providential school: School of historical thought that believes that the course of history is determined by God and that the flow of historical events represents struggles between forces of good and evil.

Quantitative history: The use of statistics in the study of history.

Quotation: A statement that repeats exactly the words of a source. Such a statement must be enclosed in quotation marks and properly documented. *See also* Plagiarism.

Reference book: A work, such as a dictionary or encyclopedia, containing useful facts or information.

Research bibliography: A list of sources that may be needed to research a topic/theme for a formal paper; includes publication information and location of the materials.

Research outline: A list of the parts of a topic/theme to be researched and a tentative ordering of these parts.

Research paper: A formal writing assignment on a specific theme that requires the reading and synthesis of primary and secondary sources; also requires documentation such as footnotes or endnotes and a bibliography.

Revise: To look over again in order to correct or improve; to make a new, amended, improved, or up-to-date version of an essay or paper.

Rough draft: The first version of a written assignment; it is polished and revised in later drafts.

Search engine: A computer program that allows the user to locate World Wide Web sites, usually by keyword or subject.

Secondary source: The findings of someone who did not observe a historical event firsthand but investigated primary evidence of it.

Short-answer exam: A test that requires brief written answers to factual questions.

Source card: The first in a series of cards created to hold (and later organize) the information from a particular source. Unlike the other cards in the series, the source card contains all the information you will need to cite that source in a footnote or list it in a bibliography.

Stacks: *See* Library stacks.

Statistics: A branch of mathematics dealing with the collection, analysis, interpretation, and presentation of numerical data; a collection of quantitative data.

Subject bibliographies: Lists of books, articles, and other material organized by subject.

Subject directory: *See* Subject index.

Subject headings: Terms used in catalogs, such as the *Library of Congress Subject Headings*, to describe the contents of a library's or a Web site's materials.

Subject index: A list, organized by subject, of links to Web sites.

Table: A systematic arrangement of data in rows and columns.

Take-home essay exam: A test usually consisting of one or more short essays that are to be prepared outside of class.

Textbook: Often the principal reading in an introductory course; usually supplemented by other, more specialized materials.

Theme: A narrow part of a topic chosen or assigned for research. A theme sets limits on the area to be investigated and suggests the kinds of questions to be answered and the points to be made. *See also* Thesis.

Thesis: A clear statement, usually appearing at the beginning of an essay or research paper, that informs the reader of the central argument or claim the writer intends to make about the theme. The thesis results from the narrowing of your theme. *See also* Theme.

Topic: A broad subject area chosen or assigned for research.

Topical organization: A research paper that is organized by topic.

URL: Stands for "Uniform Resource Locator." A URL is the electronic address of a Web site or Web page.

Web browser: Software that interprets hypertext markup language (HTML) and displays embedded graphics and multimedia; allows the user to view a variety of content on World Wide Web sites.

Word processing: The creation of documents, such as notes and research papers, by computer programs that allow great flexibility in editing.

World Wide Web: Part of the Internet that uses hypertext markup language (HTML) to connect texts, including images and sound, by means of embedded links.

Writing outline: Framework for a research paper that lists thoughts and ideas in an organized manner and acts as a guide for writing a rough draft.

Yearbook: A book published yearly containing a report or summary of statistics or facts.

Acknowledgments (continued from p. iv)

From *World Civilizations,* Eighth Edition, Volume I, by Philip Lee Ralph et al. Copyright ©
1955, 1958, 1964, 1969, 1974, 1982, 1986, 1991 by W. W. Norton & Company, Inc. Used by
permission of W. W. Norton & Company, Inc.

From *The World since 1500: A Global History,* Fourth Edition, by L. S. Stavrianos, 1976.
Reprinted by permission of Prentice Hall, Inc., Upper Saddle River, N.J.

Index